Inside Accou
Volume I

Manchester University Press

Inside Accounts, Volume I

The Irish Government and Peace in Northern Ireland, from Sunningdale to the Good Friday Agreement

Interviews by Graham Spencer

Manchester University Press

Published by Manchester University Press
Altrincham Street, Manchester M1 7JA
www.manchesteruniversitypress.co.uk

British Library Cataloguing-in-Publication Data
A catalogue record for this book is available from the British Library

ISBN 978 1 7849 9418 1 hardback
ISBN 978 1 5261 4916 9 paperback

First published 2020

Typeset by Servis Filmsetting Ltd, Stockport, Cheshire
Printed in Great Britain by TJ International Ltd, Padstow

In memory of Dermot Gallagher

Contents

Notes on interviewees

SEAN DONLON was Ambassador to the United States (US) from 1978 until 1984 before becoming Secretary General of the Department of Foreign Affairs. He was later Special Adviser to the Taoiseach, John Bruton, before becoming Executive Vice President of the aviation company GPA and a non-executive director of companies in the insurance and aviation financing sectors. Sean was Chancellor of the University of Limerick from 2002 to 2008 and more recently represented Ireland, Denmark, Lithuania and Kosovo as an Executive Director on the Board of the European Bank for Reconstruction and Development in London. He is Chair of the Press Council of Ireland.

NOEL DORR is a retired Irish diplomat. He served as permanent representative to the United Nations (UN) and Irish representative on the Security Council (from 1981 to 1982), Irish Ambassador in London, and Secretary General of the Department of Foreign Affairs. He represented Ireland on the official-level working groups that drafted the European Union (EU) treaties of Amsterdam and Nice. He has written books on Ireland and the United Nations. His most recent book, *Sunningdale: The Search for Peace in Northern Ireland*, was published by the Royal Irish Academy, Dublin, in November 2017. He is a member of the Royal Irish Academy and has an honorary doctorate from the National University of Ireland, Galway.

DERMOT GALLAGHER was one of the Irish Government's negotiating team at Sunningdale in 1973 before working in San Francisco, at the UN headquarters in New York and in London. In the early 1980s he was seconded to Brussels as Deputy Chef De Cabinet with the European Commission and was later appointed as Ambassador to Nigeria. He became Irish envoy to Washington from 1991 to 1997 and was then Secretary General in the Department of the Taoiseach until 2001, when he became Secretary General of the Department of Foreign Affairs. He retired as

Secretary General in 2009 and was nominated as Chairman of the Garda Siochana Ombudsman Commission. He was also appointed Chairman of University College Dublin Governing Authority.

MICHAEL LILLIS joined the Irish Department of External Affairs in 1966. As Counsellor at the Irish Embassy, Washington, DC from 1976 to 1979, he was involved with John Hume in establishing the 'Four Horsemen' lobby (Speaker O'Neill, Senators Kennedy and Moynihan and Hugh Carey, Governor of New York) who inspired the President Carter Initiative on Northern Ireland of August 1977, the first position by a US President independent of the UK Government. As Diplomatic Adviser to the Taoiseach 1982 and negotiator of the Anglo-Irish Agreement with the UK (Mrs Thatcher's) Government from 1983 to 1985, he was also the first-ever Dublin Government official to be permanently based in Belfast, Northern Ireland (from 1985 to 1987) as first Irish Joint Secretary under the Anglo-Irish Agreement.

DR MARTIN MANSERGH, a former diplomat, was Northern Ireland political advisor to three Taoisigh: Charles Haughey, Albert Reynolds and Bertie Ahern. In the early stages of the peace process he acted as back-channel to the republican movement. He contributed to the negotiation of the Downing Street Declaration and the Good Friday Agreement, particularly the constitutional accommodation. He was subsequently an elected Senator, TD (Member of the Dail) and Minister of State.

DAITHI O'CEALLAIGH joined the Department of Foreign Affairs in 1973. He served in Moscow, London, Belfast, New York, Helsinki and Geneva as well as in headquarters in Dublin. He spent six years as Ambassador in London, from 2001 to 2007, before retiring in 2009. Since then he has been Director General of the Irish Institute for International and European Affairs, from 2010 to 2013, and Chairman of the Press Council of Ireland, from 2010 to 2016.

TIM O'CONNOR is a former senior Irish diplomat and former Secretary General (Chief of Staff) to the President of Ireland. He worked with the Irish Department of Foreign Affairs from 1979 to 2007 and was a senior official of the Irish Government negotiating team in the talks that led to the Good Friday Agreement in 1998. Thereafter he was the lead negotiator in the talks to identify and establish the cross-border bodies provided for in the Agreement. From 1999 to 2005 he was the Inaugural Southern Joint Secretary of the North–South Ministerial Council, the institution created by the Good Friday Agreement to oversee cross-border co-operation on the island of Ireland. He was Consul General of Ireland from 2005 to 2007, and from 2007 to his retirement from civil service in 2010 he was Secretary General to the President of Ireland. In 2018 he was appointed by the Irish Government to be its representative on the Independent Reporting Commission, whose mission is reporting on efforts to end paramilitarism in Northern Ireland.

SEAN O HUIGINN worked as a career diplomat in the Irish Foreign Ministry between 1968 and 2009, serving successively as Consul General in New York and as Ambassador in Saudi Arabia, Copenhagen, Washington, Berlin and Rome. He worked directly on Northern Ireland issues as Counsellor at headquarters in the late 1970s, and as Irish Joint Secretary of the British–Irish Intergovernmental Conference (from 1987 to 1990). He was deeply involved with the peace process as Head of the Anglo-Irish Division of the Department of Foreign Affairs (from 1992 to 1997) and as Ambassador to Washington (from 1997 to 2002).

Acknowledgements

This book would not exist without the patience and help of those interviewed. I want to thank each individual for accommodating my persistent and, no doubt, annoying requests for interviews and for the candid and open way in which each volunteered information and recollections about efforts to achieve a peace settlement in Northern Ireland. Each person was interviewed at least three times before their testimony was edited down into one single interview. Apart from the interviewees I want to thank Aaron Edwards, Lincoln Geraghty, John Grieve, Sue Harper, Chris Hudson, Jim Kenny, Chris Maccabe, Seamus Mallon, Jim McAuley, Connal Parr, Kevin Spencer, Pamela Spencer, Pip Sutton, David Trimble and particularly Lynn Evans. The book, though, is dedicated to Dermot Gallagher, who died in 2017.

Brief chronology of the Troubles and origins of the peace process

February 1967	Formation of the Northern Ireland Civil Rights Association.
October 1968	The Derry Civil Rights March.
August 1969	Arrival of British troops in Northern Ireland.
August 1971	The introduction of internment.
January 1972	Bloody Sunday.
March 1972	Introduction of direct rule.
December 1973	Sunningdale Agreement.
May 1974	Ulster Workers' Council strike.
December 1974	Provisional IRA (PIRA) declares a ceasefire to conduct talks with British Government.
May 1981	Republican Bobby Sands dies on hunger strike. Nine other republicans die.
October 1981	Hunger strikes come to an end.
June 1983	Sinn Fein obtains 13.4 per cent of the vote in Northern Ireland.
1985	Anglo-Irish Agreement.
November 1987	PIRA kills eleven people and injures many more at a Remembrance Sunday service in Enniskillen.
January 1988	Social Democratic and Labour Party (SDLP) leader John Hume meets Sinn Fein leader Gerry Adams.
October 1988	British Government imposes broadcasting ban on Sinn Fein and other groups linked to paramilitaries.
March 1989	Gerry Adams comments on the need for a 'non-armed political movement to work for self-determination'.
November 1989	Northern Ireland Secretary Peter Brooke states that the PIRA cannot be militarily defeated and that talks could follow an end to violence.

November 1990	Peter Brooke states that the UK has 'no selfish strategic or economic interest' in Northern Ireland. Brooke goes on to say that 'It is not the aspiration to a sovereign, united Ireland against which we set our face, but its violent expression.'
March 1991	Talks begin, chaired by Peter Brooke. Talks end when the Intergovernmental Conference, which emerged from the Anglo-Irish Agreement, is resumed. The talks focus on Strand One only and the process of talks is constructed along the lines of three strands: relations in Northern Ireland, relations between Northern Ireland and the Republic of Ireland and relations between Dublin and London.
February 1992	Sinn Fein publishes the document Towards a Lasting Peace in Ireland, setting out a political peace strategy.
May 1992	Strand Two talks chaired by Patrick Mayhew on North–South relations are launched in Dublin and last until November. The Ulster Unionist Party attends but the Democratic Unionist Party does not.
April 1993	John Hume and Gerry Adams make a joint statement about Irish people as a whole requiring a right to self-determination. The statement is made after Gerry Adams is seen visiting the home of John Hume in Derry.
October 1993	Ten people are killed when a PIRA bomb explodes in a fish shop on the loyalist Shankill Road.
November 1993	Secret communications between the PIRA and London are revealed.
December 1993	Downing Street Declaration is released stating that Irish unity would require 'double consent' support of majorities in both parts of Ireland and that no constitutional change would occur without the consent of the majority of the people in Northern Ireland.
January 1994	President Clinton agrees a visa for Gerry Adams to visit the United States.
June 1994	Loyalists kill six Catholic men at a bar in Loughinisland, Co. Down.
August 1994	The PIRA announces 'a complete cessation of military activities'.
September 1994	The British Government lifts the broadcasting ban on Sinn Fein.

October 1994	The Combined Loyalist Command (an umbrella body for the Ulster Volunteer Force, the Red Hand Commando and the Ulster Defence Association) announces a ceasefire.
February 1995	British and Irish Governments release the Frameworks Document.
March 1995	Northern Ireland Secretary Patrick Mayhew reveals a three-point plan to try to remove PIRA weapons in advance of talks, making decommissioning a key condition for reaching agreement.
May 1995	Sinn Fein meets British Government Minister Michael Ancram after exploratory dialogue with senior officials.
July 1995	Drumcree parade becomes flashpoint of the marching season after members of the Orange Order are prevented from marching through a nationalist area.
November 1995	President Clinton visits Northern Ireland.
January 1996	The Mitchell Report is published. It canvasses for elections to roundtable talks and stresses a commitment to non-violence as a basis for participation.
February 1996	The PIRA ends its ceasefire with a bomb in Canary Wharf, London, killing two. Sinn Fein is excluded from talks.
May 1996	Elections take place to decide participants at talks. Sinn Fein gets 15.5 per cent of the votes but does not take part, having not made the necessary commitment to non-violence. The PIRA ceasefire is not renewed. Talks take place in Castle Buildings, Belfast and are chaired by Senator George Mitchell.
June 1996	The PIRA plants a bomb in Manchester city centre.
July 1996	Drumcree creates a stand-off, but police allow marchers to complete the route. This is followed by major rioting.
April 1997	The PIRA creates hoax bomb alerts in the UK, targeting motorways and the Grand National horse race.

Parties, organisations, offices and key documents

Parties

Alliance Party
Democratic Unionist Party (DUP)
Fianna Fail
Fine Gael
Northern Ireland Women's Coalition (NIWC)
Progressive Democrats
Progressive Unionist Party (PUP)
Sinn Fein
Social Democratic and Labour Party (SDLP)
Ulster Democratic Party (UDP)
Ulster Unionist Party (UUP)
UK Unionist Party (UKUP)

Organisations

Combined Loyalist Military Command (CLMC)
Independent International Commission on Decommissioning (IICD)
Independent Monitoring Commission (IMC)
Irish National Liberation Army (INLA)
Irish Republican Socialist Party (IRSP)
Police Service of Northern Ireland (PSNI)
Provisional IRA (PIRA and/or IRA)
Real IRA (RIRA)
Royal Ulster Constabulary (RUC)
Ulster Defence Association (UDA)
Ulster Defence Regiment (UDR)

Offices

Department of Foreign Affairs
Department of Justice and Equality
Department of the Taoiseach
Foreign and Commonwealth Office
Ministry of Defence
Northern Ireland Civil Service
Northern Ireland Office (NIO)

Key documents

Sunningdale Agreement 1973
Anglo-Irish Agreement 1985
Downing Street Declaration 1993
The Frameworks Document 1995
The Good Friday Agreement 1998

Introduction

This book of eight wide-ranging interviews conducted between 2014 and 2017 with Irish senior civil servants comprises the first of a two-part collection that explores political attempts to bring the Northern Ireland conflict to a close. Beginning with Sunningdale in 1973 and concluding with initial stages of the peace process (Volume II deals more substantively with the dynamics and activities of the peace process), the interviews seek to reveal the complexities and difficulties of trying to draw the political parties in Northern Ireland towards acceptance of a peace agreement and how the challenges that arose were faced. This first volume concentrates on early efforts to develop a political accommodation through Sunningdale and the Anglo-Irish Agreement of 1985 before then focussing on the formative years of the peace process that emerged through confidential dialogue in the late 1980s before taking on more formal political shape and momentum from the early 1990s.

The relevance of Sunningdale and the Anglo-Irish Agreement provides a context for understanding initial attempts at peace-building that, to an extent, created foundations for the peace process that followed and that stand as concerted attempts to end the conflict that emerged in the late 1960s and became commonly referred to as the Troubles. Unlike the peace process of the 1990s, Sunningdale and the Anglo-Irish Agreement did not engage the extremes of republicanism or loyalism. In the case of Sunningdale, work to forge a settlement was undertaken largely by the moderate strands of nationalism and unionism but undermined by the more extreme strands of loyalism and republicanism that were excluded from participation and refused to acknowledge any advantage in the possibilities of power-sharing. Further, by not confronting the destructive forces of extremism that were set on destroying Sunningdale, the British Government shared responsibility for its demise, and the potential for partnership government in Northern Ireland ended until the chance for greater co-operation between the British and Irish Governments arose in the 1980s. During that intervening period thousands were killed in the conflict and many more thousands injured. Sunningdale had opened the door to a possible accommodation but had fallen because of no real support from those outside the moderate parties of nationalism and unionism and because of disinterest on the part of the British Government in developing a power-sharing arrangement.

Potential for the involvement of Dublin in the affairs and workings of Northern Ireland at Sunningdale brought to the surface unionist fears about the possibility of Irish unity and British inability to decisively counter or assuage those fears (Bloomfield 1994; Currie 2004: 225–281; Devlin 1993: 172–290; Hennessey 2015; Kerr 2011; McDaid 2015). But a backlash from the more fundamentalist strands of unionism (Rees 1985: 90–91) was further compounded by a change in British Government from Conservative to Labour in 1974. Then, incoming Labour Prime Minister Harold Wilson added to the difficulties by mooting a possible withdrawal from Northern Ireland, which served only to exacerbate unionist panic about possible British treachery and an end to the Union (Craig 2010: 182). Hindered as it was by a range of electoral, legal and political factors, along with differing interpretations between the British and Irish Governments about core principles such as 'consent', the collapse of Sunningdale nevertheless stood as a marker for later peace efforts by highlighting the need for a joint Dublin and London approach to bring about stable government within Northern Ireland based on equality and partnership (Dorr 2017: 379–392).

The internal turmoil of Northern Ireland, made worse by a loyalist workers' strike in 1974 designed to bring Sunningdale down (Anderson 1994), along with the inability of the British and, to a lesser extent, the Irish Governments to defend the initiative by acting against the excesses of such resistance, effectively ended efforts to confront the Northern Ireland problem until Dublin and London began tentative re-engagement in the early 1980s, becoming involved in dialogue and negotiations that led to the Anglo-Irish Agreement in 1985 (Aughey 2011; FitzGerald 1991: 494–575; Lillis and Goodall 2010; Moore 2015: 298–342; Owen 1994; Spencer 2015a: 33–54). The situation in Northern Ireland in the intervening period since Sunningdale had worsened, with nationalist anger at the death of republican hunger strikers in 1981 galvanising growing republican demands for retaliatory action against the British. At the same time, and seeking to capitalise on support for the Provisional IRA, Sinn Fein tested the political waters by successfully getting iconic republican Bobby Sands elected as an MP in March 1981, two months before his death from starvation in protest against British criminalisation of republican prisoners.

Fears in Dublin that the political growth of Sinn Fein would legitimise violence and de-legitimise the democratic process found consistency with fears in London that a more confident and better-organised Provisional IRA would present a growing security threat. This stimulated British and Irish thinking about how to resist both possible outcomes (something which, for the British, was made real by the Brighton bomb of October 1984, when the Provisionals killed five at a Conservative Party conference, narrowly missing Margaret Thatcher, whom many republicans blamed for the deaths of the hunger strikers). Against this background, and in an attempt to confront the growing threat of militant republicanism, Thatcher committed to a process of dialogue and negotiation between her senior officials and Irish officials, out of which Dublin acquired a 'consultative' role in the affairs of Northern Ireland.

Unionist resistance to the Anglo-Irish Agreement and its perceived influence in expanding Dublin's involvement in Northern Ireland was less successful than Sunningdale, due to the Agreement's having been directly negotiated between the two Governments. Further, authority for the Agreement, as a binding international treaty, was imparted over and above the objections of a hostile unionist population. Ironically, the British would later encourage the unionists to become involved in negotiations to address the potentially corrosive impact of the Agreement and this would be used to draw them into the peace process that developed.

Clearly, there are evident dangers in reading Sunningdale and the Anglo-Irish Agreement as part of some chronology that organically morphed into a peace process, but we should not assume that these two moments were without influence. They offered principles and stood as markers and structures that would inform later attempts to reach a settlement. The following chapters bring into focus the problems of trying to reach an accommodation without involving the protagonists of conflict, and highlight tensions and contestations between the two Governments on the extent of Irish participation in Northern Ireland. They address how the prospect of an internal settlement facilitated by the moderates in Northern Ireland was then followed by a bilateral process of negotiation by the British and Irish Governments that largely excluded those moderates, before a process of inclusivity based on participation by the two Governments and all the Northern Ireland political parties together was acknowledged as the more favourable approach to making peace.

As with a comparative study on British official perceptions and encounters in the peace process (Spencer 2015a), this book is not concerned with the long and complex history that has defined the contours of political tension and violence in Ireland and about which many fine studies already exist (Bew 2007; Bourke and McBride 2016; Bowyer Bell 1993; Coogan 1995; English 2006; Fanning 2013; Ferriter 2015; Foster 1988; Hennessey 1997; Jackson 2003; O'Malley 1997; Patterson 2006; Townshend 2013; Walsh, 2015). Moreover, although the testimony here may inform historical narratives, the emphasis is less on the dynamics of Irish identity and Anglo-Irish relations and more on the practicalities and activities of peace-making.

These days the peace process in Northern Ireland seems to have become a template for conflict transformation and resolution. It suggests a map by which to stop violence, based on advancing democratic structures as an alternative to military ones. As such, this offers interest for those who might similarly wish to understand the actions of ending conflict as a mapping or cartographic exercise. However, in this case such an outlook risks ignoring the circumstances, conditions and efforts that preceded the peace process (as well as downplaying how conflicts are conditioned and influenced by differing and indeed shifting social and political expectations). For those inclined to think the trajectory of the peace process through a cartographic perspective that uses historical chronology to frame explanation of moments and developments there arises a likely tendency to miss the creativity, imagination and application needed to end conflict that hinges on the unexpected, the spontaneous, the peripheral and the psychological. These interviews are intended to highlight such dynamics and so to depict history more as an expression of personal activity and relations than of grand governmental positions or matters of ideological conviction (both of which, I admit, are not without importance).

A successful peace process relies on eradicating violence as a legitimate means by which to achieve political goals, but even here understanding that process ostensibly in terms of practical and political steps misses the power of psychological attachment, building trust, interpersonal relationships and informal conversation, and on this more analysis is needed. Admittedly, enquiry about such areas presents a trickier and perhaps less productive terrain of investigation for the political scientist or historian, but it is essential in helping us to understand how a commitment to violence can change to become a commitment to non-violence. Bringing a conflict to an end (if indeed an end is what it is) requires dealing with the messier, less predictable aspects of human interaction and the responses that emerge from such interaction. The interviews in this book bring to light the difficulties of managing such outcomes.

At the broader political level, it is clear that the transition within violent groups towards recognising the value of negotiations to support power-sharing and democratic renewal (Spencer 2008; 2010; 2015b; Taylor 1997, 1999) was, for both Governments, about trying to turn exclusive political differences into a struggle over inclusive political differences (an approach very much informed by the thinking and activities of SDLP leader John Hume (Hume 1979; 1996: 79–144)). The formal architecture to facilitate this was a three-stranded framework of interlocking mechanisms designed to bind relations between the protagonists closer together. Through the formation of new institutions in Northern Ireland, a series of North–South arrangements between Northern Ireland and the Republic and tighter collaboration between Dublin and London, a context for decision-making was created that enabled all political parties to maintain cultural and national allegiances in relation to social and political ambition. The possibilities of the peace process, in its architecture and purpose, were contested as a matter of democratic principle and not, as had previously been the case, as a matter of privilege and power extended by one community over another, with violence being used to oppose that imbalance. Interdependence achieved through mechanisms to ensure power-sharing provided the necessary framework for negotiations and the Good Friday Agreement that resulted in 1998.

Irish influence in developing the peace process can be traced to Charles Haughey's administration in the 1980s and the idea that the Northern Ireland problem could only realistically be resolved through a 'totality of relationships' (Kelly 2016: 316–355). However, the formative momentum for driving a peace process came later from Albert Reynolds, who, during his role as Taoiseach from February 1992 until November 1994, based his 'formula for peace' (Duignan 1996: 103) less on the formal nature of negotiations and more on an unconstrained motivational impetus to drive a 'peace initiative' using self-determination and consent as core components (Reynolds 2009: 204).

The role of the British in contributing to this process took hold under John Major's Government and benefited from the creative efforts of Peter Brooke, who, as Secretary of State, publicly stated in November 1989 that the British Government would be 'flexible and imaginative' if the IRA were to end violence (Bew and Gillespie 1999: 229), before following a year later with the comment made at a local constituency event that the British had 'no selfish strategic or economic interest' in Northern Ireland and would not stand in the way of a unified Ireland if there was majority consent for this (Bew and Gillespie 1999: 242). The respect between Major and Reynolds proved important for melding a joint approach, and the memoirs of both men are testimony to the mutual regard that came about because of this (Major 1999; Reynolds 2009). There might be some comparison to be made here with the later relationship of Ahern and Blair, which was also highly respectful, close and convergent, but the Reynolds–Major partnership never had the longevity or dynamism that the Ahern and Blair relationship had and was more restrained, at least for Major, by internal political matters of concern which curtailed his ability to move decisively or as quickly as Reynolds wanted. That said, the Major–Reynolds relationship paved the way for a formal political process, and the possibilities and aspirations of that collaboration took form in the Downing Street Declaration released by them in December 1993.

That text reiterated the importance of the 'totality of relationships', as articulated by Haughey, with the British committing to 'encourage, facilitate and enable' a settlement 'through a process of dialogue and co-operation based on full respect for the rights and identities of both traditions of Ireland', and stipulated that any agreement might 'take the form of agreed structures for Ireland as a whole, including a united Ireland achieved by peaceful means' underscored by self-determination, consent and democratic participation (Bew and Gillespie 1999: 282–285). A Forum for Peace and Reconciliation was proposed in the Declaration, to take effect in Dublin (and was officially opened in October 1994), so that parties could consult about what a political accommodation might look like and get used to the cut-and-thrust of political exchange in a new power-sharing environment; but its main function was to provide an opportunity for republicans to acclimatise to the expectations and forces of political debate and negotiation that were to follow. The Declaration further established that the British would not be 'persuaders' for a unified Ireland as many nationalists and republicans wanted, but 'facilitators' for an 'agreed' Ireland.

After the Downing Street Declaration a succession of moves took place, including involvement by the United States, granting Gerry Adams and senior republican Joe Cahill visas to enter the United States to sell the benefits of the peace process; followed by PIRA and loyalist ceasefires in August 1994 and October 1994, respectively. Then the Frameworks Document released by the British and Irish Governments in 1995, setting out the parameters and responsibilities for negotiations, led to a number of meetings between republicans and loyalists, with senior British and Irish officials, to try to assess possible commitment to a negotiations process and adherence to core principles as established in the Downing Street Declaration and Frameworks Document. President Clinton visited Northern Ireland in November 1995 to offer American blessing to the process and, under the chairmanship of Senator George Mitchell, talks took place based on exclusively peaceful participation. What followed, however, were a series of tensions and acts of low-level violence, culminating in the Canary Wharf bomb of February 1996 when the PIRA ended its ceasefire in objection to what it saw as foot-dragging on the part of the British (republicans needed to see tangible and decisive progress in talks, and quickly, if support for the peace process was to continue and morale was not to decline). Negotiations then effectively stalled until Tony Blair was elected as British Prime Minister in May 1997. At that point, and along with newly elected Irish Taoiseach Bertie Ahern, a fresh impetus came into play that led to the Good Friday Agreement of 1998.

The journey from Sunningdale, through the Anglo-Irish Agreement to the start of the peace process is addressed through the eight extended interviews in this book. In Chapter 1 Sean Donlon comments on his involvement and experience at the time of Sunningdale and highlights how missed opportunities led to a further twenty-five years of violence that made political accommodation harder to achieve. Donlon talks of the personalities and conversations that informed the environment at that time, offering detail on his relationship with John Hume, as well as on Irish attempts to engage more productively with nationalists and unionists in Northern Ireland in order to make power-sharing work. Donlon also positions Sunningdale in relation to later efforts to end conflict and presents a picture of missed opportunities, intransigence, lack of will, British apathy and Irish indifference, all of which were considerations to be taken into account in the later Anglo-Irish Agreement negotiations and the peace process itself.

Noel Dorr also talks about Sunningdale and the path to the Anglo-Irish Agreement in Chapter 2, and how key concepts that informed negotiations established a foundation for accommodation that influenced later attempts to build peace. Dorr reflects on how an 'Irish dimension' was created to make the Irish integral to resolving conflict and how building tighter relations was essential to giving the Irish a greater role in the affairs of Northern Ireland. How that involvement was developed and how this created a momentum for engagement that led eventually to the Good Friday Agreement of 1998 informs Dorr's commentary, which offers a pathway from Sunningdale to the Anglo-Irish Agreement and highlights the importance of concepts and frameworks in the thinking and formation of governmental strategy.

In Chapter 3 Michael Lillis presents a comprehensive picture of the strategy and tactics used to bring about the Anglo-Irish Agreement. Lillis points toward the significance of a small and tight team used to forge successful relations and how his productive relationship with British civil servants David Goodall and Robert Armstrong proved critical in bringing negotiations to a positive conclusion. Lillis also talks about the importance of trust and intensity as drivers in a negotiating situation, and reaching an accommodation in a process that British Prime Minister Margaret Thatcher was instinctively opposed to but nevertheless supported. Lillis then elaborates on meeting Sinn Fein leader Gerry Adams some three years after the Agreement, when Adams was contemplating what challenges republicans would have to deal with, were they to engage with the British in a negotiating process.

Chapter 4 summarises what happened before and after the Anglo-Irish Agreement and expands on the difficulties experienced by the Irish in trying to monitor developments and civil rights violations in Northern Ireland. Daithi O'Ceallaigh paints a picture of carrying out this work prior to the Anglo-Irish Agreement in a hostile environment of unionist resistance, and of later being made largely unwelcome by Northern Irish civil servants who remained opposed to the Anglo-Irish Agreement. Setting the later peace process in a context where closer involvement in the affairs of Northern Ireland took place against a backdrop of considerable unionist recalcitrance, O'Ceallaigh then goes on to talk about how his involvement as Irish Ambassador in London during later stages of the peace process required dealing with tricky issues such as policing and how such issues were managed to support power-sharing. His interview is a personal account of, and reflection on, the difficulties experienced in moving from the violence of the early 1980s into a peace process and then bringing that process to a successful conclusion. His interview provides a narrative about the importance of deepening relations and trust with the British as well as the necessity of momentum for facilitating closeness with others.

In Chapter 5 Sean O hUiginn, the key Irish architect of the Downing Street Declaration of 1993, talks about the foundations of the peace process and the need to understand competing psychologies as integral to the tensions and dynamics of progress. O hUiginn expands on the conceptual areas of the Downing Street Declaration and the importance of creating language to converge zones of difference. He comments on the complexity of key principles and the Downing Street Declaration as an enticement for entry into talks, and ruminates on the essence and centrality of text as a motivating force for movement and engagement. O hUiginn also explains how early problems in the peace process, such as the British decision to impose decommissioning as a precondition for republican entry into substantive negotiations and the Canary Wharf bomb of 1996, which ended the PIRA ceasefire of 1994, were received and dealt with. This wide-ranging interview moves from detail and conceptualisation in the peace process to the practicalities and outworking of that detail and conceptualisation, and adapting to changes and shifts as they occur. Ultimately the interview highlights the value of pragmatism, creativity and strategic thinking and how each proved central to the process and progress of negotiations.

Martin Mansergh played a central role as back-channel contact with republicans prior to their formal involvement in negotiations, and his interview in Chapter 6 provides detail on meetings with republicans to assess the possibility, first, of committing to a peace process, and second, of adhering to the expectations of non-violence as the basis of that commitment. Here Mansergh comments on his secret meetings with republicans at the behest of Charles Haughey in 1988 and elaborates on his long engagement with leaders such as Adams and McGuinness, as well as talking about personality differences, reading republican messages and explaining the tendencies of republican thinking to appreciate respective concerns and motivations.

The Forum for Peace and Reconciliation set up as part of the Downing Street Declaration and launched in Dublin in October 1994 was used to try to provide an opportunity for those who had little knowledge of multi-party negotiation to get a sense of what such engagement might feel like and what expectations and compromises might be expected in such an expansive process. In Chapter 7 Tim O'Connor talks about the Forum (which was suspended and never resurrected after the Canary Wharf bomb of 1996) and his observations of Sinn Fein, who were using the Forum to adjust to the practicalities of multi-party negotiation (even though the unionist parties, apart from the Alliance Party, abstained from attending) and who used this opportunity in turn learn to hone their message and communicate their position more effectively when it came to formal roundtable interaction. O'Connor also comments on the expectations and pressures of negotiation and dealing with adversaries to reach compromise. He argues that the need to reach a 'sufficient consensus', not just internally but with the other negotiating teams, is essential for progress and creating trust. He also highlights the value of building networks and the importance of design if internal disputations are to be successfully constrained and overcome.

In Chapter 8, the final chapter of this book, Dermot Gallagher reflects on how dialogue was conducted and influenced and describes the dynamics that shaped and informed the journey towards political agreement in 1998. Gallagher also talks about the role of the United States under Clinton and the pressure to try to get Clinton to grant Gerry Adams a visa so that the advantages of a peace process could be sold to the republican base there. The symbolism of such a move also meant that Sinn Fein could be presented as a serious political force on the international stage, and so a credible player in the process. Gallagher comments on the significance of developing trust in order to build confidence and expands on the tensions between pragmatism and principle that influenced the dynamic of negotiations. Gallagher talks broadly about the challenges of the peace process and how the main intention was not only to draw republicans into the political arena (key though that was) but also to locate a diversity of competing political concerns within a framework of core principles and values.

Each chapter is a self-contained extended interview (although I prefer to call each a conversation) and each person was interviewed at least three times. Although the interviews seek to examine specific areas of expertise and experience there are a number of common points of interest which run through them all. Given that developing peace tends to be an iterative process, there should be no surprise that some repetition across the interviews is necessary to illustrate the collective approach adhered to. A range of areas such as text and context, formality and informality, momentum, space and leverage, symmetry, reciprocity, dissonance, language, symbolism, strategy, ambiguity, clarity, relationships, trust, patience and persistence emerge in the course of the interviews, reflecting the complexities and challenges of interaction. But with such specificities common points of interest frame each interview and provide the threads that link the interviews collectively: What were nationalists and republicans and unionists like to work with and how did they view the problems? What was the Irish relationship with the SDLP like and what differences were evident in how the British Government worked, as compared to the Irish Government? Were the Americans important? How was language used and adapted? How significant were documents and texts in comparison to dialogue and conversation? How does the relationship between principle and pragmatism work? How did creativity come into play, and how were unforeseen consequences and events managed? How important was it to avoid surprises? How necessary is reliance and resilience, and how do intensity and application change in relation to shifting circumstances? These are the kinds of questions that interested me and informed the approach to interviewing.

The truth revealed in the interview is not the truth of documentation, which can be conveniently contained and categorised by way of dates, choreography and the more precise nature of text itself, but relies on the more fluid interplay of experience and memory. In that sense, the interviews here are reflections on encounter and experience. No doubt there should be caution in merely accepting the 'experiential narrative' as any more reliable or authoritative an account than another source (English, quoted in Hopkins 2013: 66), but perhaps one way of further assessing the credibility of personal testimony is through interviewing a number of others about the same things and to consider responses not just individually, but in the light of the collective narrative that results. Although the interview fascinates because of its potential to elicit both personal (emotion) and institutional (policy and strategy) memory, the limitations of recollection and questions about the reliability of testimony are ever present. Yet, acknowledging that, as an important historical source the interview remains indispensable, and not only for uncovering what people did, why and how, but because the stories that emerge offer us 'truths, of the subjective and intersubjective kind' that cannot be found in the archive. Such stories can only be 'revealed in the manner of telling', and as inner dialogues of lived experience they reveal the encounter with the self as well as with others (Coetzee and Kurtz 2015: 63).

Invariably, interviews reveal two obvious lines of interpretation. One is where responses articulate what is remembered as important and the other is where responses seek to avoid talking about what is important by talking about something else. It is hard to see in the context of the interviews that follow where responses fall into the latter category. I cannot remember one occasion where the interviewees refused to answer a question, answered by talking about something else or asked for questions in advance. Inevitably, too, because respondents did not know the questions in advance there was far less chance (especially in the spontaneity of the moment) for them to contrive a response which acted as an avoidance of the question asked. Additionally, the value of some repetition in questioning across a range of players, as here, is an insurance against individual attempts to use the interview to construct a favourable and distorted version of events for self-promotion. Since the responses exist as a public record it is unlikely that any individual would get away for very long with fabrication or misrepresentation. Because of that I take the responses of all those interviewed in this book to be accurate, sincere and honest recollections. Any differences should not be seen as making any one account more or less credible or valid than another, but as part of the fabric of experience that informs relationships and different ways of recalling those relationships.

The interview is a process of both assumption and discovery. The question assumes that because something happened other things must have happened too; but, because of not knowing what those other things are, the interview offers an opening to a new understanding, and so a possibility of greater reflection. The inference of the question is therefore an enticement to find out more about relations and intentions which the archive alone is unlikely to bring to light. The interview is a human interaction, an engagement and a tension between the known and the unknown, the expected and the unexpected, the predictable and the unpredictable, the interviewer and the interviewee.

Arguably, the civil servant is less concerned with the potential pitfalls of the question than is the politician, who tends to see a question more as a trap that can have damaging consequences if not handled properly. The question for the politician is an opportunity to not only stay on message but to repeat, reinforce and make more convincing that message. Once the politician leaves office, however, he or she is invariably more candid about what really happened, as so many political memoirs reveal. Although politicians need to know the detail of the situation they are involved in, it is also apparent that at the highest levels they should have a motivational aim which strives to be cross-cutting in appeal across oppositional constituencies and where the specificities of process support that imperative. The civil servant knows that too, and, although not suspect to the publicity fallout that politicians are, must still understand the aims of the strategy being pursued and provide intelligence, analysis and input which is focussed on serving that end.

Most of those interviewed here were involved over decades in the search to bring conflict to a close. Their testimony merits attention over that span of time. In all cases I am intrigued to know how respondents saw moments and experiences in relation to events as they unfolded and how they dealt with each in terms of an overall strategy. But what the interviews also reveal is the importance of teamwork and the collective approach. The effectiveness of negotiations and the success of a settlement is surely an outcome of this common purpose and the intensity of engagement that arises because of it. Above all, the peace process was a process of human relations. It was about individuals and groups. It was about the one and the many. This book is concerned with the interplay of such forces and what happens in the spaces created by them. The interviews that follow are individual *and* collective accounts of that reality.

A note on style

While some respondents preferred to talk about the Provisional IRA, others opted to talk about the Provisionals, or the PIRA. This is the same organisation. Any reference to other strands of republicanism will be identified as such. Also, the Frameworks for the Future text published in 1995, although consisting of two parts and called the Framework Documents, is more commonly referred to as the Frameworks Document and that will be the title used throughout this book.

References

Anderson, D. (1994) *14 May Days*, Dublin: Gill and Macmillan.

Aughey, A. (2011) *The Anglo-Irish Agreement: Rethinking Its Legacy*, Manchester: Manchester University Press.

Bew, P. (2007) *Ireland: The Politics of Enmity 1789–2006*, Oxford: Oxford University Press.

Bew, P. and Gillespie, G. (1999) *Northern Ireland: A Chronology of the Troubles*, Dublin: Gill and Macmillan.

Bloomfield, K. (1994) *Stormont in Crisis*, Belfast: The Blackstaff Press.

Bourke, R. and McBride, I. (2016) *The Princeton History of Modern Ireland*, Princeton: Princeton University Press.

Bowyer Bell, J. (1993) *The Irish Troubles*, New York: St Martin's Press.

Coetzee, J. M. and Kurtz, A. (2015) *The Good Story*, London: Harvill Secker.

Coogan, T. P. (1995) *The Troubles*, London: Hutchinson.

Craig, A. (2010) *Crisis of Confidence*, Dublin: Irish Academic Press.

Currie, A. (2004) *All Hell Will Break Loose*, Dublin: The O'Brien Press.

Devlin, P. (1993) *Straight Left*, Belfast: The Blackstaff Press.

Dorr, N. (2017) *The Search for Peace in Northern Ireland*, Dublin: Royal Irish Academy.

Duignan, S. (1996) *One Spin on the Merry-Go-Round*, Dublin: Blackwater Press.

English, R. (2006) *Irish Freedom*, Basingstoke: Macmillan.

Fanning, R. (2013) *Fatal Path*, London: Faber and Faber.

Ferriter, D. (2015) *A Nation and Not a Rabble*, London: Profile Books.

FitzGerald, G. (1991) *All in a Life: An Autobiography*, Dublin: Gill and Macmillan.

Foster, R. (1988) *Modern Ireland 1600–1972*, London: Allen Lane.

Hennessey, T. (1997) *A History of Northern Ireland 1920–1996*, Basingstoke: Macmillan.

Hennessey, T. (2015) *The First Northern Ireland Peace Process*, Basingstoke: Palgrave.

Hopkins, S. (2013) *The Politics of Memoir and the Northern Ireland Conflict*, Manchester: Manchester University Press.

Hume, J. (1979) 'The Irish Question: A British Problem', *Foreign Affairs* 58(2): 300–313.

Hume, J. (1996) *John Hume: Personal Views*, Dublin: Roberts Rinehart Publishers.

Jackson, A. (2003) *Home Rule*, Oxford: Oxford University Press.

Kelly, S. (2016) *'A Failed Political Entity'*, Newbridge/Co. Kildare: Merrion Press.

Kerr, M. (2011) *The Destructors*, Dublin: Irish Academic Press.

Lillis, M. and Goodall, D. (2010) 'Edging Towards Peace', Issue 16, *Dublin Review of Books*.

Major, J. (1999) *John Major: The Autobiography*, London: Harper Collins.

McDaid, S. (2016) *Template for Peace: Northern Ireland 1972–75*, Manchester: Manchester University Press.
Moore, C. (2015) *Margaret Thatcher, Volume Two: Everything She Wants*, London: Allen Lane.
Mowlam, M. (2002) *Momentum*, London: Hodder and Stoughton.
O'Malley, P. (1997) *The Uncivil Wars*, Boston: Beacon Press.
Owen, A. E. (1994) *The Anglo-Irish Agreement*, Cardiff: University of Wales Press.
Patterson, H. (2006) *Ireland since 1939*, Dublin: Penguin Ireland.
Rees, M. (1985) *Northern Ireland*, London: Methuen.
Reynolds, A. (2009) *Albert Reynolds: My Autobiography*, London: Transworld Ireland.
Spencer, G. (2008) *The State of Loyalism in Northern Ireland*, Basingstoke: Palgrave.
Spencer, G. (2010) 'Managing a peace process: an interview with Jonathan Powell', *Irish Political Studies* 25(3): 437–455.
Spencer, G. (2015a) *The British and Peace in Northern Ireland*, Cambridge: Cambridge University Press.
Spencer, G. (2015b) *From Armed Struggle to Political Struggle: Republican Tradition and Transformation in Northern Ireland*, London: Bloomsbury.
Taylor, P. (1997) *Provos*, London: Bloomsbury.
Taylor, P. (1999) *Loyalists*, London: Bloomsbury.
Townshend, C. (2013) *The Republic*, London: Allen Lane.
Walsh, M. (2015) *Bitter Freedom*, London: Faber and Faber.

1

Sunningdale and the problem of power-sharing: an interview with Sean Donlon

Graham Spencer: *Can you give me some background on your involvement in Northern Ireland?*

Sean Donlon: When the Troubles started in late 1968 the Irish Government was not administratively structured in any way to deal with the situation. The older generation of politicians thought they knew it all themselves because they had been involved in the 1920s and since some of them came from Northern Ireland they didn't feel the need to have any professional Civil Service assistance. The Department of Foreign Affairs was essentially told it's not a foreign policy matter; Northern Ireland is part of the national territory therefore it is not appropriate for you to be involved in it. The fact that it was an Anglo-Irish matter, and therefore a foreign policy matter, did not seem to impinge very much, so there was no one in the Department of Foreign Affairs who was dealing with the situation in Northern Ireland. That is, until a middle-level councillor called Eamonn Gallagher, who was from Donegal, started spending regular weekends with his sister in Letterkenny. His sister happened to be friendly with a Derry family called the Desmonds who were very close to the Humes and through that connection Eamonn Gallagher met John Hume in August 1969 and began to do analytic reports which he gave to the Head of Foreign Affairs, Hugh McCann, who gave them to Paddy Hillery, the Minister, and Jack Lynch, the Taioseach. But it took about six months of Eamonn doing these weekend visits and reports before Jack Lynch decided it might be helpful to appoint him full time to the position, so in the spring in 1970 Eamonn became the first official of the Department of Foreign Affairs to be given an assignment relating to Northern Ireland.

I got involved in August 1971 when internment was introduced. I was happily in post in Boston, where I was Consul General, when I got a phone call from Foreign Affairs the morning internment was imposed asking me to return to Ireland and go to Northern Ireland and collect information relating to the circumstances in which internment was introduced. I had been chosen apparently because I had no family connections with Northern Ireland, and had indeed never been there, probably typical enough for a Southerner in those days of my generation. I rented a car in Dublin, drove to Belfast where the only appointment that had been made for me was to go to see Paddy Devlin on the Shore Road in Belfast, and Paddy would introduce me to other people who might be in a better position to help. As we now know the circumstances surrounding the introduction of internment were pretty vicious, with the use of torture, inhuman and degrading treatment, and through a network that I built up of solicitors, doctors, community groups and, particularly, priests I was able to assemble quite a bit of information which became the basis for the human rights case which the Irish Government launched in November 1971 against the British Government under the European Convention on Human Rights.

My network built up fairly quickly for one or two reasons. I had been a clerical student in Maynooth from 1958 to 1960 and in those days Maynooth was the national seminary for the whole island, where, by 1970–71, the ordination class was in virtually every part of Northern Ireland. I could knock on a presbytery door and if I didn't find somebody I knew from my Maynooth days my connection would be sufficiently well established to allow me immediate access. Very often the Irish parish priest and his curates were well plugged in to the community, so if I wanted information through reliable sources they were extremely helpful to me, and particularly people like Father Denis Faul in Dungannon, Father Raymond Murray in Armagh and Father Brian Brady in Belfast. The only instruction I had been given was not to have any contact with anybody who was involved in violence, so therefore I had no direct contact with the IRA. But I have no doubt the IRA were approached, particularly by Father Brian Brady, to ensure that they did not put any obstacle in the way of my work, and indeed to hope for a level of co-operation from the IRA prisoners and the IRA internees who had been lifted in August. I had no particular problem, but I had no political mandate to deal with the IRA either. My mandate in Northern Ireland was gradually extended as Eamonn Gallagher moved on to other things such as getting involved in Ireland's application to join the Common Market and then eventually becoming a Commissioner in Brussels. So from the spring of 1973 my mandate was extended basically to monitor and assess the political situation in Northern Ireland.

And at that point there was still no contact with the British?

Very little contact with the British other than for what might be called 'protest related matters', for example, Bloody Sunday, when we withdrew our Ambassador from London, and although there was contact on that sort of issue with the Foreign Office there was no dialogue in any serious sense. There was an attempt at dialogue in 1971 when Ted Heath was Prime Minister and the situation in Northern Ireland was bad. Jack Lynch had two meetings with Heath in September 1971. One was a bilateral meeting involving simply Dublin and London and the second was a trilateral meeting involving Brian Faulkner and some other people from the unionist side, but both of those meetings led nowhere and there was no follow-up. You then fast-forward, where the objective of Irish Government policy now became the abolition of Stormont because we had lost confidence in the ability the British had to reform it, so we felt it had to go. We were heavily influenced in that by our relationship with the SDLP, which had been formed. There had been informal associations between Devlin, Fitt, Currie, Hume, Cooper and O'Hanlon, who were the six original members of what became the SDLP, and the initial contact through Eamonn Gallagher. Jack Lynch came to the view they were a reliable interlocutor and I certainly continued that contact. I was in regular communication with all the leading SDLP people and I was reporting back to the Irish Government. My reports essentially summarised my conversations with individuals so that I could enable the political masters to make up their own mind based on what I was being told.

Where were the seeds sown? Was there a turning point when unionists started to become involved in talks with the SDLP, and what were the factors which led to the British getting involved in discussion with you?

It was when Stormont was prorogued in March of 1972. Having achieved that objective we then began a dialogue with the British. Initially it was Paddy Hillery dealing with Willie Whitelaw, and then that translated into conversations at official level between people like myself and British representatives in Laneside, which had been established in 1969 as a centre for London-based officials to monitor the situation in Northern Ireland. The British had a very professional approach. They had MI6-types, Foreign Office-types and security-types monitoring the situation and I suspect it was their information that led the British to conclude that there is no future in relying on Stormont. But there were lots of factors such as Bloody Sunday at the end of January, the failure of internment, which manifestly had led to massive recruitment to the IRA by people who would never have contemplated joining the IRA, the use of torture and what was euphemistically called 'interrogation in depth'. All of that led to the emergence of very significant hostility on the part of the nationalist community towards Britain.

When you first met British people and when you first met the unionists what was their attitude towards you? Where they hostile or did they recognise there had to be negotiations to try and achieve power-sharing?

First of all, I did not meet any unionists until the summer of 1973, when I began to meet British representatives in Northern Ireland, and it was actually quite comical. My personal relations with them were quite good, it was open and we traded information. I would arrive back in Dublin to find that the British Ambassador had gone to see the Minister for Foreign Affairs to object to my presence in Northern Ireland on the grounds that I was not accredited in the UK and I had no immunities, so therefore they could not guarantee my safety. I had discovered only in recent years, when I had chance to dig into records in Kew, that in 1972–73 the British regarded me as the Head of Irish Intelligence in Northern Ireland, which had the implication that my role was a security one. In essence, it was a political role with security as an element, but I had no security background. I had no training of any description and I certainly had no brief in relation to security matters other than in so far as security impacted on politics. I didn't know at the time who, if anyone, on the Irish Government side was involved in security matters, but it was probably someone from army intelligence. However, I don't think they had a very active presence in Northern Ireland. I had no contacts on the unionist side. That happened only when you had the British Green Paper and White Paper proposing power-sharing with an Irish dimension and then the Assembly elections. My closest contact became John Hume, who had been an approximate contemporary in Maynooth. I had met him in Boston when I was Counsellor-General when he came out in 1970 to talk to various people there. Certainly he was my primary contact among SDLP people and it was John who suggested to me that after the Assembly elections we needed to go for power-sharing talks with North–South institutions and that somebody from Dublin had better start talking to the unionists. John Hume set up my very first meeting with Brian Faulkner and, accompanied by Dermot Nally from the Taioseach's Office, we went to see him late September–early October 1973, just before Sunningdale.

So the decision by Faulkner and the unionists to get involved in power-sharing discussions essentially came through conversations between Hume and Faulkner?

Well it came initially because the British Government had laid it down as their recipe in the Green Paper, and then in the White Paper. Once Stormont was prorogued the British were very active in coming up with policies, and that is where people like Ken Bloomfield came into it.

What was the SDLP attitude towards the Irish Government? Did they expect you to do more for them or did they find you interfering? What were relations like?

I think relations were constructive. Each side recognised that it needed the other side. For an Irish Government to have a Northern Ireland policy at all it had to have the support of nationalism in Northern Ireland and, from the SDLP's perspective, to gain credibility in London and internationally, they had to have credibility with the Irish Government. There were times when Dublin's policy was not just influenced by the SDLP but was formed by the SDLP, and there were many occasions through the 1970s into the 1980s where, if you're looking for Irish Government policy, you basically take the SDLP's policy.

Were they talking even then about self-determination, consent and power-sharing?

Yes, the principles that Hume had set out as far back as 1964 in the *Irish Times* and which are framed in the SDLP constitution. Not exactly the words Hume had used in 1963–64, but their commitment to the principle of consent was key. The principle of power-sharing was also important, and somewhere down the list of objectives they also included the coming together of the people of Ireland. They never used the word 'reunification'. They always talked about the coming together of the people of Ireland, or the coming together of the communities in Northern Ireland and the people of both parts of Ireland. They were careful in their use of language. But the biggest single influence was two articles written by John Hume, published in the *Irish Times* in 1964, where he set out the principles that he thought would form the basis of an agreement. Consent was the big one, the accommodation of the two communities and agreed structures was the second one, and obviously no room for violence. One can certainly trace some of the language of Sunningdale back to Hume's articles in the *Irish Times*. One very important feature is that he never changed his position. You could say that was a negative and that he was inflexible, and although he certainly was on the principles he wasn't inflexible on the detail. The same principles that were in Sunningdale were in the Hume–Adams dialogues, the Downing Street Declaration and the Good Friday Agreement, and they came from Hume. In the *Irish Times* articles what he was saying posed a challenge to Irish Government policy, which at that time was sterile. It had nothing to show. What Hume did was open people's eyes to you've got to look at what our policy is and what it is achieving. He said the policy hasn't achieved anything so I am now putting an alternative policy. Hume's influence on FitzGerald was important. FitzGerald took his thinking on Northern Ireland from Hume, and although Hume can't take one hundred per cent credit for the formulation of that policy he can take one hundred per cent for selling it and having it implemented. It was first set out by a man called Donal Barrington way back in 1957–58, and that heavily influenced Hume. Barrington was a lawyer who became a Supreme Court judge and a judge of the European Court. He was one of the original thinkers of his generation.

Were the SDLP instrumental or central to the thinking of the Irish Government on these issues or was it more about what was coming from you to them?

I would go so far as to say that from 1970 onwards, and certainly from 1971, the Irish Government's policy was in effect made by Hume. Sometimes Hume would put a proposition to people in Dublin. I know of no situation where any Irish Government or any senior Irish politician in those years from, say, 1969–76 tried to influence Hume or didn't accept what he was saying.

What about Hume's relationship with Gerry Fitt, as he was leader? How did Hume become the central character?

Gerry Fitt, and I say this in a spirit of generosity, not otherwise, wasn't an intellectual. Gerry was a good grafter, particularly at Westminster. Don't forget he had been an MP from around 1966 to 1967. He knew how to work Westminster in a way that Hume did not, and in particular Gerry had very good relationships with the British Labour Party and people like Kevin McNamara, who had started off a campaign for democracy some time back in the 1960s. Gerry had his role, and the reason he was leader was because he was the only MP when the party was being founded, so it would have been invidious not to make him leader. But he and Hume fully understood their respective strengths and weaknesses. Gerry knew and accepted that Hume was the intellectual leader of the party. Sometimes there were tensions because there were times when Gerry Fitt, in particular, thought that Hume was too green.

Yet these people who came from the education sector tended not to write things down. How did things start to appear on paper and the nailing down of formal positions begin?

Going back to the formation of the SDLP, people in Dublin, including myself, were basically helping them to do things like draft their constitution, and in the summer of 1971, following the introduction of internment, the SDLP withdrew from the Northern Ireland Parliament and set up something called the Alternative Assembly of the Northern Irish people in Dungiven. It was people like me who drafted the constitution for the Alternative Assembly. I remember roping in a colleague who was Chief Clerk for our Dail to help me draft the rules of procedure, so anytime they needed, in those years, a bit of bureaucratisation or writing, that sort of thing was done essentially out of Dublin. However, the policy was clearly one that Hume had articulated.

Can you talk about when you first met the SDLP and how decisions were made about the core concerns and what the Irish would and would not do?

Well the SDLP in those days was six people, Fitt as leader, Hume as deputy leader, Austin Currie, Ivan Cooper, Paddy Devlin and Paddy O'Hanlon. That was the core group. It wasn't a cohesive group in terms of policy making. The thinking for that was done primarily by Hume, with some independent thinking from Austin Currie. The technique Hume developed was that he would take the group somewhere for a weekend, where basically he would sell his approach to the others. Sometimes they would nibble at the edges and get slight amendment, but essentially it was Hume's policy and they frequently met, in Dungannon and Toomebridge, but most often in Donegal, to work on this. Very little was put on paper because none of the original SDLP people had been accustomed to any form of bureaucracy, so I would normally attend at the venue where they were meeting but I would not attend the actual think-in session, which might last from ten in the morning to four in the afternoon. Usually there was a good dinner and a bit of drinking and a bit of a sing-song and I would participate in that and chat to the members of the party. I would get a fairly good picture of what it was that they had been discussing and what it was they had agreed. Hume knew that I was documenting that with a view to informing the Irish Government, and particularly the Minister for Foreign Affairs and the Taoiseach of the day, whether it was Jack Lynch, Paddy Hillery or, subsequently, Liam Cosgrave or Garret FitzGerald. The SDLP rarely documented anything. The best guide you would get to the development of their policy would be in Hume's speeches. The SDLP built up quite rapidly in the period before Sunningdale. There were elections in Northern Ireland in June of 1973 and that was the first time when you could really say there was a cohesive SDLP. They had a General Secretary called John Duffy and they had an office in Belfast. They were also reasonably well funded, mainly by private individuals and supporters in Dublin, but not the Government.

In those early discussions that led into Sunningdale did you talk with the nationalists or the unionists about the IRA or loyalism and how each could be 'turned off'?

Yes, the conversations particularly with Brian Faulkner and with the SDLP had, as one of the objectives, to detach people from the use of violence on both sides. That was always a topic, not least because the British kept that on the table as the primary objective, and it didn't matter who was in office from 1969 onwards, their goal was always to deal with violence. They were less concerned about the political situation than they were about the violent situation because they were the people who had to send in the army and were picking up the tab, which was huge, because when the violence started compensation was being handed out like confetti at a wedding. If you look at the bills in 1969 and from 1971 to 1973, when the bombing campaign was at its height, the British were paying compensation almost overnight, to the point where eventually we had to ask them if they knew what they were doing. The PIRA were frequently being asked by people whose businesses were running down if they would mind blowing those businesses up, and particularly if it was a big hotel or retail business in an area which was not doing well. The number of hotels being blown up probably at the request of the owners was especially notable, and within weeks they had a compensation cheque.

Was it Ken Bloomfield who coined the term 'the Irish dimension' in the Green and then White Paper?

It was.

You must have been fascinated by what that term might mean. What was the reaction in the Irish Government to this expression 'the Irish dimension'?

We were encouraged by British policy as set out in the White Paper. We didn't know exactly what the British had in mind but we interpreted it as our Council of Ireland. So we were sufficiently intrigued by that phrase to translate it as being equals in a Council of Ireland. We began to develop practical ideas as to what a Council of Ireland should be, but that only began the summer before Sunningdale. I think we started to work seriously on that and had conversations with the unionists from September 1973.

Did you see Bloomfield's paper?

Yes, we did.

What was the Irish reaction to it?

Generally, the Irish view was that it was very well intentioned to start with. Ken Bloomfield's relationship with Dublin went back quite a bit. He had been involved as a junior official in the first-ever meetings between Lemass and O'Neill, so was regarded as a unionist, yes, but a unionist who had a good appreciation of what nationalism was and what nationalists were thinking. We knew that a piece of paper which had been written by Ken Bloomfield would be positive. We might disagree with some of the sentiments in it, but most of Ken's document was translated into the Green Paper and then became a White Paper, and that formed the basis for the Northern Ireland elections in June 1973.

Were you surprised by this discussion paper? Did you think there were things in there you could get something out of?

We were pleasantly surprised by the acknowledgement that there had to be an 'Irish dimension'. That was a significant breakthrough. Don't forget, up to the prorogation of Stormont the British politicians, including prime ministers and foreign secretaries, were telling Dublin Northern Ireland is none of your business. That was the theme of the initial conversations between Heath and Lynch, and there was a particularly nasty conversation on the side at the Olympics in Munich, around 1972, which was poisonous. Heath just hammering on with this is none of your business, this is our problem, leave it to us. And, of course, to come back to your question about the American influence, the State Department in particular was heavily influenced by the British. In fact, even when I was Ambassador in Washington, starting from 1978, I never dealt with the State Department. There was no point, you might as well as have been dealing with the Foreign Office in London.

Words like 'executive' and 'harmonising' became part of the language. What is the difference between executive and harmonising in the context we are talking about?

In an executive you merge functions. For example, if you take inland waterways, you set up one body North and South and put inland waterway administrations into this one body so it has the executive authority to do what is needed. Harmonising is where you leave the executive functions where they were but you set up some sort of group that would ensure the same policies or the same type of policies were formulated on both sides.

It sounds like an executive role is essentially a harmonising role by other means?

You would have to have harmonising to have executive functions.

Was it the word harmonisation that terrified the unionists?

What terrified the unionists was the extent of the proposed powers to be given to the Council of Ireland. Almost everything was thrown into it.

And yet Faulkner accepted this?

Yes, under pressure from the British.

Was he haemorrhaging support from the start?

I think that by the end of December it was clear that, in a formal sense, he did not have the support of the unionist community. He was a very weakened unionist leader, going into Sunningdale. Now we didn't necessarily see that at the time, but I think he was negotiating from an extremely weak position and unfortunately we all put pressure on him. The SDLP put pressure on him, the Irish Government put pressure on him and, most tellingly, from his point of view, the British Government put pressure on him.

So you think the Irish put too much pressure on him?

Yes, of course. Dermot Nally on the last night of Sunningdale did a numbers calculation on how many points each delegation won. Now you might argue with his calculations but essentially the Irish Government got pretty well everything it wanted, the SDLP got everything it wanted, but Faulkner got almost nothing. He got a wishy-washy statement from us about the constitutional position of Northern Ireland, he got almost nothing on security and nothing on extradition, and they were three big topics for him.

What skills did the unionists bring to the negotiations?

The unionists at least had a tradition of dealing with bureaucrats, including people like Ken Bloomfield. By this stage he had no involvement. Up to Sunningdale the civil servants in Northern Ireland were unionists by tradition, by commitment, by background, by backbone, so the unionists had that backing, whereas the SDLP didn't and it relied on Dublin. There are only two internal reports of Sunningdale, in my view, that are good. Dermot Nally, who by now had become Secretary to the Government in Dublin, did a very good report which is available in the Dublin archives, and a man called Phillip Woodfield on the British side did too, although it was not quite as complete a report. But there is no agreed report, there is only an agreed communiqué, and don't forget Sunningdale was not an agreement. Sunningdale was a press release which was intended to lead to an international agreement that never happened.

And yet it's always called the Sunningdale Agreement?

Yes. It was a joint communiqué and a press communiqué which was intended to form the basis for subsequent negotiations for an Anglo-Irish Agreement.

Why was it called a communiqué?

Because it wasn't an agreement, it was too raw. There wasn't enough time even to produce the language for an international agreement.

If it had become an agreement would it have changed that much from the communiqué?

No, although I think it would have been polished. The idea was that it would be registered with the United Nations because that is what gives it status as an international agreement. So the objective was to do that, and I recall discussions on timing about that. The objective was to get it done before the summer break. In other words, we were allowing about six months to polish it but there were some very complex topics to be polished, such as how were we going to deal with the matter of the status of Northern Ireland on which, in fact, there was no agreement. As you know, there were parallel texts. It was a novel thing for a communiqué to have separate positions expressed in the same document. I have never seen that since.

Would you say that the communiqué was constructively ambiguous?

Most of it was not ambiguous. Most of it, with the exception of the bits on the status of Northern Ireland, was clear, but there couldn't be agreement on the status of Northern Ireland because the British were not going to accept our position, which was that Northern Ireland is part of our jurisdiction.

Who drafted the communiqué on the Irish side?

That was very complicated. Sunningdale was not a group negotiation. Sunningdale was five or six rooms and each room had a different topic, extradition, security co-operation, the status of Northern Ireland, human rights and the Council of Ireland. Each room had its own negotiation. As I said, the two people who pulled it together were Dermot Nally on the Irish side and Phillip Woodfield, who was a Home Office man, on the British side. Woodfield was definitely a security-oriented person, so he and Dermot Nally were the people who pulled together the outcomes from the rooms.

So did you have five teams?

Yes.

How many in each team?

Each team on our side had a politician and two or three civil servants.

So what did you deal with?

I dealt with North–South co-operation, but I suppose my main role was doing a lot of drafting for the SDLP because they had the political ideas and they had figured out what they wanted, but they didn't have the capacity to translate their stuff to paper. I had been doing that for the SDLP in the all-party talks in Belfast up to September before Sunningdale.

On those five areas were the participants asking how each area would work in relation to North–South relations?

No, they were separate and some of them became very narrow, but that was needed.

So there was an SDLP and unionist team in each room?

There was an SDLP team, a unionist team and an Alliance Party team and a Dublin Government team and a British Government team, some of who had never previously been involved in that sort of stuff. The British would have had a Foreign Office man who was probably an expert in international law on extradition, and we would have had an expert from our Attorney-General's Office on the same area. But, of course, the unionists, the SDLP and the Alliance didn't, so some of the negotiations were very uneven.

Presumably both the SDLP and the unionists were learning the art of negotiation because previously they had not had to do any?

They started to learn the art of negotiation after the elections in June of 1973 when Faulkner led the Unionist Party and Gerry Fitt led the SDLP and Oliver Napier led the Alliance Party. Once the summer was over, in September, Willie Whitelaw started pulling them together, although initially it started with bilateral conversations with each of them and then he had them sitting down together.

Who was drafting for the unionists?

Ken Bloomfield and Maurice Hayes, but the Alliance were better equipped. They had a lot of middle-class lawyer-types, but in any event they were minor players, and I don't say that with any disrespect because at some stages in the negotiations they were key. Initially, for example, they were supposed to have two full ministries in a new Government of Northern Ireland and at some stage that got diluted and they went along with that. Bob Cooper became a sort of a Junior Minister, so they were very helpful. But the SDLP and the unionists had no experience in negotiation.

Was it counterproductive for Heath to take Whitelaw out and replace him with Francis Pym? Most from that time seem to have great regard for Whitelaw?

Absolutely, but additionally we thought that Heath was jealous of Whitelaw's achievement and that therefore he wanted him off-side. I became convinced of this because he had done such a good job in this difficult situation and then Heath brought him back to deal with the unions. Heath wasn't the sort of personality who could bang heads together over a beer and sandwiches. He would almost do the wrong thing and send for claret and smoked salmon, whereas Willie Whitelaw had shown a remarkable capacity in Northern Ireland to pull together, even though initially we all thought he was very partisan on all sorts of things. In fact, he was very persuasive in both talking to the SDLP-types and the unionist-types. Pym was completely lost. He did not even have time to read the briefs. My memory of him was wandering around Sunningdale, coming to me and saying 'Now who are you and what are you doing?' But then he would ask me 'But who is that?' and I would actually have to say 'That is Roy Bradford, he's one of the senior people on the unionist side.' He didn't know anybody. It was a disaster. Don't forget that at this time we were watching the disintegration of the Lebanon and how a country which was once stable, wealthy and attractive could disintegrate because of civil war. We had absolutely no doubt that without the British presence in Northern Ireland there would be chaos which would spread in Ireland and Britain. In the autumn of 1973, in probably the first really serious conversations with the British in the lead-up to Sunningdale, we did a lot of groundwork at Civil Service level preparing for not just the Irish dimension but as back-up work for the SDLP. They had no experience of government or bureaucracy or documentation, so a lot of the preparation for Sunningdale was in helping the SDLP to translate what was in their head into documentation.

Was Heath's grasp of it as good as anybody had?

It was good enough given that Sunningdale overran the timing that had been allowed for it. It was to have finished on a Saturday morning at the latest and Heath had an official visit from Rome. He had the Italian Prime Minister coming and it was important. Heath left Sunningdale roughly at lunchtime on the Saturday to go to the airport to greet the Italian Prime Minister and take him to Chequers or Downing Street, settle him in, then come back. So he was missing for four or five hours and during that time there was nobody to lead on the British side. Pym was still wandering around in his double-breasted suit trying to figure out who was who, so everything was suspended for five hours.

Did you try and develop any communication with Paisley at that point?

Yes, we tried that even before Sunningdale and he rejected it. I would cold-call Paisley occasionally and say I'm from the Irish Government and could we meet and have a chat and the answer was usually no, but at some point after Sunningdale he would say 'No I don't see you have any role in this. However, I will be in seat 1A on the flight from Aldergrove to Heathrow so if you get seat 1B we could have a chat,' and I did that twice. The chat on his part was full of good humour. He thought it was a great joke and he would say 'How much is this costing the Free State?' But there was no serious communication even though it was very affable. I was not surprised when he developed the relationship with Martin McGuinness, because of the chat I had with him in those two very brief encounters.

Did the collapse of Sunningdale give credence to the IRA argument that unionists don't want to share power?

Strangely enough the IRA–Sinn Fein people never focussed as much on the unionists as they did the British. Their focus was always 'Brits out' and then we can deal with the unionists, so in my experience, at that stage, they never seemed to be focussing their attention at all on the unionists.

Whitelaw had met the IRA at Cheyne Walk in 1972. Do you think that was an influence in the background for the British? That they realised the IRA would continue to pose a considerable problem and therefore the best strategy would be to bolster the moderates to try and isolate them?

That was my speculation all through the 1970s, but it's confirmed by documentation that the British always kept in touch with the IRA. There was never a period when the British did not have a channel of communication. There were brief periods when they relied on intermediaries, but, in fact, the line was always open. If either side ever wanted to enter into serious conversations each side knew who to talk to on the other side, whereas the Irish Government had no contact. John Hume entered into conversations with the unionists and the IRA and he reported to us then that the IRA had no political intentions or political ability and so there was no point in talking to them. In fact, John didn't talk to the IRA again until he began his conversations with Gerry Adams in the late 1980s.

Was it apparent, at the same time at Sunningdale, that recruitment into the IRA had dramatically intensified post-Bloody Sunday?

The phases of recruitment into the IRA were the introduction of internment in August 1971, which brought a huge boost to recruitment not least because (a) it was badly handled, (b) many of the wrong people were picked up and (c) a lot of torture and degrading and inhumane treatment was used to interrogate people. Word of that spread very quickly and that was a massive boost to IRA recruitment, so that was the first wave. The second wave was obviously after Bloody Sunday, which was seven months later, and then you probably didn't have another equally successful, from the point of view of the IRA, wave until the hunger strikes of 1980–81. But Bloody Sunday did give them a huge boost, as did the introduction of internment.

Was there any attempt while Sunningdale was going on to convince them that it would be a good move for them to call a ceasefire? Was there any attempt to influence them on that from the Irish Government?

No. As far as I know there was no contact with the IRA directly or indirectly in that period.

Do you think that the violence of the IRA was a factor in drawing the Irish Government into recognising the need for engagement with the British? If the IRA had not been active would there have been Sunningdale?

I wouldn't quite categorise it in that way because of the general disturbance in Northern Ireland from late 1968 onwards when the Irish Government had to get involved. Even before the IRA really emerged, and particularly the Provisional IRA, the Irish Government was in some sort of contact with the British Government, so I don't think that was the driver of the conversations between Dublin and London. The driver was the very severe disturbances in Northern Ireland.

Did you get negativity from republicans in the South about your involvement with Sunningdale? What were the internal tensions?

It's very important to emphasise that we had no contact with the republican movement in that whole era. The only opposition to Sunningdale in the South was one TD (Member of the Dail) Major Vivian de Valera, who objected on complex constitutional grounds to the Sunningdale arrangements. Generally speaking there was an overwhelming support for the Sunningdale arrangements, but I emphasise we had absolutely no contact with the republican movement. I felt I would have been fired if I had opened up a line of contact with the republicans.

When Sunningdale fell apart the violence got worse. Did you expect that?

I didn't expect it to be as bad as it was. First of all, the IRA upped their game and then the loyalists upped their game. I don't think we expected that. What we expected was that we would attempt another variation of Sunningdale, but Wilson and others in his Cabinet blocked that. I was inclined to think that even if Wilson was going to behave stupidly that some of the intellectuals in his Cabinet would hold him back. To find that Roy Jenkins was supporting him was a big surprise.

Did the SDLP continue to engage with the Irish after Sunningdale? Did any elements in unionism continue to engage with the Irish, or did that break off?

The relationship with the SDLP was very close to the point of intimacy before, during and after. The relationship with unionism became difficult because it began to fragment, but we were given the task of opening up lines of communication with all shades of unionism, except those who were involved in violence.

One gets the impression that Sunningdale started to unravel before it really got going. Do you agree?

Sunningdale was beginning to unravel at the end of December, and the reason we knew it was going to unravel was because Brian Faulkner, when he came back from Sunningdale, went round the various unionist organisations and by the end of December there was a Unionist Council meeting at which the Sunningdale arrangements were overwhelmingly defeated. Faulkner bravely carried on for the next few months but he had no support, even within his own Cabinet. People like Roy Bradford, who was one of his senior colleagues, betrayed him and began to plot the downfall of Sunningdale before the first executive meeting had taken place.

Looking back on the period, and with hindsight, what could have been done to head that off? Should such people have been incorporated in discussions more? Would that have made any difference?

Well, don't forget that the unionists to the right of Faulkner, including Paisley, were invited to Sunningdale, and that's forgotten. Faulkner had agreed in principle to power-sharing and a Council of Ireland and Paisley was invited when letters were sent but never responded. He turned up at Sunningdale, but at the gates to protest, not inside to participate.

Do you think that the British Government should have acted much more quickly on the Ulster workers' strike?

Yes.

What were the Irish saying and doing about this at the time?

Usually it came down to practical things. We pressed the British to make sure that power continued to be generated in Northern Ireland, but the power stations were in the hands of extreme loyalist-types. The sewage facilities, and indeed all the public services, were controlled mainly by unionists who did not support Sunningdale. So we tried to persuade the British at a pretty early stage to bring in the necessary expertise in the British Army to run power stations, but don't forget the British Government had changed in February 1974 and the Sunningdale Agreement was basically negotiated by Ted Heath and his colleagues. Wilson was never committed to it.

There was a body, the Loyalist Army Council, set up to resist the Council of Ireland, was that so?

It was set up to resist Sunningdale. To be fair, it could be accurate that the element of the Sunningdale Agreement that the loyalists focussed on was the Council of Ireland. They were not that concerned about power-sharing. They didn't like it, but their focus was on the Council of Ireland, and, in retrospect, I can say we over-cooked the Council of Ireland. We asked a senior civil servant in Dublin to flesh out what a Council of Ireland should be, and within three or four months he came back with a document after wide consultations and he had a Council of Ireland with about 25,000 staff, mainly with civil servants from both sides who were performing functions which should be transferred into a Council of Ireland, like waterways and rail links North and South. It was a frightening document even for us in Dublin who were sensitive to loyalist and unionist views. I was certainly worried when I saw the document. I was also worried that it might leak, and if it did it would have looked as if Dublin was taking over a lot of the administration of Northern Ireland when all it intended to do was transfer many of these functions from ministries in Belfast down to this new structure in Armagh which would have been the headquarters for the Council of Ireland. Anyone looking at the document would have said this was clearly intended to be the document for a united Ireland.

Did you think or believe that Articles Two and Three would be a problem at some point, even if not then?

I think we knew from the beginning, and certainly the lead-in to Sunningdale, that Articles Two and Three were a problem, but the political view taken in Dublin and, incidentally, supported by London was that this was not the time to have a referendum to change Articles Two and Three because the situation was too volatile and if we went for a referendum to change Articles Two and Three we probably wouldn't win it.

What do you think about that now?

I think that was right. We would never have carried an amendment to Articles Two and Three in 1971–72 because the situation in Northern Ireland was so bad and, in general, the view in Dublin, and the populace for that matter, was there was massive discrimination remaining in Northern Ireland, unionists were still on top and the Brits were not behaving in a balanced way because they were essentially backing the unionists. There would have been no hope, and even fast-forwarding to 1985, in the negotiations leading to the Anglo-Irish Agreement, one of the points contemplated in Dublin was let's go for a referendum, and I'll never forget the conversation which took place between Peter Barry, who was Minister for Foreign Affairs, and Geoffrey Howe, who was Foreign Secretary, where Howe said something like 'You haven't a hope of carrying that referendum so don't put it on the table. It will wreck everything.' You had the extraordinary situation of the Irish side being prepared to make an offer, but the British reading of Dublin politics was probably accurate, although I do think the combination of a good Anglo-Irish Agreement, plus the personal input of people like Garret FitzGerald and Peter Barry, would have carried. Charles Haughey, of course, as leader of Fianna Fail, would not have supported it.

What happened when Sunningdale ended? Was that effectively it until the Anglo-Irish Agreement, and what happened in that intervening period? Was there any attempt to resurrect it?

There were lots of attempts to do something within Northern Ireland, in other words to do another version of power-sharing. The idea of an 'Irish dimension', or Council of Ireland, was more or less parked because it had become clear pretty well to everyone in Dublin that the bloated Council of Ireland was not a runner and because it would have had both executive and harmonising powers.

Is it the case, as Maurice Hayes suggests, that Faulkner had to downplay the fall of Stormont in unionism more generally and that while the SDLP were trying to play up the Council of Ireland Faulkner was trying to play it down?

At that stage it's important to remember that the SDLP, in an attempt to save the Sunningdale arrangements, agreed to ditch the Council of Ireland, and that's often forgotten, but because it came very late Sunningdale collapsed. The SDLP came to Dublin and said to save the arrangements and power-sharing we will have to dump the Council of Ireland. The Irish Government said fine, if that's what it takes.

Was it rejected by the unionists?

At that stage Sunningdale was gone, even though technically it was still there.

Did the SDLP put that on the table at that time?

Yes, they did.

As a hindsight point, if Heath had been re-elected and was in power for another few years do you think it would have worked?

I think it could have worked, yes, and if there had been a Thatcher-type in politics in Britain I think it could have worked. It needed a very firm commitment with the ability and the willingness to do whatever was needed to protect whatever had been agreed. Wilson was completely hostile, in effect.

The consensus seems to be that Wilson has to take much of the blame for letting it collapse, and of course Paisley and the workers' strike, but do you think the Irish could have done more at that point or was it gone?

Not based on my advice. At the end of Sunningdale and by the end of December I will never forget coming back from Northern Ireland for a New Year's Eve party in Garret FitzGerald's house and breaking the news to him that Brian Faulkner had just lost an internal Ulster Unionist Council vote and I predicted that that was the most important leg of the Agreement gone. It needed to have a unionist leg and thereafter there was not much point in the Irish doing things, but we did agree, at the SDLP's request, to dump the Council of Ireland section of Sunningdale in an attempt to save it and, as I said, that is often forgotten or overlooked.

Was that a temporary dumping?

I don't think we defined whether it was temporary or permanent. It was done in an attempt to save the arrangements, but it was far too late. That was almost at the end of the workers' strike. Could we have done more? Yes we could have done more on things like extradition, but the lawyers in Dublin said we could not go any further than we had gone in relation to either extradition or the more central question on the status of Northern Ireland as defined in the Constitution. There was no point at that stage in having a referendum to change the Constitution, which is what happened after the Good Friday Agreement.

Was there any talk at that time of Articles Two and Three going?

There was talk of it, but there was no confidence on the Irish side and, incidentally, no confidence on the British side that we could carry that, and if you look at the

Anglo-Irish Agreement in 1985 part of that was to amend the Constitution when we felt there was a good prospect of winning a referendum.

Who is to blame for the Sunningdale collapse?

There are a number of factors but I would put Harold Wilson at the top.

Can you give to some background to how the rumours that Harold Wilson was considering withdrawal came about?

We discovered that Wilson was thinking of unilateral withdrawal from two British journalists who kept in regular contact with both sides. John Cole in particular had very good contacts within the British Labour Party and he regularly visited Belfast and Dublin, and in the usual trading of information he would meet people like me. I would give him information and he would give me information and by June of 1974 we were scared like hell about the prospect of British withdrawal, and I mean really scared.

Was this a prospective policy that was doing the rounds or was it just known by a very small group?

It was known by very few people because it was a very, and even in British terms, radical way of thinking.

Had the British put this to you?

No, it was leaking to us.

Do you remember when you first heard about this and what your reaction was?

Yes, terrified. Don't forget, at about the same time we had had the Dublin and Monaghan bombings. I think more were killed in the Dublin and Monaghan bombings even than the number killed on the day Lord Mountbatten was killed and the eighteen soldiers at Warrenpoint. I could certainly see what would happen if the British withdrew from Northern Ireland. Inevitably there would be an upping of violence on the loyalist side and the republican side and it wouldn't be confined to Northern Ireland. If you look at Robert Armstrong's notes trying to persuade Harold Wilson that his view was not the correct one he made exactly the same point about

Britain. That is, we already have bombings here by the IRA so how much more can we expect if we withdraw precipitously from Northern Ireland? We will have all sides using violence.

Do you think if Wilson had acted on the strike it would have made a difference?

Yes. I think the British will was broken by that strike, but if they had tackled the strike earlier there was a chance that the Sunningdale arrangements, not a guarantee, might have survived. In particular, we pushed them very hard to maintain power and we knew that could be done by putting the army into two power-generating stations in Northern Ireland.

Looking back at the calling of the general election in 1974 one must surely think this was a bad decision for a range of reasons, but more obviously because the parties were going to begin going into rhetorical mode which wouldn't help power-sharing. Did you at that point try to discourage the election in 1974? What was the Irish reaction to it?

You have to understand that you could not get involved in situations like that. If you start getting involved in other people's domestic political arrangements you lose all political credibility because then they begin to reciprocate. Wilson was elected in February and I became convinced that this was trouble. Indeed, in the month of January we were pressing very hard with the British. They were also pressing hard on us in relation to security co-operation, where they felt that because we had got Sunningdale and had had many of our principles incorporated into the communiqué so we should up our security co-operation. There was a lot of activity between London and Dublin in the month of January and February. You had the change of government but, by then, Northern Ireland support for Sunningdale on the unionist side was waning.

Did you think that it was going to cause trouble?

Yes, because we never trusted Wilson. Wilson had deceived the Irish Government when as leader of the opposition in 1972 he asked for meetings with the Irish Government. Everything was laid on for him, police escorts etc. and he met the then Taoiseach, who was Jack Lynch, as well as the Minister for Foreign Affairs, Paddy Hillery. Everything was done, but what we didn't know was that the real purpose of his visit was to meet the Chief of Staff of the IRA, who he did meet. So we thought that was not the behaviour of an honourable man. And any records we had of conversations, say between the Irish Ambassador in London and Wilson, didn't offer us any comfort about either his knowledge of, or genuine interest in, what was happening in Ireland.

When Sunningdale collapsed did you carry on communications with Wilson? What did he say to the Irish and what did the Irish say to him?

Right through the strike we were in touch almost on a daily basis with the British Government, including at that level. I think you will find, and I presume they are now released, there were frequent letters signed by Liam Cosgrave to Wilson saying put in more troops to keep the power stations open and to keep the roads going, things like that. I was travelling in Northern Ireland and I would get back as far as Dundalk and dictate my reports on a confidential line from the police station in Dundalk back to Dublin, so we had daily reports. I could see with my own eyes the roads being blocked by the strikers, that public transport was at a standstill, milk deliveries were blocked and food deliveries into Catholic areas were blocked. All these things were reported back to Dublin, who would react usually by taking it up with Number 10.

Did it sour relations with Britain?

It certainly soured relations with the Labour Government. If you look back from Sunningdale at constructive relations, with the exception of Blair, this seemed to occur more with Conservative Governments: Heath, Thatcher, Major, and I find that interesting.

So Labour has historically been less willing to address the Irish problem?

With the exception of Harold Wilson all British leaders in my time took the problems of Northern Ireland and Irish relations very seriously. Some of them were in a position to do something about it and some were not. Callaghan was not because he didn't have the numbers in the House of Commons and he became dependent on independent republican MPs for votes, so his hands were tied. But the Irish Government knew Callaghan well. Thatcher's relationship was also good on Ireland and John Major ditto. No, I think the rogue Prime Minister in all of that was Wilson. All the others recognised that Britain had a duty to deal with this problem.

Looking back on that period, do you think there should have been a small Irish team that, as Sunningdale was taking place, were talking to the opposition in London? Should there have been more concern and action on the possibility of collapse?

Yes, probably, but because we didn't trust Wilson we couldn't bring him into our confidence. My experience was the British were very good at using what they called the Privy Council relationships to brief the opposition on what is going on, but I think Heath didn't trust Wilson and they did not seem to have any kind of relationship.

Was the European context of influence or value at this time?

Yes, because there was the additional factor that from 1973 onwards British and Irish ministries met regularly in Brussels, and that should not be under-estimated.

Can you say more on that?

On 1 January 1973 when Britain and Ireland joined what was then the Common Market there was a very elaborate system where there were meetings at head of government level, ministerial level and senior Civil Service level, so for the first time since 1922 British and Irish officials were meeting regularly and that gave an opportunity for the sort of conversations which were unscripted and informal which enabled people to get to know one another. This was extremely effective, and it was Ted Heath and Jack Lynch when we both joined who established quite a good working relationship. Certainly, subsequent heads of the two Governments, as well as foreign ministers, established excellent relationships because of the EU.

Do you think the European context was as important as the formal and focussed discussions on Northern Ireland that took place in Northern Ireland?

I think it was very important in establishing a climate of trust. There were differences along the way in the Anglo-Irish relationship but there were differences against a background of trust and confidence from each side in the other and that obviously had not existed when the Northern Troubles started in the late 1960s. There were still aspects of British policy or activity that we didn't trust. We were concerned, obviously, about their continuing contacts with the IRA. And we were particularly concerned about aspects of their security policy and collusion between British security forces and loyalist paramilitary organisations, which was a huge issue in the 1970s. You will also see from the records that both Jack Lynch as an outgoing Taoiseach and Liam Cosgrave when he became Taoiseach frequently raised the matter of collusion with their British opposite numbers, and I don't know when it stopped, but certainly it was rife in the 1970s.

What about America, did they do anything in the background of Sunningdale?

No.

Was there an international dimension to this where other countries tried to assist?

There was an attempt on the Irish side to get EU people involved, and I remember that Garret FitzGerald tried to get a former Luxembourg Prime Minister, who was President of the Commission in Brussels, involved, but that this came to nothing. At that stage there was no question of getting any serious American involvement. You are looking at a very disturbed period in Washington. You had Watergate, Nixon's departure, Ford coming in and so on. American involvement started with Carter because people like Tip O'Neill and Ted Kennedy had now become influential and quite powerful in Washington. Carter was new to Washington politics and had come up from Georgia. Obviously a number of people had tried to get the Americans involved on the side of Irish nationalism and you can go back to Parnell, Pearse, de Valera and in more recent times Frank Aitken or Sean McBride, all who tried to get the Americans to support the Irish nationalist position in different negotiations but never succeeded. We switched the line of approach in the 1970s after the collapse of Sunningdale, realising that we needed help and there were two possibilities here. One was getting the EEC on side and the other was focussed on getting the United States to the table. We made the breakthrough in August of 1977 when we got Jimmy Carter to issue what, for us, was a key statement saying that it was in the interests of the US to work with the two Governments to get a peaceful solution in Northern Ireland, and he held out the carrot that in the event of such an agreement being achieved the US would back it. We got that statement in 1977 mainly thanks to people like Tip O'Neill, Ted Kennedy and Pat Moynihan, who were important figures in Washington. Carter was new to Washington and had no background in there and didn't fully understand how it worked, but luckily they were all Democrats. Once we got that statement from Carter in 1977 our objective was now on the record to make sure that successive presidents commit to that document. Carter was succeeded by Reagan. Luckily, we were successful in getting him to commit, and then so on with Bush and Clinton, which turned out to be a very important factor when it came to the Good Friday Agreement, when the Americans were enormously helpful in getting Sinn Fein across the line and in keeping the British on side.

Does that mean that from 1977 the Americans were putting a lot of money into Northern Ireland?

No, they didn't put money in until the Anglo-Irish Agreement of 1985.

So from 1977 to 1985 what was going on?

Well, we were keeping the Americans fully informed on the various efforts that the British Government was making. There was the Northern Ireland Convention and there were two or three attempts to create structures in Northern Ireland, which we followed closely, where we kept the Americans fully informed, and I suppose we were putting pressure on the Americans to keep asking the British what they were doing about Northern Ireland. We were not asking the Americans to support the Irish Government's position but simply saying to them that when the President meets a British Prime Minister please do ensure that Ireland is on the agenda. We now know that in every bilateral meeting after 1977, no matter who was President and who was in Downing Street, Ireland was on the agenda. Ireland was an important element in the conversations between Reagan and Thatcher.

Was the perception in the Irish Government, and indeed did it continue after Sunningdale, that by bolstering moderate nationalism and with support from a pragmatic unionism the loyalists and the IRA would effectively be isolated and neutralised?

Yes, that they would be side-lined. And certainly on the nationalist side we had a very strong impression that if we could show significant progress, and if the SDLP got their hands on significant power, that this would lead to a weaning away of support from the IRA. We were probably wrong, but, even if we were right, a number of things continued to happen that built up support for the IRA. People I knew, and had known in Northern Ireland since 1971, who started by being totally opposed to the IRA, by the late 1970s to the early 1980s were so frustrated with elements of British policy they could not see long term. Dublin could see long term, but if you were living in Northern Ireland you couldn't be expected to see long term. The behaviour of the British Army lifting people even after internment had been abolished, the introduction of the special courts, the use of the UDR, which was a re-vamped version of the old 'B' Specials, all these things contributed.

Were you of the mind that the situation had somehow changed precisely because the Irish dimension was introduced, and in that sense once it was on the table it would not be retracted even in the cold years of violence that followed?

No. What we wanted to maintain and what we did maintain, what always had to stay on the table, was a role for the Irish Government. If it did not have to be a Council of Ireland, or an Irish dimension as defined in the 1970s, it had to be an acceptance that no matter what was going on it had to involve the Irish Government, and obviously that was cemented in the 1985 Agreement.

Did the British still believe in that and agree with it even after Sunningdale failed?

I think they did. They didn't formally acknowledge it but the nature of consultations between Dublin and London was such that it was a tacit acknowledgement that nothing could happen without involving the Irish Government. Now that didn't mean there would always be agreement, but the Irish Government would at least have to be involved, otherwise, as far as the British was concerned, we would never be able to carry the nationalist community in Northern Ireland.

Just as Sunningdale was a lost opportunity, the Anglo-Irish Agreement was an extension of the psychology of bolstering the moderates to isolate the extremes and that carried on from Sunningdale, but at what point do you recall this approach being reversed and the decision made to draw the extremes into the middle?

That came from Hume–Adams. Hume was heavily criticised when he came up with the idea.

Do you remember when you first heard it mooted?

Yes, but I was out of the system. I left the Irish Government system in 1987 and moved into the private sector, but I kept in touch with Hume and would spend some time in Donegal in the summer. Hume was now taking a house in France for six or eight weeks in the summer and he persuaded me and my late wife and children that we should transfer from Donegal to the south of France. We went down there and I remember walking on a beach in France with Hume when he proposed this possibility. It was either the summer of 1990 or 1991 and, as we know, he had already started his conversation with Adams by then.

Did he ask you to meet Adams with him?

No. He asked me to meet Adams when I went back into the Government when John Bruton became Taoiseach from 1993 to 1997 and when it was felt that John Bruton needed some sort of advisor on Northern Ireland because he had no background in it. I went back, and one of my first trips in 1994 was to see Hume and he brought me to see Adams, and that would have been February or March.

Who attended?

Just myself, Hume and Adams.

What did you make of Adams and the interaction between Hume and Adams at that time?

Adams was very reserved, not at ease, and it was my first time meeting him, and probably everything he knew about me would have been negative in the sense that he knew that in the US I had campaigned against any support for the IRA. I had been involved in ensuring that he would never get a visa to enter the US, so he was barely civil to me at that first meeting with Hume, but it was clear that he was in awe of Hume.

How many meetings did you have?

I had one follow-up meeting and then I met Adams with larger groups when he began to bring delegations down to Dublin, but I never developed a personal rapport with him.

After the initial meeting did Hume talk to you afterwards and suggest you should not worry about the reaction of Adams?

No, John just wanted Adams to get to know me because he thought I was a key figure in Dublin, which was an exaggeration because I was an advisor to John Bruton. I did not resume the bureaucratic function that I had had in the earlier years. That remained with people like Sean O hUiginn and later there was a formal channel of communication opened by the Bruton Government with Sean O hUiginn from Foreign Affairs, Tim Dalton from the Department of Justice and Paddy Teahon from the Taoiseach's Office. They were the trio who were appointed as the point of contact for Adams and Sinn Fein.

When you had that conversation with Hume on the beach in France, do you remember what he actually said and how you reacted to it?

Yes, what he said was we have been at it for twenty-five years, we have tried everything and nothing has worked. He argued that one of the reasons nothing has worked is because an important group of people are outside the tent rather than inside. I remember he talked about the difference between a cactus and a caucus and he said on a cactus all the pricks are on the outside. He said we've got to transmute or convert from having a cactus structure to a caucus structure, and my reaction was that this won't wash and people in Dublin and London would not support him on that. But eventually, as we know, he succeeded in persuading people in Dublin and London and Washington.

I assume that that view was influenced by two years of private meetings with Gerry Adams, but was he thinking primarily about the IRA or was he thinking about the loyalists too? Did he think that the loyalists would just fall away if the IRA did so?

Yes, I suspect his view, and certainly it was my view, was that the loyalist paramilitary organisations were a reaction to the IRA, so if you were able to wind down the IRA or bring the IRA in from the cold then there was a reasonable possibility that the loyalists would follow, and that's what happened.

Do you think that even then he foresaw that this change might lead to the end of his party as the dominant force of nationalism in Northern Ireland?

I don't know the answer to that. I doubt he would have planned that, but unfortunately what happened was that just as Sinn Fein were brought in Hume began to show symptoms of what became his very serious illness. He became a much weakened man from the late 1990s onwards. I could see it because I knew him well, but for many years many people didn't. But we must remember that Hume is the man who changed the Irish agenda, and by that I mean the agenda for Irish nationalism and even Irish republicanism. He also persuaded republicans of two things. You will not achieve your objective through the use of violence and you will have to accept the principle of consent. He sold that in the same way as he successfully sold that to political parties in the Republic way back in the late 1960s–early 1970s. He sold it to Gerry Adams and Sinn Fein in the early 1990s.

2

Fermenting the Irish dimension – Sunningdale to the Anglo-Irish Agreement: an interview with Noel Dorr

Graham Spencer: *Can you provide some background to the talks and contacts that led to Sunningdale?*

Noel Dorr: Let me start by saying that when the Troubles broke out in Northern Ireland in the late 1960s both Governments reacted badly. The British Government more or less said it's no business of the Irish Republic, which was an independent country, and the Irish Government tended to blame everything on partition. It took a few years for them to both understand the realities of Northern Ireland. There were various exchanges between Taoiseach Jack Lynch and British Prime Minister Ted Heath and in the middle of 1971, following the introduction of internment, Ted Heath had a meeting with Brian Faulkner, the Northern Ireland Prime Minister, at Chequers. Jack Lynch was not at that meeting but he sent an open telegram to Heath which more or less asserted a role for the Irish Government. There was a good deal of acrimony at that stage. Early September 1971 Heath met with Lynch at Chequers and at the end of September there was what was called a Tripartite Conference involving Heath, Lynch and Faulkner. The process I am describing is the gradual involvement and acceptance of the Irish in relation to Northern Ireland. It started with the British Government rejecting any role for the Irish Government on the basis that all that had been more or less settled in 1921 but, over time, the British came to realise that it was necessary to involve the Irish. That took shape in a Green Paper called 'A Paper For Discussion in Relation to Northern Ireland', published by the British Government in 1972.

What was the Irish reaction to this discussion paper, and did you try and change it?

The British thought the Republic was a foreign country and had no business interfering in the jurisdiction of the UK, and that was said in so many words at meetings.

One particular aspect of Irish policy in the early 1970s was to assert a role for the Irish and to say that this was not finished business from the 1920s but was still a problem. The second theme of Irish policy at that time was that the system of devolved government in Northern Ireland was not suited to a divided community. It was essentially modelled on the Westminster system where the winning party takes all. In Northern Ireland every election was basically about the border, and this was created in such a way that a unionist majority would tend to vote through their fears and the minority would vote against the Union. There was also permanent unionist government that wasn't suited to a divided society and that was a second theme addressed by the Irish in the 1970–71 period. First of all, there was a meeting after internment was introduced which, in the view of the Irish Government, was very badly handled and exacerbated the problem. In his open telegram to Heath, Lynch asserted his role, and there was an acrimonious public exchange between Heath and Lynch about that telegram. There wasn't a great deal of substance achieved at the tripartite meeting that followed, but the statement issued at the end was that the two Governments would maintain contact on all aspects of Northern Ireland, which was quite a contrast to the position the British Government had taken before. The gradual understanding of both sides was epitomised and given particular shape in the Green Paper. That paper recognised, or it seemed to accept, the argument the Irish Government had been making, which was that the parliamentary and governmental system of the devolved government in Northern Ireland was not suitable and that something better would have to be found. It also had a new phrase, 'the Irish dimension', which became quite important. This more or less meant that the connection with the Republic and the wish of a minority in Northern Ireland for a united Ireland made Irish involvement intrinsic to the problem. In my view, this was a recognition that it was no longer simply a claim by the Republic on Northern Ireland, which was the way it was often depicted because of our Constitution and Articles Two and Three, but that you had to recognise that a very substantial minority were dissatisfied with the whole settlement of 1920–21 and were hoping one day to have Irish unity. That was encapsulated in the phrase 'Irish dimension' and the need to accommodate this dimension in any future settlement.

Were you given a steer before on this term 'Irish dimension'?

The term was newly coined in the document but it was very much in line with what the Irish Government had been pressing for nearly two years with the British. It was another way of saying that the connection with the Republic or the role of the Irish Government was a part of the jigsaw. It was also a kind of tacit recognition that Northern Ireland, which was becoming acute through violence, was a legacy to both countries and the result of a very complicated interaction through centuries of history. After Bloody Sunday in January 1972 the British Government had come to see that they had to start by getting new structures and institutions into Northern Ireland. What they had come to accept was that the system of government there was not good enough and so Stormont was prorogued in March 1972, with Northern Ireland coming under direct rule thereafter. The problem for the British Government was to find a new way of creating devolved government, and they began to accept the thesis of the Irish Government that a new system of government had to somehow accommodate the minority as well as the majority. That led to the idea of partnership government, which came to be called 'power-sharing'.

What role did the Irish Government have here?

They certainly had a role in what I would see as two of the basic ideas in that paper: the Irish dimension and partnership government. I don't know exactly whether there was some brief advance notice that the paper would be produced, but it certainly fitted with the developing relationship between Dublin and London. Of course, there were other things in the Green Paper too. There was a proposal for a plebiscite in Northern Ireland on whether they wanted to join the South, which the Irish Government was not too happy about because it thought that a straight yes or no vote would only show what everybody knew, which was the majority and minority positions, so there was some unease and disquiet about that from the Irish side. But the Green Paper became the basis for the lead-up to Sunningdale and the effort to lead the parties in Northern Ireland into a power-sharing Executive.

Were the Irish talking to the SDLP at this point? What were the discussions outside the immediate British–Irish axis?

Yes, they were. When Lynch met Heath in September 1971 he was clear that he wasn't the agent of the SDLP and he couldn't represent them but he was nevertheless reflecting what he believed their views were. At that particular point the SDLP had withdrawn, they were not taking part in talks. They were, if you like, stuck on the problem of internment, and they were not co-operating with British Government talks. They had earlier withdrawn from Stormont and were having difficulties going in to talks. Lynch's response to Heath was to say that he didn't represent the SDLP and was not speaking for them, but to make it clear that they were not going in to talks while the situation continued.

What impact did Bloody Sunday have?

It had a huge effect. It was an absolutely traumatic event for most of Ireland. Certainly in the Republic it's well known that there were visible emotions, with marches and protests to the British Embassy. In Britain it also produced a very substantial effect, although not the same effect that a similar shooting in Birmingham or Manchester would have produced. I suppose it also confirmed the idea that the British had to take control of the security forces, and it showed that the situation was a mess. I believe that it had a particular effect on Ted Heath and that in the following months he began to read up and brief himself very much on the Northern Ireland problem.

When it moved towards formal discussions and talks about Sunningdale, in the Council of Ireland discussions, what were the Irish trying to do, because in the final document there are words like 'harmonising' and 'consultative' in relation to the Irish role?

The SDLP and the Irish Government did not want what was called an 'internal settlement'. They believed it was necessary to 'prop up', if I might use the term, whatever new institutions were created between the communities in Northern Ireland by a North–South link, and that was the Irish dimension. It's an image of a three-legged stool, where two legs would be the parties working together in Northern Ireland but you need the third leg to make the whole thing stable, otherwise it becomes a purely internal settlement which the minority in Northern Ireland were not prepared to accept because that would mean an aspiration for Irish unity or a change in the situation is no longer there. The SDLP, as representatives of the minority, needed proper support, and the Irish and British Government recognised that.

I keep coming back to the phrase 'the Irish dimension', which was probably intended as a vague general phrase. I'm saying that it was recognition, in principle, that Northern Ireland couldn't be dealt with in a closed system, that there had to be the external aspect, some kind of link with the Republic, and the way that all took shape was under Willie Whitelaw, who was Secretary of State. He had a conference in the middle of 1973 with parties that were willing to take part in the emergence of new structures. The unionists under Brian Faulkner, the Alliance Party under Oliver Napier and the SDLP under Gerry Fitt met and agreed in principle on forming a joint Executive on power-sharing. The agreement of the SDLP was conditional on further development of a structure for a North–South connection which was to be given effect in the Council of Ireland, so it was a provisional agreement on a power-sharing Executive. The formal purpose of the Sunningdale Conference, which took place in

December 1973, was to work out that Irish dimension as part of the whole package, and once that had been agreed then the Executive was formally constituted.

Were the SDLP sceptical of the Irish role? Did they work cordially with the Irish, or was there some tension there?

I think that while the Irish Government wasn't representative of the SDLP their approaches were quite similar. If you are saying, when an Executive was formed in Northern Ireland and ministers appointed, that a particular minister might have been jealous of holding on to some function, rather than transferring to a Council of Ireland, then I suppose there might have been a bit of that on the part of the Irish Government. I think that was more the exception than the rule, though.

How many meetings do you recall between the initial Green Paper and the final Sunningdale Agreement itself?

It wasn't, to my memory, a continuous process of officials meeting at intervals of every few weeks as you had in the 1980s for the Anglo-Irish Agreement, but there were various exchanges and meetings over 1973. Remember, both Governments had become members of the European Union from January of 1973. It was not the EU at the time but the EEC, and that had a very important effect because representatives from both Governments were now meeting regularly in Brussels in the form of the Council of Ministers and there was an easier relationship developing. Previously, meetings of British and Irish ministers would have been a big event and rare, whereas now it was a routine matter and not just for the Minister for Foreign Affairs or the Foreign Secretary in Britain, but other representatives from other departments. Over the following years it did make the contacts much easier for people meeting outside as well as inside councils and in addition to other formal, preparatory meetings.

Do you remember how many drafts Sunningdale went through before it was finalised and what the Irish changed or amended?

I don't think the Sunningdale Agreement emerged from a process similar to that under which the Anglo-Irish Agreement emerged in 1985 because in that case there was a process of gradual refinement of text over a long time. The Sunningdale Agreement essentially emerged at the Sunningdale Conference. Brian Faulkner claims in his book *Memoirs of a Statesman* to have been the originator for the proposal of a Council of Ireland, although he would have wanted to focus it much more on security matters, and he makes that claim that he was the first to propose a Council of Ireland. However, there were proposals from October 1972 and an appendix summary of the proposals from all of the main Northern Ireland parties that were involved at that stage. They all have some version of a Council of Ireland in mind, conceived in different ways as a link between North and South.

Was the Council of Ireland and the consent principle the two main locks for the Irish?

Yes, and the third part was partnership in government, or power-sharing. The idea of the consent principle was, if you like, to put a floor under unionist fears and assure them that they were not going to slide into a united Ireland against their will. The Irish Government went as far as it could, given the constraints of Articles Two and Three of the Constitution, and so, as long as those Articles remained, the Irish Government had to be wary of running foul of them. Subject to that it wanted to go as far as it reasonably could to assure the unionists that there was no wish to force them against their will. The parties in Northern Ireland, or those willing to participate, had agreed in principle to establish a power-sharing Executive given effect through what then became the Council of Ireland. So you have the three elements of consent, partnership in government and the Irish dimension. Underlining it all, of course, was the idea of security and co-operation, and that leads you on to the policing issue, which was not resolved at Sunningdale. It was more or less thrown forward to a Law Commission, with representatives of the British and Irish Governments trying to come up with a solution on extradition. Policing was fudged at Sunningdale. The real disagreement was between the SDLP, the unionists and the British Government on the question of policing. The SDLP wanted some kind of link between the police and the new Council of Ireland, while the unionists wanted policing to be devolved to them and to be a matter for the Executive. The British Government was very wary of devolving policing to an Executive though, given their experience of what happened before Stormont was abolished.

Before we come to the Ulster Council workers' strike and the Paisley backlash against Sunningdale, what was the thinking about the IRA at the time? Was there any back-channel involvement with the IRA?

Well, first of all there had been an episode of talks and a ceasefire in 1972 when Whitelaw got them together in Chelsea. That petered out and went nowhere, so there was an effort by the British at that time to talk and then it stopped. On a more general note I think the underlying idea was to try to get all moderates, all people who were willing to keep to politics, to come together and devise structures within Northern Ireland, between North and South and with the British Government, to reduce violence to a minimum. So you get the maximum degree of support for political institutions which will promote reconciliation coming together and working together. You don't try to determine the future outcome in detail, you let the future take care of itself, but you hope that by doing all that you gather together everybody of goodwill who is willing to work politically despite their disagreements, and you let the institutions work in a benign way over time in the hope that this will isolate people who are determined to make violence work. You then try to act forcefully and strongly through security-force measures against those involved. So the basic idea was to minimise the support. If you like, it was all predicated on the idea that the violence in Northern Ireland on both sides was not some absolute aberration which nobody could understand, it was the expression in extreme form of the emotions of fear on both sides of the community, so the more there was fear in the community the more emotions rose between both sides and the more they would tolerate or even support people who gave expression to that emotion in the form of violence. That was true on the loyalist side as well as the republican side.

So why did it not happen?

If you are asking why Sunningdale failed, the conventional view is that the Irish Government overloaded the proposal for a Council of Ireland and that was too heavy a weight for Faulkner to carry with the unionist party, so it collapsed and fell. I do acknowledge the Irish Government may have had exaggerated ideas of the size of the Council of Ireland and the numerical importance of it, but I think that is too facile an explanation of why Sunningdale fell at the end. I would see four or five different reasons. One is this, that people forget that Sunningdale was only the first part of a two-part conference. It was the stage where the principles and the broad ideas were worked out, but there was to be a second, formal stage which was a conference at which an agreement would be signed. The Sunningdale communiqué itself says that agreement would be registered at the UN as an international agreement and that a formal second stage would take place once the details of the Council of Ireland had been worked out. Unfortunately, the second stage never took place, so all that we have is a communiqué, not an agreement, issued by the first-stage conference. We have in that communiqué the idea of a Council of Ireland, the broad lines, but none of the detail. The second point is that Ted Heath called an election in February 1974 for reasons not connected with Northern Ireland. However, the election obviously extended to Northern Ireland as part of the UK and that meant that voters there who were perhaps apprehensive about what was coming were asked to vote in effect on the Sunningdale settlement at a stage where it was still in its raw state, without having exactly worked out what this Council of Ireland would be and how it would work. I liken it to someone making a judgement on a building while the scaffolding is still around the building. You had only the skeleton outline of it, so, if you like, it was the worst possible time to ask the voters to make a judgement on something within a month or two of the Agreement while fears were still there. A third reason was that, as a result of the election that Heath lost, a new Labour Government under Wilson came to power which had no integral involvement in Sunningdale, and it wasn't their thing. I don't mean to say they were against it, but it wasn't their settlement, whereas Heath and Whitelaw had been quite enthusiastic and involved. If you have an opposition politician who comes to office he may say well that is okay and we don't disagree, but he doesn't have the deep commitment to it.

Another important thing was that the Irish Government immediately after Sunningdale were suddenly blocked from speaking out strongly in favour of it because of a court case in Dublin undertaken by Kevin Boland, an Irish former Fianna Fail politician, who challenged what had been done at Sunningdale. He claimed that the Irish Government were acting contrary to Articles Two and Three. Once you get to the courts in both Britain and Ireland people are precluded from commenting on something while the case is ongoing, and because of this the Irish Government could not make any big statements in support of Sunningdale, which was needed at that time. There needed to be strong political statements both North and South to get across to the public that this was a real chance for a settlement. The Irish were blocked on this because they were advised by their lawyers not to say anything until this court case was over. The Attorney-General of the time and others were at pains in the court case to challenge Boland's allegation that this was a settlement which betrayed the Irish Constitution. It was fine for the court case to play down the political significance of what was done, but what was needed for political reasons was to play it up and say to everyone this is a settlement worth having. Remember, the IRA and the loyalists continued their violence, and then you had the loyalist strike and the British Government reacted weakly. So the whole thing became impossible and the new Executive fell apart in May 1974.

Did the court case in Dublin add extra fear to the Paisleyites and the loyalists because they were reading this situation and stoking the view that there was real intent to absorb Northern Ireland into the Republic?

It may have, but I tend to emphasise another angle on more or less the same thing, which is that it blocked the Irish Government from acting politically to boost the Sunningdale outcome. What was needed was for everybody who was involved to come back and play up what they had achieved, but the Irish Government, through its lawyers, was playing it down. I don't know how far that got across to people like Paisley but I suppose it's like two sides of the same coin in that if they found this negative, the Boland case certainly stopped the Irish Government from being positive. My sense is that Faulkner was saying he needed support but the Irish Government felt blocked from speaking out to provide that support.

Why was it called a communiqué instead of, say, Agreement Part One?

Because it was just a communiqué, it wasn't a formal agreement. It gets called the Sunningdale Agreement precisely because it was a part one of a formal agreement. I think it says in the course of the communiqué that a formal agreement would be reached in due course, and there is a reference somewhere to once set up the Agreement would go to the UN for ratification. I should also add that the Irish and British Governments had different legal and formal positions in relation to the status of Northern Ireland. The Irish wanted to reassure the unionists on the consent principle but they were constrained as to how far they could do so legally and constitutionally without the changing the Constitution, which itself would require a referendum in Ireland. The British Government were also expected to not stand in the way of a united Ireland if a majority in Northern Ireland so wished it. In a plebiscite earlier in 1972 one of the questions to the Northern Ireland electorate was do you wish Northern Ireland to become part of a united Ireland?

It was indeed a most unusual procedure for a government to ask the population in part of its own territory if they wished to belong to another country or not. So they had already recognised this and made it known that if a majority in Northern Ireland wanted to unite with the rest of Ireland then the British Government would support it. There are two parallel declarations set out in the text of the communiqué, with the British Government's declaration and then the Irish Government's declaration. However, there are significant differences between the two statements. They both had the same intent of reassuring the unionists that consent of a majority would be necessary for any change in status, but the Irish Government did not feel free to formally recognise the status of Northern Ireland as part of the UK. The Irish Government's declaration focussed on change in status without spelling out what the status was, while the British Government felt it had to spell out what the status was; so you had the Irish Government fully accepting and solemnly declaring there could be no change in the status of Northern Ireland until a majority desired it and you had the British Government saying it would remain British policy to support the wishes of the majority in Northern Ireland if, in the future, a majority should indicate their wish to become part of a united Ireland.

When Sunningdale was brought down, what was the Irish reaction?

In April 1974 I was assigned a new function as Political Director, which in practice was the head of the international and political division dealing with foreign policy co-operation within the EEC. In April 1974 I ceased to be as deeply involved, so I don't have the same intimate knowledge of what happened thereafter because I was dealing with other matters. My sense, however, is that there was no real belief or effort to revive it at that stage. It was seen as the disintegration of our hopes, and a rather bleak period followed for several years.

Was there a blame game afterwards?

To some extent there was. People like Conor Cruise O'Brien, who was in the Irish Government and indeed the spokesman of that Coalition Government, was the spokesman on Northern Ireland matters as well as being Minister for Communications, and in his later writings he attributed a lot of the blame to the overplaying of the Council of Ireland on the Irish side. In his view this was too heavy a weight imposed on Brian Faulkner, who lost support after Sunningdale. In turn, the Irish side generally tended to blame the weak reaction of the British Government to the loyalist strike and believed that they should have reacted more firmly.

Would it be fair to say that after Sunningdale things never really happened until the Anglo-Irish Agreement in the mid-1980s, or were things going on between those two periods?

The opposition of the more extreme elements in unionism to Sunningdale was really as much against power-sharing as it was against the Council of Ireland, so putting all the blame on the Council isn't quite right. Nor is it correct to say nothing happened until the Anglo-Irish Agreement. There was a period in 1975–76 when there was apprehension on the part of the Irish Government that Harold Wilson was seriously thinking about withdrawal. Even though the long-term hope was for a united Ireland achieved by agreement, with consent and peace and so on, the idea of a precipitant British withdrawal would have easily intensified the prospect of civil war. When Charles Haughey became Prime Minister in 1979 he set himself to meet with Mrs Thatcher and develop a relationship and he had a first meeting with Mrs Thatcher in May 1980, followed by a second meeting in Dublin Castle in December 1980. I was involved to some extent in the discussions which he had with officials in the weeks before his first meeting, and the idea he wanted to press was to develop the 'East–West link', the relationship between Dublin and London that came to be encapsulated in the phrase 'the totality of relationships'. In a simplistic way the intention was to develop partnership within Northern Ireland between the political parties, develop a link between North and South in Ireland, and that the British Government would benignly and benevolently be helpful towards this.

So the East–West axis was neglected?

The British Government were quite prepared to see the maximum degree of agreement that could be achieved in Ireland without insisting on an institutional role. They had, of course, the role of a sovereign government and they had to be responsible for Northern Ireland, but the concepts at Sunningdale did not build in an institutional East–West link corresponding to the North–South link which they were aiming for in a Council of Ireland, which corresponded to partnership within Northern Ireland. Haughey's tendency was to stress that the issue of Northern Ireland was the legacy to both islands of a complex interaction and that because of this there needed to be a strong East–West relationship. But this needed a focus on going beyond Sunningdale. The first meeting in May 1980 went very well, and this was the famous occasion when Charles Haughey presented Mrs Thatcher with a silver teapot and a silver spoon. He gave her a quite valuable gift which she seemed to appreciate, and it was a very positive meeting. He came out of a private meeting with her on that day full of enthusiasm, saying they had agreed to meet again later in the year, and they did so in Dublin Castle. At the first meeting they met privately after lunch when officials were not present before engaging in a more formal setting. Haughey was intent on using that meeting to establish a relationship and he believed he had done that.

At the second meeting I think it went further, and his idea of the totality of relationships, advocating the need for a commissioning of studies between officials, was another way of developing the relationship. But after the second meeting several things went wrong. For one thing the Irish side oversold what had been agreed. I think there was a lot of talk at the meeting of institutional relationships, and there was a tendency on the Irish side to talk that up as constitutional, which would have been seen as a coded way for talking about the status of Northern Ireland within the UK. Mrs Thatcher was quite angry about that and complained to Haughey when they met again at a European summit a short time afterwards. Further, over the following year the hunger strikes took place and there was a lot of bad feeling on the Irish side about the way she handled that.

Then there was the Falklands War, where initially the Irish Government supported the British in the UN Security Council on calling for a withdrawal from Argentina, but as the conflict developed they called for a meeting of the Security Council at a difficult time for the British, omitting any reference to the previous resolution which Ireland had voted for. This was seen by the British as a backing away, although it may have been more of a blunder than a deliberate move. That said, it caused a lot of bad feeling and the relationship between Thatcher and Haughey soured over the following couple of years, although in her memoirs she tends to show a degree of regard for Haughey. This souring had an important unforeseen effect because the studies undertaken about the relationships continued between officials in the Cabinet Office in London and the Department of Foreign Affairs in Dublin, and out of that emerged the talks that led to the Anglo-Irish Agreement.

So when relations were soured between Haughey and Thatcher over the Falklands there was still a kind of strand of discussion or dialogue going on? The totality of relationships was still alive?

It was still alive and the studies continued, but then there were several quick changes of government in Dublin, with some three Governments within a period of two years. Nevertheless, from the studies some documents were published which became the seed-bed out of which the talks developed that led to the Anglo-Irish Agreement.

Would you say Haughey really needs some congratulation in the sense of forging this idea of the East–West relationship that became crucial not just for the Anglo-Irish Agreement but, of course, what happened later on with the Good Friday Agreement?

I think that's true, but I should put in a caveat or qualification here. I was essentially a civil servant, a diplomat, and in the British and Irish system civil servants continue even when there is a change of government. The tendency of a politician or a minister who's in government and then in opposition would be to emphasise the degree of difference and change between one government and another, whereas the tendency of your average civil servant is to see more continuity there. So I tend to see a certain thread of development over several decades which led eventually to the Good Friday Agreement.

To what extent did the hunger strikes impact on relationships?

I think the hunger strikes had a very important effect, and the phrase used later in the negotiation of the Anglo-Irish Agreement was 'alienation'. That was the strong theme of Garret FitzGerald, who believed that the creation of martyrs was throwing support to Sinn Fein and republicans who were still engaged in violence or connected with violence, and that was a dangerous development. In his view that support was now leaking away from people who were using and wanted to use only political means to make progress.

Armstrong and Goodall insist that Thatcher did not like the word 'alienation', which she saw as having Marxist tones?

The word comes indirectly from Hegel through Marx, but the phrase is normally associated with Marx and she didn't like that. She may not have liked the particular word but she agreed that something had to be done. Her focus would have been on security co-operation, but she eventually signed up to the Agreement, which gave the Irish Government an institutional role in relation to direct rule for as long as there was not agreement on a devolved government through partnership within Northern Ireland.

What was the earliest moment you can recall when there was talk or tentative discussion about the possibility of negotiations that might lead to the Anglo-Irish Agreement?

That would have been in 1983. The initial contacts were made between David Goodall and Michael Lillis, and then Robert Armstrong came over to Dublin, probably early 1984. It's hard to specify exactly when the talks process began, but the latter part of 1983 and early 1984 seemed the key initial periods.

Do you recall any moments that led to that? Why then, and what was the context surrounding that moment?

Garret FitzGerald set himself to convince Mrs Thatcher that it was necessary to do something in relation to Northern Ireland and that inaction was likely to lead to increased support for Sinn Fein, and not only in the North but in the South, so it was dangerous to do nothing. Her inclination might have been to leave what was bad enough well alone because her friend Airey Neave had been killed, and she may have felt that any actions in relation to Northern Ireland were not productive. That was the context. Talks took place between officials on both sides, and in that context Michael Lillis and David Goodall met. That was the way the first tentative soundings started and that subsequently led to more substantial contact with Robert Armstrong and more organised talks in 1984–85.

Would it be too simplistic to suggest that the underlying aim of those talks and the Agreement was to bolster the political ground for the SDLP while marginalising Sinn Fein?

It wasn't directly intended just to bolster the SDLP. It was driven by a strong conviction on the part of Garret FitzGerald that the situation was deteriorating and that support for violence was growing after the hunger strikes. The minority were quite isolated and things were getting more and more difficult and he was seriously worried that this would result in much greater support for a party which was at least affiliated to those engaged in violence. His fear was that if Sinn Fein gained a majority of the minority in future elections they could claim to be the voice of the minority, and this at a time when they were still connected with the IRA. The SDLP, which had been seen in America as the elected representatives of the minority looking for a solution by peaceful means, would now become a minority of the minority, so to speak, and Sinn Fein would be the voice of the majority of the minority, and that would lead to a situation which would be more and more difficult. Indirectly one could say that the aim was to bolster the SDLP and boost democracy through a peaceful settlement in Northern Ireland rather than accept a slide towards more violence and further alienation of the population.

Do you remember the way the Agreement was constructed? Did it reflect the chronology of the negotiations?

A descriptive phrase which I think applied to these negotiations was 'successive approximations'. Obviously we had to deal with different aspects at different times and we did not have a framework in advance. We were working through what became the whole agreement and created it from scratch. But there were different drafts and we would argue over a draft and then come back with a better version, so it really was a matter of 'successive approximations', that is, working bit by bit towards an agreement. Of course, we had to do it in sections on security or devolution etc. and it was only in the latter part of the negotiations in 1985 that the pieces began to come together. We were concerned about 'confidence-building measures' going into the communiqué rather than the draft Agreement. For a full appreciation of what was agreed you will need to take the two documents together, that is, the Agreement and the communiqué.

What parts of the negotiations were the most difficult?

Obviously policing and symbols, but particularly dealing with questions about the unionists not being forced into unity. The phrase used in the briefing documents in a press conference after the Agreement was something like 'We come to this Agreement with different title deeds', meaning that the Irish Constitution still had Articles Two and Three as a claim on Northern Ireland until a majority there wished for change and that it would involve a referendum in our jurisdiction to try to remove those Articles. If opposition grew to that and Sinn Fein and others conducted a campaign against it and the referendum was lost, then that would entrench and reinforce Two and Three, so in order to win a referendum it was necessary to counterbalance it with a deep settlement in relation to Northern Ireland. The British did not believe that such a deep settlement was really feasible at that time, so everything short of that was to be done in Article One of the Agreement to give reassurance to the unionists.

Did you discuss what the implications of this Agreement might be without involving the other parties in Northern Ireland?

I should say that as a preface to that on the Irish side we couldn't be sure how the Agreement would be received and, in a way, when the Agreement was announced it was a matter of which side would say it was a betrayal and which side would welcome it, because it played into the zero-sum game. Both sides were very well aware that Sunningdale had been pulled down as a result of the electricity workers' strike and by the strong reaction on the part of the unionists, and both sides saw the Agreement as one between the two Governments which couldn't so easily be pulled down. On the other hand, the Agreement was also seen as the British Government wanting some kind of restored government on the basis of power-sharing or partnership. The long-term aim would have been a devolved Assembly and Executive of the kind we more or less have now, so built into the Anglo-Irish Agreement was that if devolved government were achieved and unionists accepted that, then perceptions of an intrusive role by the Irish Government in the internal affairs of Northern Ireland would diminish step by step. The Irish were not trying to spite the unionists or score over them. We were genuinely trying to find something that would bring the minority in from the cold, get them to support democratic politics, let the Irish Government speak as their surrogate voice unless power-sharing was agreed and they were able to speak for themselves through their democratic elected representatives.

Two things interest me in this period. One is the proposal of the five-mile no-man's-land strip across both jurisdictions to enable each to make incursions in the pursuit of terrorists and the other is Thatcher's 'Out, out, out' speech. What are your thoughts?

I don't think that idea would be very easy to implement. You are simply moving the border on each side a bit and have the same problems. I cannot be specific about when it arose in the discussions and how seriously it was considered, but I don't think it was ever a runner. The New Ireland Forum, which was a detailed and extended conversation among nationalist parties North and South, that is to say Labour, Fine Gael and Fianna Fail and the SDLP, on establishing a base position for Irish nationalism in regard to Northern Ireland, was important though. The Forum Report came out in May 1984 and contained the preference for a unitary Irish State and possible ways of implementing it. The solutions were a united, a single Ireland, a federal-confederal Ireland and joint authority, all of which were not acceptable to the British Government. However, what was important was the broad principle which set out that both communities in Northern Ireland had to be accommodated in a way that they would be comfortable with and their identity had to be preserved. The general consensus was that the Forum would be open to other ideas that would help with progress, and that became the basis for the Anglo-Irish negotiations; but gradually, as the negotiations went on, it became evident that full-scale joint authority wasn't on as far as the British side was concerned. What did emerge was agreement to a role for the Irish Government in relation to direct rule, which was described later as 'more than consultative but less than executive'.

What does that mean?

It was a way of encapsulating the Irish Government having the right to put forward views and proposals in relation to Northern Ireland until there was devolution on a basis of 'power-sharing'. It was also said that every effort would be made to achieve agreement, so there was a formal right given by the British Government that its direct rule procedure would involve henceforth an ability of the Irish Government to put forward views and proposals and that both sides would be committed to try and find agreement. To give effect to that there was to be a Permanent Secretariat in Belfast as a day-and-night channel between the two Governments and a regular meeting of a body called the Anglo-Irish Intergovernmental Conference. There would be regular meetings of the body every six weeks or so, and that was a way of giving effect to an involvement of the Irish Government which was more than consultative and less than executive.

It was spelled out in the Agreement that the sovereignty would remain, so that's why it was less than executive but it would be just short of that, something more than consultative. After the Report appeared I was asked to present it to the British, and I went to see Robert Armstrong and drew his attention to these options, and he led me to understand that the British Government would not be able to accept any of them. In July 1984 Garret FitzGerald and Mrs Thatcher met at a European summit in Fontainebleau, and it was clear then that specific proposals in the Forum Report would not be acceptable to the British too. By the time you come to the summit meeting at Chequers in November 1984 it was quite clear that the specifics in the Forum Report were not acceptable but that we were continuing to negotiate to achieve something that met the general requirement of contributing to political progress.

The situation was that Mrs Thatcher and Garret FitzGerald, after the summit, gave separate press conferences. She gave hers in Downing Street and he gave his in the Irish Embassy, and although there had been difficulties at the summit it wasn't all that bad, but she gave her press conference some time after five and we, in the Embassy, had sent a middle-level official to report back on what she had said in time for Garret FitzGerald's press conference, which was to be broadcast live straight into the six o'clock live television news in Dublin on RTE. As it happened, the famous 'Out, out, out' comment came after he left, so when Garret went to give his press conference at six, and I was sitting beside him as Ambassador, he didn't know that she had said this. I don't think she meant it in a bad sense, in fact she had to be reminded of one of the proposals and said in a very flat way 'That is out, that is out, that is out', but the consequence and the unintended result was that the Irish television audience saw Garret FitzGerald not responding at all, so the contrast for the audience was very sharp and there was a general feeling that he had been humiliated. I suspect that people around Mrs Thatcher told her she had unwittingly damaged Garret FitzGerald, and he was obviously hurt by it but he did not react as other politicians might have. He didn't show extreme public anger, and this image of his suffering may have been helpful later because Thatcher was asked to make up for the damage done. Certainly the negotiations continued and were not derailed by that.

Can you think of an example where the British moved significantly to accommodate the Irish?

It's the whole Agreement. The Agreement gave the Irish Government a role in relation to direct rule in Northern Ireland, which was in sharp contrast to the position the British Government took in the late 1960s and early 1970s when the Troubles broke, and then you had the British accepting a formal role for the Irish Government in putting forward views and proposals and a commitment to make every effort to achieve agreement in matters which bore directly on the internal affairs of Northern Ireland, so that was a major move. The officials, I think, met thirty-six times, both in formal discussions across the table and informal, when we met at dinner or over a meal where discussions were less inhibited.

Was the informal as important as the formal?

Yes. I think informal moments and discussions when people are less inhibited and more frank enables the psychology to work differently, allowing for a better understanding of deeper emotions that are moving people. If you get into an argument people are less inhibited than in a formal negotiation and both sides can come away with a better understanding about what really matters to the other side and why they are taking this position or that position.

How many people on the Irish side were involved in this?

I think five or six. The ones that I recall specifically were Dermot Nally, who was the Cabinet Secretary who was the leader of our group, Sean Donlon, who was, as it would be called now, Secretary General of the Department of Foreign Affairs, Michael Lillis, who was Assistant Secretary in charge of the Anglo-Irish division, Andy Ward, who was Secretary of the Department of Justice and Declan Quigley, who was the senior official in the Attorney-General's Office here, and myself, who was the Irish Ambassador in London. On the British side Robert Armstrong was the Cabinet Secretary and David Goodall was Deputy Cabinet Secretary at the time, and Robert Andrew, who was head of the Northern Ireland Office.

The time period from initial contacts through to the final Agreement was eighteen months, is that correct?

Between eighteen months and two years, depending on when you start counting in 1984.

Did you know what you wanted the Agreement to end up looking like, not just in terms of the issues and core principles but in terms of scope and limitation as well?

It's difficult to say, but at an early stage in 1983, early 1984, the idea of some kind of joint authority or joint approach to Northern Ireland would have been the general idea on the Irish side, and it took shape eventually as the role conceded to the Irish Government. The idea of joint authority was a vague aim that just wasn't on. The phrase at the time by Sinn Fein and others was 'Brits out', but this was now more a case of 'Irish in'. You couldn't simply treat Northern Ireland in isolation without being aware that a substantial minority there were looking in another direction and that an Irish Government had to be a part of the solution.

How did the nationalists and Sinn Fein react to the Agreement, and did they react in the way you expected?

It was touch and go as to how the nationalist politicians would react. The reaction of people like Seamus Mallon was very important. The last month or so before the Agreement we were not quite sure which side would welcome it and which side would reject it and what would be needed to bring the minority in Northern Ireland along to democratic politics, as well as could the unionists live with what we had done? We were kind of trusting that the British had measured that aspect, and we might have measured the minority aspect, but it was still hopeful. We had no certainty as to what either side would do. We assumed that Sinn Fein wouldn't accept it and, as we know, the opposition here under Charles Haughey rejected it as a betrayal, but Fianna Fail politicians would see that as a misjudgement and foolish. There was a general sense that an agreement was progress as well as an important stepping-stone towards a settlement later. There was a lot of uncertainty in the month beforehand as to who is going to rubbish this and who is going to think this was a good thing.

Would it be unreasonable to say that if the impetus of the Anglo-Irish Agreement was to prevent the political advancement of Sinn Fein, it failed?

Yes and no. I don't think it would be reasonable to say that as a general statement. My judgement is that the Anglo-Irish Agreement was of seminal importance on the road to the peace agreement that eventually emerged with Good Friday in 1998. Although Sinn Fein opposed it very strongly when it came out it had an effect on their thinking and they came to see eventually, through a long, slow process promoted by John Hume and others, that this was a way of making progress by political means. Equally, on the unionist side it was strongly opposed by unionists who were vehemently against what they called a 'diktat', but they couldn't pull it down because it was made between the two Governments; it didn't depend any more on the agreement of the parties in Northern Ireland, although it had an accommodation for that. On both sides you had a long-term 'fermenting effect' of the Agreement where, on the Sinn Fein side, it gradually persuaded them to come in from the cold provided there could be a much larger negotiation in which they could speak for the republican position once they had abandoned violence. On the unionist side it was so opposed that they were that much more open to an alternative, and therefore in the late 1980s and early 1990s various efforts were made and gradually, as the 1990s went on, they began to take part and eventually, out of that, comes the Good Friday Agreement.

Did you discuss the possibility that the unionists were going to go through the roof on this and it was better that they went through the roof than the nationalists?

There was, I should mention, in the course of the negotiations a time when some thought was given to possible change in the Irish Constitution. because Articles Two and Three were seen as a claim by the Republic on Northern Ireland. In fact, that wasn't an accurate way to describe them. They were rather subtly drafted by de Valera in 1937 in such a way that the national territory was the whole island of Ireland, but then you had another Article that said 'Pending the re-integration of the national territory the jurisdiction of the Irish Government shall be limited to what is in effect the Republic', so you had a kind of broad statement about the Irish territory as a whole island and then you had a drawing-back from it when, and until, the island is reunited, so the jurisdiction of the Republic is limited. The Irish Government at the Sunningdale Conference in 1973 had felt constrained by that and therefore had to insist that it had to be done as two parallel declarations in order that neither would have primacy, because the Irish Government were afraid of a constitutional challenge in the Irish courts under the Constitution. When it comes to the Agreement of 1985 the question of a possible change in those Articles was considered during the negotiations by both sides; and both sides, having considered it, backed away.

Haughey was critical of the Agreement when it was signed, but when he became Taoiseach did he try to destroy it?

Not at all. On the contrary, he wanted it to work. He was critical of it when it was first adopted and agreed in 1985 and he sent his spokesman on foreign affairs, Brian Lenihan, to Washington to lobby against it. I think there were a number of people in Fianna Fail who did not like that approach, and it didn't work anyway. I would say that it was largely driven by political motivation. In other words, where the duty of opposition took over, but I think it was a misjudgement by him and I suspect that privately he may have been a bit surprised about what had been achieved. Certainly, when he came to office his formal position was that it was an agreement entered into by the previous Government and therefore as a legal matter he accepted it, so there was continuity and he wasn't going to repudiate something by a previous Government. That was the formal position, but I think the reality is he wanted to make it work at that stage.

Was there a consensus from the Forum on the ultimate aim being Irish reunification?

The merit of it was that it brought the opposition in and tied them into a whole series of principles. The disadvantage of it from the point of view of the Government was that in order to achieve agreement it was necessary to become rather greener in its aims than they would have wanted to be, because while everybody would subscribe to the idea of hoping some day there would be a united Ireland there is a very different view whether it is realistic to even talk about it in the immediate future, and the focus was not on that, and it was not that they were repudiating it, because it was a long-term hope that some day it would happen. How do you end the conflict? The Forum Report was fairly advanced by the standards of Irish nationalism, with developed principles about recognising the identity, the culture and the ethos of the unionists as well as the nationalists. The more typical old Irish nationalist thing would not have had that much concern about unionists, but this was quite broad minded and quite positive, and even equally saying there are two identities in Northern Ireland, two ethoses, two cultural identities and so on.

Was it coincidental that the Forum talks started before the talks on the Anglo-Irish Agreement?

I think they started probably the previous autumn, the autumn of 1983. I would guess they would have started by September of 1983. So they were underway in 1983 and then into 1984. The first meeting was on 30 May 1983. The Report was released on 2 May 1984, effectively a year later. That was part of the build-up.

State papers suggest it was advisable to try and avoid talking to Thatcher about the substance of the text and manage her support by emphasising the moment as a window of opportunity. Do you think that Thatcher had a grasp on the detail of the text?

I think that was purely a tactical point in so far as you talk about focussing not on the substance of the text. That whole issue of managing Margaret Thatcher is strange. You have read volume two of the Charles Moore biography, I take it. The chapter there on the Anglo-Irish Agreement is quite interesting. I think it probably draws a good deal on David Goodall's private memorandum, but there is a key sentence there which I think explains a good deal about Margaret Thatcher; at least, the sentence that I thought reflected well said something like 'She had a great ability to allow other people to do something which she might have been seen in principle to be opposed to.' Now I don't believe that she was fooled in any way, she went along with it and she knew what she was doing. She raised difficulties at times and proved quite tough, but the idea that she was just managed into it was not quite right. The point about whether to talk about the substance on the British side was that it would be more or less on the basis of private advice, that if you want to get anywhere with the Prime Minister don't start pushing this. If you are in a continuing negotiation and you are trying to make the thing work and both sides are meeting regularly and talking to each other and one side says you are focussing too much on the detail, you would be much better to focus on the big picture, or else don't focus on the big picture, but on the detail, you consider that. She knew perfectly well what she was doing at all stages and she may have balked and been difficult at times but they certainly did try to smooth the relationship, and the idea that she was blind to what was happening was wrong. I remember at the stage where the Agreement was more or less ready to go, in the weeks before 15 November 1985, the officials on the two sides prepared a question-and-answer paper running to thirty-five pages for each Prime Minister for the press conference that they would be giving after the Agreement was signed, in order to prepare them to answer the different questions that might be thrown at them. This was a more or less agreed text and both had it before they went into the press conference, so you had officials managing the various criticisms or questions and both sides had an agreed text to work from on the answers they gave. Mrs Thatcher, before she went in, had to study this so she was not walking into something she didn't know about.

Did the SDLP see the text before it was released?

Yes and no. There was close contact but Hume did not brief his colleagues in the SDLP and it was only in the very late stage, close to the actual signature, that the whole party saw it. Hume was certainly kept abreast in general terms, maybe not of each detail, but he was certainly aware all along. I gather his colleagues did not realise exactly what would happen and were only briefed a few days before the Agreement appeared.

Were you concerned with the vehemence with which the unionists attacked the Agreement, or was it just batten down the hatches and say nothing?

I remember being at the House of Commons when the Agreement was being debated and it received overwhelming support, something like 490 to 50 or 60. I also recall Harold McClusker, who was a unionist MP, being very hurt by the Agreement. There was obviously a concern about the vehemence with which they opposed it, but also some degree of assurance that it was now between the two Governments and it was not something that could be pulled down as Sunningdale was with the Ulster workers' strike, and a reliance on Mrs Thatcher's determination to carry through what she had agreed. In the long term the Agreement was very important because the unionists disliked it so much that they were desperate to find an alternative and so were open to something to replace it. That became the basis for the talks which took place in the early 1990s.

Do you also think that the unionist anger was part of the reason why republicans became interested in it, because if unionism is up in arms then perhaps republicans would start to think this is of interest to them?

I am afraid you are right, and part of the problem in Northern Ireland for many years has been the zero-sum game, that is, the belief in one community that whatever the other community gains they lose, whereas I would like to think that it was to the benefit of both. But there is a sense that at least it's possible if the nationalists had repudiated it the unionists might have seen something in it. There is sadly that sense where what you lose we gain, and what we lose you gain.

3

Political imagination and the Anglo-Irish Agreement: an interview with Michael Lillis

Graham Spencer: *What is the earliest moment you can recall when you were asked to make contact with British official David Goodall on an Anglo-Irish talks process?*

Michael Lillis: It was in 1983 and it followed intensive discussions within our own team, which was led by Garret FitzGerald but also included Peter Barry, Dick Spring and Michael Noonan. There had been very careful, prudent renewal of contact between the two Governments when, after the breakdown between Thatcher and Charles Haughey, there was no communication. We had an Ambassador in London and he was able to talk to the Foreign Office but there was no real communication about the problem of Northern Ireland. There was no dialogue between the Prime Minister and our Taoiseach or anybody else. A couple of months after FitzGerald was elected he called me in Brussels, where I was based, and asked me to come back. At this stage the connection between Dermot Nally and Robert Armstrong had been sort of institutionalised in something called the Anglo-Irish Intergovernmental Conference, which had been set up by Haughey and Thatcher a couple of years before when Haughey had the famous 'teapot' meetings, but which had been effectively frozen. This was carefully renewed. Things had been awful between Dublin and London, largely because of the position that Haughey took on the Falklands, which was ludicrous. We had no national interest whatever in taking the position we did on the Falklands and, in particular, no moral interest, so there was no reason for us to intervene on that. There was no pressure on us to take a line on this but Haughey wanted to make her life difficult because of the way she handled the hunger strike, which had caused him a lot of problems. In the border counties support for the hunger strikers was strong and, indeed, two of them were elected to the Dail. The concern we had when FitzGerald was Taoiseach was to get into some kind of serious discussion with the British about the North. FitzGerald and I had many conversations about this but the answer we came up with was that the only thing Thatcher was interested in was security. She had no interest in justice, discrimination, alienation or any of the issues which were really serious for the nationalist community at that time. She was pro-unionist and that was her whole instinct. The people she surrounded herself with in the Tory party, such as Enoch Powell and Airey Neave, were also so strongly unionist that there was no point in talking to them. So the problem that we were facing was how to get a dialogue going which she would tolerate and support.

What we were looking at, then, was a possible breakdown not just in the North but in the South as well. We had seen signs at the height of the hunger strikes that people could be stirred to a point where there would be confrontations with the police, with loss of life and follow-up protests and funerals, as part of a cycle of frustration and more anger. One could actually envisage a situation developing where there would be the beginnings of loss of control by the Government. We had seen some signs of that in the previous years but it was moving in that direction very strongly. We had this institutional inheritance of the Intergovernmental Conference, and then a subsidiary body of that, for which I was the Irish co-Chairman. David Goodall was the British co-Chairman but the agenda for meetings was very banal, to put it mildly. I had a general kind of instruction from FitzGerald to use this as an opportunity to try to bring home to the British how dangerous the situation was and how out of control the situation seemed to us, but also how little ability or inclination they seemed to have to do anything about it. We were losing our authority in the South, and in the North the younger members of the Catholic community were drifting very solidly towards Sinn Fein and the Provisional IRA. We saw that direction as very bad and one where it wasn't going to help the nationalist people at all. This was what I was supposed to communicate, and I had no difficulty in doing it because I was travelling to the North regularly and was horrified with what I was seeing. I was being told by responsible people like John Hume how dangerous things were getting, and so I was trying to initiate the argument that this was not going to get better unless there was a very strong, palpable and real Irish dimension in the lives of people that they can see and virtually touch. My suggestion was to move our security people into nationalist areas, and although it was a fairly far-fetched idea I felt it was necessary as part of a process to involve our courts in the legal system, because the nationalist community had completely lost confidence in the fairness and acceptability of the court system in the North. What we were suggesting was mixed three-man courts on both sides of the border for crimes that were associated with, shall we say, political inspiration. Goodall was certainly taken aback by this approach.

Initially we had a good long walk along the canal in Dublin after one of the Intergovernmental meetings and kept going back and forth to discuss this. Goodall certainly had difficulty in believing that this was coming with the authority of the

Taoiseach. The idea to broach was that I should go to the Cabinet Office in London. Goodall was very questioning and sceptical as to whether this had FitzGerald's blessing. In turn, he pursued the issue of whether we would be prepared to do something about Articles Two and Three by way of balancing any change. I said that this was possible but it would depend on what was on the other side of the equation, because the Government just couldn't go out and say to people, against a backdrop of chaos and tension, let's just recognise that Northern Ireland is now fully a part of the UK. We needed dual involvement. Goodall went away from that first conversation and then came back within two weeks. He was very specific in his questions about what together we might be prepared to do and what might be wanted. At that stage he did not make it clear to me that the specific areas I was advocating change on, that is, that we should have our security people in nationalist areas and particularly the courts system, were going to be accepted. What he did do was convey that the ideas were being studied very seriously, including by the Prime Minister.

What do you mean by being studied very seriously?

The impression he made on me is that he was taking the ideas I had launched with the authority of Garret FitzGerald and was relaying them back. He was coming back to me with questions which arose from his interactions with Robert Armstrong and the Prime Minister, although I didn't know who else at that stage. We took a bit of heart from that and, although we didn't think this was guaranteed to get us anywhere, at least something was happening which was being taken seriously at the level of Margaret Thatcher.

Was this confidential?

Totally. I didn't tell anybody in the Government about this except Garret FitzGerald, who wanted it to be played under his instructions. Within about a month, as is inevitably the case with these things, it had worked its way around to the people that needed to be told on our side. What I have read about this and have had confirmed since is that Goodall was instructed to check with other departments, notably the Northern Ireland Office, about the ideas, which were generally dismissed and became known as 'Lillisisms' – in other words, crazy, unthinkable and outrageous. The funny thing was that Thatcher didn't instruct us to stop talking. But let me explain something here, I deliberately, and this again was discussed with Garret, presented these ideas in the context of security, not in the context of political debate. I specifically said this is not for any political objective but because we had a situation which was catastrophic, getting worse and was not going to stop without an Irish dimension to achieve a level of stability.

So the argument was that we were doing this for security reasons and not because of some green nationalist objective. We presented the argument to the British side as being driven by a motivation to do the right thing and not just to stop the rise of Sinn Fein, which is now generally seen as FitzGerald's main motivation. I should also say, though, that the two ideas were not mutually inconsistent.

There were two early meetings at Head of Government level. The first was when we had the presidency of the EEC and had a meeting in 10 Downing Street which we used as a cover to have some discussion following on from the Lillis–Goodall dialogue. There was an issue about a loan that was given to the European Commission and Thatcher was resistant about doing anything for these EEC 'nuts', and she said no with the entire British Cabinet present. The man at the bottom of the table was John Major, and there were just four of us, Garret FitzGerald, Dermot Nally, myself and a Junior Minister for Finance from Cork, Jim O Keefe. There was a debate between Thatcher and FitzGerald about this loan and she said no, never, so the whole thing broke up. Once she was out of the room Nigel Lawson told FitzGerald not to worry and that the British would do it. That was the way Thatcher tended to be, almost as if she was performing on television. It was my first experience of her, followed by a meeting shortly afterwards at Chequers. On both occasions FitzGerald made it clear that the ideas I put forward to Goodall were authorised by him. This was helpful, because it meant that the scepticism which was being expressed around other departments in London about the validity of the ideas and their source was actually put to bed and we could now move forward with this. From there on the British began to make serious efforts to officially respond to us. The first and very interesting response, which was dismissed, and I think too readily by our side, was the famous proposal that there could be security operations on both sides of the border.

Before we get to that proposal, was it a strategic move by FitzGerald to put you in the position to build the contacts?

Yes. We had a programme of things that we were going to do and the whole idea was to have analyses which would interrelate and overlap, such as propose interactive agencies working for both the British and Irish in such areas as medical qualifications for doctors and nurses. It was harmless stuff, but there were an awful lot of Irish doctors and nurses in those days in England, so we set up a Co-ordinating Committee agenda where we would examine each of these things. It may have appeared banal, but it was very real too. When Goodall came back over to Dublin we had quite a lively chat, which was a bit of a 'ding-dong', which is no harm with the British in my view. My argument with Goodall, whom I held in very high esteem, was that the British had to respect the sovereignty of our country in every way that we deal with each other. I said that we respected the British but they treated us like a former colony or half-colony and that we will never get anywhere until we get past this. Goodall reacted with some anger because he knew a lot about Ireland and his family are Irish. He himself was a Catholic, but his family were Protestants from County Wexford who emigrated after the 1798 rebellion and went to England, so he had a bit of a background there.

At a first meeting of the Co-ordinating Committee we had people from his Ministry of Education, the NHS and the equivalents from Ireland and we decided to try and improve the mutual recognition of qualifications between universities, which was very technical and straightforward stuff. There was no talk of Northern Ireland. But after lunch I asked Goodall if he realised how bad the situation was. Each day you had young men and women being politicised and radicalised because they were being routinely stopped by the British Army. The hatred had got so bad that there was no way we were going to avoid situations getting worse. A lot of young people were getting into trouble and ending up in jail, which was a hopeless situation for their future. I said that the British were responsible for this but so were the Irish also. After 1922 the British let a situation fester where they wouldn't even let a question be asked in the House of Commons about Northern Ireland. It was ruled out by the Speaker on the grounds that there was a Parliament in Northern Ireland, albeit it was totally one sided, and that was where such issues should be dealt with. The British had a Protestant police force, the 'B' Specials, and so all of the power was on one side. But we were also guilty because when we had a settlement in 1920–21 we just went along with it because it was seen as probably the right thing to do, and because it was as seen as probably the best deal we could get at that time. The problem, as we know, is that in allowing Northern Ireland to run its own show we basically consented to an apartheid situation. We did not push the British to deal with this problem and we didn't use any influence around the world in a real way to help. As a result, this situation blew up, and there is no question that it was primarily the fault of the British because they are the responsible power who allowed the local system to be totally discriminatory.

When you said this to Goodall, what did he say?

I was speaking as strongly as I could even though I had been a diplomat for many years. I also personally believe that the best form of diplomacy is to look the other person in the eyes and hit them hard, because if you represent a small, relatively powerless country you don't have an opportunity to get your message across too often, so you have to make sure it's registered and makes others think. If you are very nice and subtle and indirect you are wasting your time and theirs. So I gave it to him hot and heavy about Britain's responsibility. He was already conscious of that, but what I was stressing was the emerging danger. FitzGerald was concerned about not wanting Sinn Finn to overtake the SDLP in elections, but the real concern was more primitive and direct, namely that we are going to have an awful lot of violence which is going to go on and on, and that the British didn't have anything in their arsenal of instruments of power which was going to help this situation. This was very much my theory and FitzGerald backed it. I said to Goodall that Thatcher was only interested in security, so we should talk about security and what happens day in and day out for most young Catholics in Northern Ireland. I also added that the British should allow us to send our police into nationalist areas as well as our own army, that we should and would work with the British until the alienated youth and their parents instead of having an outside alien security system had a security system which their own side could live with.

Did Goodall reject that out of hand?

No, he didn't. He certainly didn't believe it could happen, but he said if we were to do something as radical as this, or something like it, it would be unlikely to happen without changing Articles Two and Three of the Irish Constitution, which laid a claim on the territory of Northern Ireland.

Do you think that Articles Two and Three were central for the British and occupied much of their thinking?

The problem with putting those two Articles into the Constitution, which de Valera did, was that it was very difficult for his and any successive Irish Government to deal with the British, since it gave them a very strong argument and weapon against co-operation. Now I had already anticipated this in my own conversations with FitzGerald and the way we worked it out was I was able to say to Goodall that Garret FitzGerald was aware about the discussions and personally supported me. I had said to FitzGerald beforehand that Goodall would hit us with Articles Two and Three and I want to be able to say to him if we get a real debate or negotiation going here we will work to change Articles Two and Three.

Is it the case that you offered to put Articles Two and Three on the table but the British said there was no point because you would never get it through a referendum?

In a sense it was. What happened is that from the very beginning they wanted to get assurances that we would deal with that. That was difficult because the Irish Government hadn't decided at that stage they would agree to this, but I said I was sure that if we got sufficient political encouragement from negotiations then we would deal with that even though I didn't have authority from FitzGerald to offer it.

What happened when you offered it?

I didn't offer it. I said in response to Goodall's perfectly predictable questions that if we were making sufficient progress it is something we could do and, by the way, would want to do. FitzGerald later confirmed to Thatcher that we were prepared to deal with Articles Two and Three if we were making progress, but that clearly we were not going to do anything if we were not making progress. Douglas Hurd, who then moved into the Northern Ireland Office, was becoming convinced that an Agreement was a bad idea and saw this as a threat because it dealt with one of the real roadblocks, possibly the biggest one, as seen from London. At one of the meetings in Chequers Hurd, in order to try to restrict the agenda of what is being discussed, came in and said 'Oh no we don't want you to do that because the worst thing that could possibly happen is that you attempt to get rid of Two and Three and fail, because that would be a disaster,' which was a plausible argument, but his real intention was to limit the agenda of the Agreement. It was very cleverly and effectively done but actually, in the end, even though we didn't deal with Articles Two and Three, we got a pretty useful agreement.

It's interesting that he should try and discourage you from trying that, because if it had come to a referendum which then collapsed one would assume there were also many who would have been happy about that?

Yes, but when the Agreement was announced there was euphoria in Dublin. Don't forget that the SDLP at that stage was the representative of the nationalist/Catholic community in the North and they were doing handstands. We could have won a referendum in November/December of 1985, I have no doubt about that. No doubt at all about that.

At the end of that conversation with Goodall, how was it left?

He expressed astonishment at the ideas but he didn't reject them, and then he said he would report back.

Did he go and discuss this with Armstrong first or did he go straight to Thatcher?

Armstrong first.

And then they went as a double-act to see Thatcher?

They did.

And they persuaded her?

Well they came back and they looked for clarification. Goodall came back to Dublin and later he and I were at a British–Irish Association conference in Oxford where we spent several hours going around the subject. A few weeks after that Goodall went back and talked to Armstrong, and then they both talked to Thatcher. She rejected outright doing anything, but she encouraged them to keep talking and the next thing that happened was that Armstrong and Goodall came to Dublin to meet with our team. I told Goodall that John Hume supported this on a totally confidential basis too. They sent a man from the Northern Ireland Office to talk to Hume but Hume wouldn't show any awareness of anything, so they thought that I was making it up. We had a real proposal, which was also the position of the British Cabinet, in the spring of 1984 after Armstrong and Goodall had been talking to people in the security area as well as meeting Dermot Nally, Sean Donlon and Noel Dorr. We were the only people in the 'know', so to speak, at this stage. In their initial delivery they said that the big British concern was what happened in the areas close to the border and that they wanted a security zone on both sides of that border with the two police forces working together, and they gave us this in writing from the British Government. They also said they would look at mixed courts, as well as possibly having the guards (our police) in nationalist areas in Northern Ireland working with the RUC. That was when Dermot Nally said we were not going to have the British Army or police in our territory and the other officials on our side said the same thing.

Was there any conversation or suggestion amongst the Irish team about British withdrawal?

No.

You say you had a number of meetings with Hume, but what was the substance of those meetings? Were you just getting his consent or was it more involved than that?

Hume was worried, almost in despair, that the situation was going to hell and we needed a new approach. He also saw that if the only way to approach it was on the basis of security or law and order in the courts then we should try it. He was not too happy about Articles Two and Three, which was a much more painful issue for nationalists in the North than for people in the South, but we were encouraged to go ahead.

In response did Goodall offer the proposal of a five mile 'no-man's-land' between Northern Ireland and the Republic?

Yes, which was a sort of crazy British proposal, although not a random one either. It was approved by the Cabinet in London and it was the first major proposal to come from London for years to say something substantive about the problem of Northern Ireland. It was wrong-headed in one respect.

But it could have led somewhere?

The difficulty for us, which was insurmountable, was as follows: on our side the police and army are fully accepted and even popular with the public. On the other side, however, for virtually one half of the population, the army is regarded as an occupying force, whilst for the other half it's regarded as 'our army' and, while the RUC was seen as 'our police force' for unionists, for nationalists it was an oppressive, foreign police force. Because of that the idea of having those people on our side of the border, when they were regarded as oppressors of nationalists in the North, was unthinkable. Even so, Armstrong and Goodall came over to the Taoiseach's Department and they made this proposal in writing. It wasn't just Mrs Thatcher and it wasn't just the Foreign Secretary, it was a Cabinet-approved proposal as well.

Did you see this coming?

No, but it was a response to what I had put to Goodall and that was put to us orally. It came as a formal proposal, and as I was listening to it I could see others were horrified. I did think however that this proposal was remarkable, because the other side of the equation was that we would be able to have our folks on the other side of the border, working in nationalist areas inside the North and not just within the five-mile limit. They talked about 'nationalist areas' inside the North, and this was put to us orally at the meeting. They also talked about nationalist identity issues and cultural issues. I thought at the time that although we had no interest in having the RUC in County Monaghan, we had nevertheless broken a mould.

Was that the first proposal from the British in relation to your point about changes to the legal and security system?

We were at the beginning of a negotiation, so we did not want to kick them out the door. But our ministers, and this is the only fundamental disagreement I had with them over those years, immediately said no, go back and tell them no deal and we don't even want to discuss it. You see, despite the best goodwill and desire to help on our side, the fact is that our governmental system is what we call 'partitionist'. Now the word partitionist in the South is an insulting term because it suggests you are somebody who doesn't really care about what's happening in the North and that you want to keep those problems isolated and not get involved. Essentially that's what most of us in the South indeed do think. There were one or two of us who thought a bit differently from that, but the overriding view was that we didn't want those troubles dragged into our territory.

What's interesting with this territorial proposition is that you have the border being looked at with a degree of flexibility by the British but this gets ditched immediately by the Irish without further exploration?

In effect you could say this was an invitation to the guards and our military to help out in nationalist areas of the North. I couldn't believe my ears, but our official reaction which came immediately was stop it, don't do it. Nevertheless, what had happened was that effectively we had the beginnings of a negotiation. My instinct and my desire was to take it further because at least the door was open to us and we had negotiations in train. So at the time, and this is something which was much overlooked by the British, who didn't take it as seriously as they should, we had the Forum Report, and the important point about the Forum Report, which was missed, was that it was a consensus which was worked out with tremendous difficulty and a great deal of battling between the constitutional nationalist parties, the SDLP for the North, and Fianna Fail and Fine Gael with the Labour Party in sessions that went on every week for over a year, producing different reports about economic matters, security matters and human rights matters. This resulted in an overall Forum Report that consisted of three illustrative proposals. In addition to the illustrative proposals we proposed you could have an integrated, or united, or federal Ireland, or joint authority in the North between Dublin and London. Importantly, Thatcher was opposed to joint authority even though we had a very strong argument that you could have joint authority which would not breach British sovereignty. Then there was another item included, which was to allow for any other idea which could help to create stability and peace. The most important part of the Forum Report was the section headed 'Realities and Principles', because it tried to describe what the real issues were that needed to be addressed in any negotiation. What it also said was you had to have recognition of the British identity of the unionist people and their rights, and identity would have to be fully accommodated in any solution. You therefore had a principle of recognising that these people consider themselves to be British and have a full right to that self-identification and that this view should be fully reflected in any final outcome. This was what we wanted the British to concentrate on, but we never really got there because I think the British, and this wasn't the fault of the officials but probably of Margaret Thatcher personally, considered the Forum Report in terms of Haughey's involvement, which inevitably meant some kind of nationalist agenda that would be extremely offensive to unionists and to herself. But what the Forum Report was saying was we should recognise unionists fully, and this was a big step forward for nationalist Ireland to concede. Unfortunately, it was ignored.

After the Irish had dismissed the no-man's-land border strip, where did Armstrong and Goodall go from there?

Well it was very difficult for them because they had gone to tremendous trouble to push this idea through their Cabinet. If you consider the Cabinet saying to these foreigners come in to our territory and help us to solve this chaotic situation, well that was a big deal. I'm sorry our side didn't see it in those terms and negotiate on from there. It was obvious that they had put a hell of an effort in to get that through and it was a big setback for them. The negotiations resumed on an agenda which was less focussed in relation to 'feet on the ground' because I suppose we felt that if we pushed forward on our personnel helping out in nationalist areas in the North, then inevitably the British were going to say if you want that, then we want to have our folks inside your territory, which we were never going to live with.

When they left, was there any further discussion of the five-mile strip?

No, that was the end of it. It was dismissed in such terms that the British could not come back to it.

What was the next phase of negotiations used for?

Dismissing that proposal certainly limited our ability on the next step, so from there on it was more about things that seemed to be possible and easier to implement. The issues from then on would be how to have a structure where we could have a role in the North and what the areas would be where we could have that role. That's very much what the Agreement deals with but, importantly, there was also a very strong interest on our side in promoting devolution on a power-sharing basis and we came up with the idea that if there was to be devolution and cross-community agreement on a sort of government system for Northern Ireland, and if the two sides agreed, for example, to discuss economic matters, then that would be taken out of the agenda of issues that the Irish Government might use as part of proposals put forward by us to the British. That was the idea we hoped would actually work, and, of course, it was revived again under the Good Friday Agreement negotiations. The same was true on other issues like policing, which we didn't get very far on, although we did have a useful text on human rights incidents and security matters. The whole thing was about trying to find a formula whereby our role would not just be about a right to be consulted. We needed a right to propose our views. And to have a structure, the Anglo-Irish structure, whereby we would both make determinate efforts to achieve agreement in the interests of peace and stability. This was difficult, given that the British weren't going to accept we should have any executive role. But what was actually achieved in the end was quite unique in international terms. Here you have a situation which is a matter of disagreement and conflict between the Governments of two neighbouring countries, territory which we claimed should be ours, a claim which London obviously rejects, but, because of the instability that has arisen, we all agree that we should have a voice in the government of that territory and that voice should take the form of our being able to make proposals and of obligatory efforts between the two diverging or opposing positions to resolve differences.

To what extent was your conversation with Goodall, Armstrong and others occupied with what may or may not happen to the Provisional IRA?

It was a key issue. Politically, and I would say even emotionally, we were not as opposed to the Provisional IRA as they were, but even more so, because we thought they were subverting a small sovereign Irish State with limited resources. These guys were getting weapons on a colossal scale from Gaddafi and US supporters, so there was a threat to the security of the Irish State. Don't forget too, we had hundreds of their members in jail in Ireland, something that Mrs Thatcher, no matter how often we told her, never seemed to be ready to acknowledge. They had killed one or two of our soldiers, a few members of the police, and intimidated a lot of people, including juries, so we were seriously and passionately opposed to them.

Is it the case that no matter what people thought of the Agreement its main message was that unionism could no longer just control the situation?

I absolutely agree that was the case. What Wilson and Merlyn Rees had done in 1974 was re-establish, by surrendering to the loyalist strikes, the veto of unionism on any proposal whatever, even one that was internal to Northern Ireland and nothing to do with us. And that was a disaster because what that said to nationalist people is that the unionists are in control here and the British Government will never face them down. That continued to be the case until the Agreement of 1985, and Thatcher deserves a lot of credit for that change.

One of the things of interest here is how you actually understood the reasoning and logic of British officials and how the British differed from the Irish in their conceptualisation of this problem?

If you look at the different attempts at solutions, starting with Sunningdale, through to the Good Friday and St Andrews Agreements, I think it's probably fair to say that the origination of the ideas came largely from the British. The idea of setting up a power-sharing Executive and the agenda that was to be worked through was very much the drafting and the initiative of officials on the British side. But the Anglo-Irish Agreement was very largely an Irish initiative and, although not entirely, most of the ideas came from us.

Were the British more interested in principles than pragmatism?

One of the things that we had to recognise was that the British were not interested in discussing principles at all. And I have come to that conclusion working on EU matters over the years, where I worked in the European Commission on British issues. Other nations have a tradition, like the French, of wanting to start with the ideas and the principles, the Cartesian kind of stuff, and then move on to see how you apply that in practice. Whereas the British have the inverse and, I think, often the wiser approach, which is to get straight into the pragmatic issues, and then if there is a principle issue there, somewhere, deal with that, but on that basis. Here we were coming up with a set of principles which should have been very attractive to them, particularly in the generous approach that was taken in the Forum Report to the rights of the unionist people, and this was fully supported by people like John Hume, who led on the issue and persuaded Charlie Haughey to go along with it. We were trying to see if we could get this as the agenda for negotiations, but unfortunately there was a sort of reluctance, almost hostility, to discussing principles. Indeed, we were told that Mrs Thatcher had no interest whatsoever in discussing principles. That was said in a way which was not intended to denigrate her, but to persuade us that we would not get anywhere with that kind of approach. It was a lost opportunity actually. Having said that, we got back into negotiation and there was a series of contacts. Everybody talks about the famous Chequers meeting and the 'Out, out, out' speech of Thatcher as being the most important moment. What was more important were the several meetings of the European Council and discussion at the time about whether the presidency should be in Dublin or Milan. If I remember correctly the presidency proceeded on an alphabetical basis. After us, in those days, were the Italians, but on all of those occasions there were separate, informal one-on-one meetings with Garret FitzGerald and Margaret Thatcher outside of the European Council, which were intense, and much work was done there.

When Goodall and Armstrong put a text in front of you, what did you notice about the way they constructed that text in comparison to perhaps how the Irish might construct it?

Thinking about that now, it was very much the style of Armstrong and Goodall not to be highfalutin, at least in the first draft. Generally, that draft addressed what they would hope to achieve as this thing moved forward, rather than containing all the flowery stuff about peace and reconciliation, which we or they would have added later. That stuff was almost common parlance at a certain stage. But so far as it went it was focussed on practical matters.

You mentioned the initial conversation with Goodall and the five-mile no-man's-land proposal, but was that the first piece of official text used?

I am open to correction, but I think it was, although it was a response to our initiative too.

Did they leave the text with you, or just read it out and take it away?

They left it with us, and what's very unusual about this is that there was an extraordinary level of personal trust in terms of behaving correctly between the two groups that were involved at that stage. Armstrong and Goodall were the only two on the British side and there were four on the Irish side, and I have to say they did take risks with us. I mean, if that text had got into the press it would have created chaos on our side, and almost certainly on the unionist side too.

Were things at that stage dripping into the press?

No.

At what time did you have to start fielding problems outside when the press got soundings of this?

It was about a year into the whole process and it was when the Northern Ireland Office was brought in. On our side we also brought in two additional advisors, both of whom were extraordinarily discreet. One was head of the Attorney-General's Office, who was brought in to help with drafting on the status of Northern Ireland and our Constitution, and the other was head of our Department of Justice. The issue of security co-operation kept coming up because there was a lot of it going on. We had 150 Provisional IRA prisoners serving long sentences in Portlaoise jail and our police were constantly coming under armed attack by the Provisionals. But the simple fact is, and I am prepared to admit this, we could have done more after we started to get close to signing the Agreement. There is no question that FitzGerald wanted to be co-operative here because we needed to get as much out of the British as we possibly could, and we did certainly improve the security co-operation but we could have done more.

Did Armstrong and Goodall help you get more out of the British because they were involved?

No question about that. It wouldn't have happened without those two individuals.

Did the process come close to collapse at any point?

Oh yes, because basically what we had was a series of drafts of an agreement. Not with all the flowery language, as I say, but of actual substance, and they would redraft our redrafts and we would redraft their redrafts, but there was more than one occasion where their redrafts of our stuff, which would have reflected instructions from the Prime Minister, would have a huge 'No' scribbled in her handwriting over the paper, followed by the question 'What do these people want?' These were insulting kinds of remarks which, although sincere, meant that they tended to come back with proposals which were frankly inadequate. The issue of our having a referendum to redraft Articles Two and Three was taken off the table, and that was around about the time of the famous Chequers meeting which led to Thatcher's 'Out, out, out' statement. There was a lot of emotion in these things, but it was not a personal issue as far as I could see. In the preceding meeting there was a long discussion between Garret FitzGerald and Mrs Thatcher, which I was present at along with Dermot Nally and Robert Armstrong, and what was clear was her constant emotional resistance to doing anything. Most of the things that we wanted she would reject in detail before coming around a bit.

What we were looking for was 'joint authority', which was not joint sovereignty, where Northern Ireland would continue to be part of the UK and its sovereign government would be the British Government, but that we would actually be involved in the British Government's decision-making process and not be limited to offering our views and having a constant process of attempting to agree them. There are models for this in various parts of the world, such as in the Lebanon, and that was what we felt would provide sufficient confidence for the nationalist people and for stability to be achieved. But Thatcher would never accept that there was any difference between joint authority and joint sovereignty, so distinctions between the two were very subtle and difficult to argue. We saw, however, that it was possible for decisions to be made at a government level by the sovereign British Government and that at a separate subsidiary level you could have a system of joint authority, but she never accepted that.

Did you run words like 'consultative', 'co-operative', 'administrative' past her to try and find an acceptable distinction on this issue?

Yes, we did. We didn't consider 'consultative' to be adequate though. Before the final stages at Hillsborough Goodall and myself tried to anticipate possible questions from the press on this and how we would answer such a question as does the Anglo-Irish Agreement give a consultative role to the Irish Government or something else? The answer that was agreed, and which Thatcher specifically agreed, was that it was 'consultative but more than consultative'. In practice it's probably fair to say that it did work out that way but the British view of it, and particularly the Northern Ireland Office view, which was extremely hostile to the Agreement once it was enacted, was that we would never be allowed in practice to have anything more than a consultative role. Thankfully, the Northern Ireland Office had been kept out long enough to not destroy the Agreement, which they wanted to do. When they were finally brought in it was at a point when it was difficult to scupper the process.

How many drafts did the Agreement go through? What did the final Agreement look like in comparison to the initial draft?

I think it was substantially different. We would have had our draft which focussed on joint authority as being the central key of the whole thing and then there would be the pushback which would have reduced our potential role, etc. The courts issue was a different matter, and in the end that wasn't Thatcher's fault. We thought for months that we were making progress on the idea of having joint courts, where courts could have jurisdiction in both areas, and Thatcher did not oppose it at any stage.

So why did it not run?

This is described in some detail in Garret FitzGerald's autobiography. Garret came from a family which has Northern Protestant as well as Southern Catholic antecedents and his Northern Protestant family was quite well off. One of his cousins was the Lord Chief Justice of Northern Ireland and we were going along nicely with most of the negotiation being done by officials, but there was a rugby match which Garret had gone to and he had invited the Lord Chief Justice. They had a discussion, and it was unwise for Garret to have done this because it was the first that this chap had heard about the proposal and he was flabbergasted, outraged. He went back and spoke to his fellow judges, who were almost all Protestants, and they approached the Lord Chancellor, Lord Hailsham, who, and I can say this without fear of any libellous counter-reaction, was probably the most anti-Catholic British politician for a generation. Hailsham said to journalist Mary Holland on the judges in Northern Ireland, 'They do our dirty work for us,' which was no more or no less than the truth, and that was his attitude. He thought it was necessary for the security of the UK to keep that sort of system in place. So when the Northern Ireland judges went to Hailsham to express their horror at the fact that this idea was going around Hailsham immediately told Thatcher to forget it.

When was the idea of mixed North–South courts for terrorist offences introduced?

If you go back to the original conversations between myself and David Goodall my objective was to respond by concentrating on the alienation of the nationalist people, and particularly the young people who were joining the Provisional IRA, by arguing for the need, if possible, of security forces from the South in the court system of the North, so that the whole system of authority that they would be interacting with would not be seen as unionist-British, which it has been for generations. That was the thesis that I put forward and, of course, even though they found it very difficult to digest, they went along with it to some extent, and that was why what we ended up with via the Agreement was that our Government would have a role in discussion of most of the issues that were governmental, and then there would be a process of resolving differences which we wanted to have taken seriously. Now the court system in Northern Ireland was run by honourable people and lawyers who were preponderantly from a unionist background. There were one or two Catholics, but they were essentially non-existent. And the whole ethos and culture was a unionist one, so that when you came into court, particularly if you were on a charge for terrorist offences, you were really dealing with people who would not give you a fair hearing, as you saw it, because the view was that they would have to deal with you as severely as possible, lock you up and do whatever they had to, and if in the process there were issues, for example, like ill-treatment, they would ignore them. We discussed two ideas. One was that we would set up 'mixed courts' for terrorist charges and have three judges for those trials, not one but three, and no jury. We couldn't have a jury because juries were intimidated by the Provisional IRA, and when we had them there were people who got shot. At that point there were Diplock courts in Northern Ireland, with one judge sitting on his own, and the entire process was predictable. We had a pretty severe system here in the South too, where an Inspector in the Guards would give as his opinion that Joe Bloggs was a member of the Provisional IRA. It wasn't always accepted as conclusive proof but it was acceptable evidence and it would result regularly in convictions here. The population in the South accepted our court system en masse, nobody questioned it, whereas a whole section of the population in the North did not accept the British court system, so the idea we had, which was very simple, was that there should be three judges, and in a terrorist trial in the South under this system there would be one Northern judge and two Southern judges and in a terrorist trial in the North there would be two Northern judges and one Southern judge, to bring in the Irish dimension. Thatcher did not kick that out either.

Is that because she saw the logic of such a proposal in security rather than constitutional terms?

One hundred per cent, but on our side, of course, it was proposed as a political objective.

So why did it not come off?

Because of Lord Hailsham, who adamantly and absolutely rejected it. I have since read and heard that he was the only member of her Cabinet whom she would never face down, and also her view was that he had an independent constitutional position as a Lord Chancellor, as well as being one of the longest-serving members of a Tory Cabinet, so he was the one person whom she would not gainsay. But there were several other elements involved too.

Did Armstrong and Goodall do everything they could to push that through?

I would say they did everything that they thought was possible, but what was against them was the fact that they knew that Hailsham was the only member of the Cabinet that Thatcher would not take on, she was in awe of him. We then took this on board, were very disappointed and backed off, but we came up with another proposal, and this was not for mixed courts but having three judges involved, because that would create a chance that their interaction would reduce the likelihood of behaving in a sectarian way, simply because they would want to be seen as professional in each other's eyes. In the end, in the press release that went out with the final Agreement there was a reference which said something like 'consideration would be given to the idea of mixed courts', even though we had been told it would not happen. We had it in the final press release as a way of saving FitzGerald's face, and also because he wanted it to happen, but there was no more progress on it. So I suppose my conclusion would be that this was a very telling example of how the British system at its heart, the constitutional system, was supporting the unionist position.

How did Armstrong and Goodall say no to you on that? Did they just say this is a non-runner?

Yes, they were actually quite candid and said she can't gainsay Hailsham and she won't.

Did you meet Thatcher yourself?

I was a bag-carrier official at most of the meetings that involved FitzGerald and Thatcher and they would be set-piece meetings in Downing Street or Chequers, or sometimes in European Council meetings. When she was told about the Goodall–Lillis discussions which really started the whole process she allowed us to continue, which was surprising even to Armstrong and Goodall. Initial engagement with Goodall was followed by a FitzGerald–Thatcher meeting in Chequers in 1983, which was where FitzGerald confirmed to Thatcher that the ideas I had been putting to Goodall had his authority. She said fine, but wanted the secret discussions to stop because she had to be able to say in the House of Commons, if questioned, that there are no secret discussions. Of course, the secret discussions continued, but that was her reaction, and at that first meeting she asked FitzGerald to introduce me to her because she was interested in the approach I had taken with Goodall.

Did you think that Thatcher would go down this road, especially given the hostility with which the republicans viewed her after the hunger strikes?

She allowed us to go that far on the basis of our recommendations. We wanted it to be much stronger, obviously, but they were the terms that we agreed. Of course, I can't answer your question fully, but I think it's a very good question because there are two sides to the Thatcher coin. There was the very hostile one, shouting, denunciating everything from violence to Europe, which she came out with all the time. She even advocated the movement of population as a solution; take half the Catholic population over to the Irish side and that would be the end of it. This is on the record, although we didn't see it. Thatcher commented that there had been some movement of population in Ireland before, to which Goodall responded 'Yes Prime Minister, Cromwell sent a lot of the people to Connaught in the West,' to which she said 'That's it, why don't we do that?' That was the woman we were talking to; but the funny thing about Thatcher was although she could be brutal and appalling she sometimes contradicted that persona. Although she denounced the Maastricht Treaty in 1992 she still pushed it. She came from Grantham, one of the last holdouts of anti-Catholicism in England, and yet she had Catholics working for her and had full confidence in them. Goodall being an example, whom she used to tease as being her 'religious advisor'. I do think though that she genuinely disliked the Anglo-Irish Agreement and that she disliked Ireland and the Irish.

There is that idea that when someone shows a vehement dislike of something they are emotionally attached to it. One wonders if the hunger strikes and the Provisional IRA's attempt to kill her with the Brighton bombing had a more profound effect on Thatcher than was known?

You could be right, and I had not thought about it in those terms. I think that there is something in that. I couldn't give you an example of her saying the sort of thing that you have highlighted, but for sure she was much more complex than she wanted the readers of the *Sun* newspaper to believe.

Did the Northern Ireland Office try and undermine the possibility of agreement?

That is an understatement. In the last months of the negotiation the Northern Ireland Office headed by Tom King, with senior civil servants and three top officials, went directly on several occasions to Margaret Thatcher and begged her stop it. And it took all of the political credit, authority and talent of Armstrong and Goodall to circumvent that. We know that because of what we have learned since, and I can assure you that is one hundred per cent true. It was reflected in the fact that once the Agreement was signed on 15 November 1985 and we started to implement it, myself, Daithi O'Ceallaigh and two other people were sent to live in a very basic building in a palace barracks in Belfast, chosen for us by the Northern Ireland Office so as to make our lives extremely unpleasant. Once we got started we tried to have a system which would be agreed at the official level, so if we had an incident or, say, a proposal to abolish some old ghetto-type block of flats in West Belfast or Derry, we would work up a proposal and give it to them. We also logged everything, so we had a common Anglo-Irish log (invented most usefully by Daithi O'Ceallaigh) where we could register a policy proposal or a question about an incident that had taken place and get a response in two days to a week. That log shows that there was a very strong volume of content that was pushed through this process by our side at that time. However, what it also shows is an inadequate volume of agreed action at the beginning, although the momentum picked up strongly after the first months. There were two middle-to-senior civil servants from the Northern Ireland Office at the ground level of the building, along with secretaries, drivers and domestic staff. There was also my opposite number, a senior Foreign Office official, who made himself available as little as possible. Despite these difficulties the system did achieve a series of substantial improvements over the first eighteen months, largely because of its own momentum and the undeniable fact of the Agreement. Examples: abolition of the Flags and Emblems Act, a new Code of Conduct for the RUC, enhanced police accompaniment by the police of patrols by the military (including the UDR), strengthening of the laws on incitement and hatred, growth of representation of the Catholic community on the boards of all public bodies and even on the Bench, abolition of several ghetto blocks of flats, consultation on policy and individual cases in the prisons and investigation of hundreds of incidents involving the security forces and civilian population. I should add that we had a series of late-night sessions with the Head of the RUC, Sir John Hermon, who showed impressive leadership in confronting loyalist anti-Agreement violence on a large scale on the streets (several hundred RUC officers and their families were driven out of their houses). We also met several times with the Colonel-in-Chief of the British Army. He and Hermon showed independence of the Northern Ireland Office both in their willingness to consult us and in their positive attitudes to the Agreement.

The difference in the tone between working with Armstrong and Goodall and then working with the Northern Ireland Office was enormous. Certain individuals did everything possible to stop it happening, including going to Thatcher behind Goodall and Armstrong's backs. We were living in this bleak place which was chosen so as to make our lives uncomfortable. Not only were our conditions of life basic and quite primitive, but we had several thousand, sometimes 100,000, loyalists outside, screaming and yelling and threatening, and next door we had the RUC car-maintenance base, where all the personnel were loyalists, demonstrating their politics under an enormous 'Ulster Says No' banner, though this was a publicly owned British Government base. We had a few rockets coming in, occasional gunfire on the building, and the worst of it all was the fact that our families in the South were watching these convulsions on television. In the period I was there, which was about a year and eight months, not one senior official of the Northern Ireland Office ever came to see us. So what was the mistake we made? We should have kept the Nally–Armstrong channel open to ride shotgun on how this thing was working out and we didn't, and I think the reason we didn't, although well intentioned, was flawed.

So once you were in Belfast, Armstrong and Goodall left the scene?

Yes, but not entirely, because we had formed friendships which all of those negotiations had created. Armstrong and Goodall obviously had excluded the Northern Ireland Office from most of the negotiations because they saw them as we did, but when we got to the point of having lodged a treaty at the UN and had a completely new scenario, we thought that these people had to go along with it, but they did everything they could to stop it working.

Can you elaborate on Reagan's reaction to Thatcher's 'Out, out, out' comment?

A little bit of background is needed here. I was in our Embassy in Washington in the second half of the 1970s, as a political counsellor, and we set up a lobbying effort called the Four Horsemen. We were working with the foremost powerful people in

Washington, Speaker of the House Tip O'Neill, next after the Vice President, Senator Kennedy, Senator Moynihan from New York and Hugh Carey, Governor of New York. This helped to put our message to the State Department and the Carter White House that it was necessary to put pressure on the British to get a move on in finding some kind of political solution and that, with Thatcher in charge, this was virtually impossible to do. The extraordinary circumstances were such that Reagan, in order to get his US policies enacted, needed the co-operation of Tip O'Neill, Speaker of the House of Representatives, so we are talking about a power game here which was kind of unique. That is, O'Neill called the shots and Reagan needed him. They got on extremely well and they had a kind of jokey relationship even though they couldn't have been more unalike politically. O'Neill was extremely helpful to us, so when we got into the negotiations the Four Horsemen put a lot of pressure on the White House. Reagan wanted to do something with social security or medical issues and Tip O'Neill actually traded some of his policy issues with Reagan in order to get Reagan to put pressure on the British.

What was the substance of that pressure from Reagan?

It was just to nudge Thatcher to do something. It was not 'do this' in particular, but there were a couple of incidences where it was 'do this'. One was on the rather appalling 'Out, out, out' comment, which she didn't even intend. She didn't know what she was doing, but the way it came across was utterly destructive and it made FitzGerald's position in Dublin impossible. I mean, Haughey just wiped the floor with him and humiliated him along the lines of you're appeasing this difficult woman and you're getting nothing for it so you are a toady and useless. After that Reagan did talk to her directly and said something along the lines of 'Can you help FitzGerald?' and that was because Tip O'Neill went to Reagan and told him to do it. It's a great story. Sean Donlon, who was close to Reagan, played a decisive part here.

Would it be reasonable to claim that the Agreement would not have been delivered without American help?

Oh that's an understatement. It wouldn't even have begun to happen. Thatcher was a hugely important figure, probably the most powerful Prime Minister since Churchill and an extremely right-wing and patriotic unionist. We have never had such a unionist Prime Minister in Britain since partition, and indeed I would say since Randolph Churchill in the nineteenth century, so it would not have happened but for America, and Thatcher herself has apparently acknowledged that. In Lord McAlpine's memoirs she is quoted as having said to him 'The Americans made me do it.'

When the Agreement was formally announced did you envisage the scale of unionist hostility?

No, but I envisaged that it was going to be rejected by the unionists. I think that was expected by our people, Taoiseach and ministers as well. Let me say a couple of things about that. First of all, I think it's probably fair to say that the fervour and the ferocity of the rejection was far greater than I had expected. However, I knew it was going to be rejected and that it would be difficult for the British and that there would be a bit of euphoria on the nationalist side in the North. It was quite clear that the SDLP, who didn't know about it until three days before the end, were extraordinarily enthusiastic, and we knew most Catholics in the North were moderates who voted for the SDLP. Those people didn't want chaos and thought this was a big step forward. They saw it as a huge development since the rejection of Sunningdale, and that rejection had created despair. Now we had Thatcher coming up with something which was surprising and which allowed the Irish Government a substantial role, so we knew the nationalists were going to be very enthusiastic. But, in turn we also knew the unionists were going to have a tough time. Having said that, we also thought that because this had been overseen by their own British Government they would not intellectually view it as losing out. But, for them, though, the idea that a Dublin Government, their enemy, would have a role in their affairs would have been very upsetting.

My view also is that after Sunningdale, when the loyalist strike had defeated the British Government in sustaining a power-sharing Executive, that from then on the unionists had been complacent and so self-confident in their view that they could reject anything, no matter what it was. That they could just say we are not going to have it and that is the end of it. My firm conviction was that this had to be confronted and that complacency, that self-confidence, had to be overturned. It didn't mean that they had to be humiliated, it didn't mean that they had to be in some way attacked, but it did mean that they could not reject anything regardless of what it was. That this had to change and the British Government had to be involved in making that happen, otherwise there would never be any progress. That was possibly the most important achievement of the Agreement, because from then on they could not play that card. I also think, had that not happened, we would never have had any of the subsequent developments, because who was the agent for making that happen as far as they were concerned? That was a shake-up that certainly needed to happen. But to be absolutely candid I did not anticipate the scale.

It is true also that we were given reason to believe that the British side had briefed the leaders of the Ulster Unionist Party, and it turned out afterwards that an attempt was made to do it under Privy Council rules, which means that you are given the briefing but you can't talk about it in public, and Enoch Powell, who was in the leadership of the party, advised the leaders not to go ahead with the Privy Council meeting, although we did not know that. I remember there were rumblings before the Agreement was signed, but we also thought that this was proof that the British had done a certain amount of briefing of the leadership, because the leadership was not going to be happy with this and we knew that. It turned out that they had not succeeded in briefing them, and that was why the action was in fact much stronger than we expected.

Paradoxically, the strength of the reaction and the form of the reaction and then the actions of the British Government to deal with the reaction were all favourable to our interest in a big way because our interest was to convey to the nationalist community and to opinion in the South that this thing was a considerable benefit to the nationalist people, who had been so completely excluded from the power system since 1921, and so the volcanic reaction of unionism was very gratifying to the nationalist people. It was not precisely what one would have strategised for, but if you have had sixty years of humiliation, as the nationalists had, you can't blame them for celebrating. Interestingly too, what happened, frankly, that did more to entrench the idea that this Agreement had changed things both for nationalists and of course unionists than anything else. Then you had the support of the US, where Reagan was pushing for it. We didn't have contact with the Provisional IRA–Sinn Fein, though, and that was unfortunate because I had always hoped that we could have found some way to have some kind of dialogue, even if in the beginning it was going to be very unofficial with them, which might lead to people thinking about a peace process. That was scotched in the first instance by what happened in Dublin.

When you say what happened in Dublin, what do you mean?

Well there was huge enthusiasm for the Agreement in the South, including public opinion, which was in favour of it by about seventy-five to eighty per cent, but Charles Haughey opposed it in the Dail. Then the SDLP, who always tried to stay in with both Fine Gael and Fianna Fail and had successfully done that since the Troubles began, went out front and condemned Fianna Fail for doing that. Of course, if Fianna Fail had publicly opposed the Agreement you would not exactly expect Sinn Fein to back it or to even be prepared to be seen to give it serious consideration, because in the spectrum of nationalist opinion FitzGerald's party, Fine Gael, was seen as the more moderate party.

Were there any positive reactions at all from unionism about the Agreement? Could or did any of them find anything favourable in the Agreement?

No.

Is it the case that you met Gerry Adams after the Agreement and that this meeting was facilitated by the journalist Mary Holland?

What happened is the Agreement was done in 1985 and I went to Maryfield, where I was the first Irish Joint-Secretary with a British guy of the Secretariat of the Intergovernmental Council. Then Charlie Haughey comes back and I left again because he didn't like me, having been associated with FitzGerald. I wanted the Agreement to be managed as well as it possibly could and I wanted to get somebody who represented Dublin in Belfast, in Maryfield, who had Haughey's confidence. I thought that was very important, so I asked to see Haughey and said the Agreement was a great opportunity for us to work something out and I think it's very important that you have somebody representing you there in whom you have full confidence. He was quite gracious about it, he said yes, but I was then sent to Geneva to work on human rights and trade negotiations. And then two years later I retired and was finished with Dublin service and I went into business. At that point I had an approach from Mary Holland, whom I knew and greatly respected. Mary had covered all the bases and was in touch with everybody, the Provos, the loyalists, the politicians on all sides, wonderful journalist and a very dear friend of mine. She was very close to the Provos, in particular Adams and McGuinness, and she came to me and said that Gerry Adams would like to have a discussion with me. This was about the end of 1989, the beginning of 1990, and I was just retired. I wouldn't have done it had I still been an official because we had a policy of not talking to the Provisionals, which I didn't totally agree with by the way. I thought we should have been talking to them, but most people would have disagreed with that. She passed the message to me and at that point Garret was moving into retirement and I went to him and said 'I would like to do this but, out of loyalty to you, I won't if you are against it.' 'No', he said, 'you are now a private citizen,' and Mary had said that the reason they wanted to have this discussion is because I might be able to give them an insight into how the British Government worked and the way it was thinking. Meaning that they were thinking of negotiating themselves and they needed to get someone to give them a bit of background from his own experience. And I had two meetings with Gerry Adams which lasted nearly two days, and a third meeting in Belfast.

Where did they take place?

The long meetings were in Mary's house.

Just you and Adams?

Yes, and it was quite amusing in some ways because Gerry had probably assumed that I was pro-British because of where he was coming from, but he was quite wrong about that. Also I had very good fluency in the Irish language, a lot better than he did, and we started for about ten minutes in Irish and then we switched to English, in which he was more comfortable. It was basically an interrogation by him of me. I started by telling him I absolutely opposed their campaign of violence and I wanted to be very clear about that and I was ashamed of it as an Irishman, and he took that quite well. He's a very bright guy and he gets a lot of credit from me for stopping the violence, which he did, because it can't have been too easy, but that does not mean I am a supporter of his, because I am not. But I do give him credit for what he has done. Then he wanted to get a feel for, and it may have been Mary's suggestion or it may have been his, what it was like to negotiate with the British, and I gave him a very full run-down and we went through the Agreement. He wasn't going to say to me that he supported it because he is too shrewd and too dug-in to do that. He wasn't critical of it at all but he was focussed on negotiating with the British; and I wouldn't for a moment claim that I had any influence on him, but I think it was a useful and interesting move on his part to talk to somebody who had a couple of years of negotiation with the British about Northern Ireland.

On each occasion you stayed with him for two days?

The first time was two days and the second time was a day and a bit. In other words, we didn't finish on the second occasion in one day and I came back the next morning and spent some time with him.

Did he take a lot of notes or was it just open conversation?

He did take some notes, yes, and I did a note on it afterwards and I gave the note to Garret FitzGerald.

Apart from wanting to know about how the British negotiate, was he offering you anything?

No, but the implication was there because why otherwise would he be wasting his time? At that time he was on the run and I actually did subsequently meet with him in West Belfast on a third occasion, and on that occasion Mary was present and drove me up, and we covered the same ground again. I don't think there was a particular crisis but he wanted to see me for another time and we had, I would say, some of the same conversation again.

Did he get into any conversation with you about the Agreement?

Yes, I went through it with him.

Did you sense he was receptive to any particular part of that?

I have to be very careful and I don't want to make a claim I can't validate, but he has never suggested that the Anglo-Irish Agreement was anything other than an entrenchment of partition. Having said that, there are so many contradictions in the positions that he takes that I am inclined to think that he did think about it. His questions showed that he had actually thought about it and possibly even had a discussion with somebody else and come back with questions which they had figured out between them, but I can't go any further than that because it would not be fair to him.

But what were the kinds of questions he was asking?

It was less about his position and more about the British Government's flexibility, their seriousness, and in particular, because Thatcher was still around, whether she had any interest in being positive. And I remember this part of the discussion, where I said I know you guys hate her, particularly because of the hunger strikes, but in my experience with the Agreement she defended it against the unionists and the unionist reaction was hysterical, with 200,000 people meeting and Paisley roaring and all that stuff, and she and the RUC actually faced down this rejection of the Agreement, which is something that Harold Wilson didn't do. Wilson gave in to the loyalist strike in 1974, so what I was saying is that if you make a deal with her, which is not going to be easy, she will stick to it.

Is there a way of telling me what you think he might have got out of that experience or what he might have taken away with him?

I think that the first thing he should have learned from that was that it's a mistake to think that the British are inflexible. Here you have a sovereign territory, there is a dispute between one part of it in two sovereign countries and this dispute has led to a great deal of misery and instability and they have made an agreement that both Governments will work together to help to reduce the problems. Now they won't go in as equals, but there will be mechanisms which oblige the actual main sovereign power to make efforts to ensure that they come to an agreement on the basis of proposals from the other. There wasn't anything like this in the world, and I remember talking to him about Kashmir in India and saying imagine if in the case of Kashmir the Indian Government invited in the Pakistani Government to deal with all the issues which arise between the two communities in Kashmir and to have not just a consultation process but a process which obliges the Indian Government to make efforts to reach agreement. You can't imagine that happening even though it is a perfect analogy. So it's a very big thing, and what I was saying is that a government has made this move, which was historic, and that if we were to do the same thing everybody on our side would say it's in breach of our Constitution, that we couldn't have the British here in Dublin telling us what they wanted us to do about this and that. So they had broken with their Constitution to make this happen, and so it would be a mistake to think they were just inflexible. That was my main point.

I read that the Anglo-Irish Agreement was both a 'come-on and threat' to the Provisional IRA. Do you concur with that, and do you think that Adams foresaw that the Agreement was going to make it more difficult for the Provisional IRA to stay in business because the possibility of change was opening up?

The difficulty with that question is that, for me, their campaign of violence was immoral. That it wasn't going to get them anywhere and that they would not achieve any of their goals. If one asks whether it was the case that the leadership of the Provisional IRA felt threatened in their own territory by their own public opinion and that the Agreement had contributed to this by highlighting the possibility of and need for a new approach, then one might say that it's logical and historically consistent that this might well have been the case. It was certainly the argument that their main interlocutor at the beginning of the peace process, John Hume, used. I was close to Hume, and from time to time he told me how he was getting on with his discussions with Gerry Adams, and I think you have to say that from that period on the evidence is that Adams and McGuinness were looking for a way out because, intellectually, what Hume and Adams agreed, while it makes sense, is in direct contradiction with the war aims of the Provisional IRA.

On the point of the discussions with Hume, are you able to say anything about what he was saying about Adams and whether he saw the republican movement shifting as a serious possibility?

Yes, Hume on two occasions showed me a piece of paper to do with the constitutional position and self-determination and how you defined the sovereign self-determination of the people of Ireland, North and South, and the additional language that you had to have there to bring along the unionists, and he had worked this out himself and was in the process of selling it to Gerry Adams. My observation, for what it's worth, is that Hume was excited about it. He thought Adams was buying it, and indeed Adams did buy it, as the Hume–Adams declaration showed. I think it was ingenious and involved a huge effort from Hume and Adams to sell that. Hume worked intensely on that and believed that it was going to resolve both the conflict and Gerry Adams' problems more than almost anything else.

Was the possibility of a peace process ever mentioned in the aftermath of the Anglo-Irish Agreement?

I was hoping against hope perhaps that there was some way we could reach out to Sinn Fein. The problem at the time, though, was the violence of the Provisional IRA. If that had stopped there would have been hope. I don't know for what, but at least people would stop killing each other. The British were doing terrible things in some areas, as were the loyalists, but the source of the tit-for-tat was the Provisional IRA, so how was there any possibility of getting them to stop was a very important consideration in my mind. There was a provision which outraged a lot of people, of course, that was not in the Agreement itself but in the measures that supported the Agreement, which became part of the whole process. Those measures included undertaking a review of prisoner sentences where, if for a period violence was to abate, then that would be taken into account in a review of sentencing. In the discussion of all of that our view, which we tried hard to persuade the other side with, was that the hunger strikes had been defeated by the families of the hunger strikers. The last hunger strikers were taken off the strikes by their families, not by the Provisional IRA, who wanted them to continue, and there's no doubt about that. That families don't want their kids to spend their lives in jail was something we were urging on the British with a lot of support from people within the community, notably Father Denis Faul, and we wanted the British to make an announcement a couple of months after the Agreement that there was going to be a review of prison sentences and that the approach to the review would be influenced by the level of violence that was taking place. We were hoping that the families of prisoners would go to the Provisional IRA and say we want to get our guys out.

4

Tightening Anglo-Irish relations: an interview with Daithi O'Ceallaigh

Graham Spencer: *Can you tell me about your involvement in the peace process?*

Daithi O'Ceallaigh: The use of the term 'peace process' to describe the changes which have taken place in Northern Ireland is too confining as it has come to focus exclusively on the inclusion of Sinn Fein in the process following the Provisional IRA ceasefire in 1994. There are other elements which don't necessarily come under this confining term 'peace process' that are central to the changed situation of Northern Ireland, such as the relationship between the Governments in London and Dublin. The building of trust, confidence and respect between the two Governments was central to the process. Also important is the attention paid by the Irish Government from 1983 onwards to the politics and administration of Northern Ireland. That was something new for London, the unionists, as well as for the Northern nationalists and for us in the South too. I was involved from November 1977 to August 1982 when I was the press officer at the Embassy in London during very difficult days. The murder of Airey Neave, the murder of Lord Mountbatten, the hunger strikes, extradition and the Falklands War were all difficult issues at that time. I came back to Dublin in 1982 and later that year I was moved into the Anglo-Irish division to work on Northern Ireland, largely with the nationalists. I did that job from then up to the signature of the Anglo-Irish Agreement in November 1985. When we signed the Agreement, an Anglo-Irish Secretariat was established at Maryfield, just outside Belfast, and I was the deputy on the Irish side under Michael Lillis. Michael and I were in Belfast from December 1985 to July–August 1987, when he went off to Geneva and I went off to New York as the Consul General for six years, where I remained peripherally involved in Northern Ireland matters. I went from there to Helsinki and I came back to Dublin in 1998. When Dermot Gallagher went to the Taoiseach's Office in 2000 I replaced him as Head of the Anglo-Irish Division. I went to London as Ambassador in 2001 and spent six years there until August 2007. The relationship between London and Dublin was vital for the process.

There were conscious efforts made by a number of Irish Governments to get involved with the British rather than standing back from direct engagement with the British or with Northern Ireland, as had been the case traditionally. From the early 1980s in particular, the Irish Government tried to develop relationships with the British. The FitzGerald Government felt it was incumbent to try to help nationalists and Catholics in Northern Ireland to resolve their problems with the Northern Ireland State in a political way by achieving changes in policies and administration rather than through the use of violence as followed by the Provisional IRA. The FitzGerald Government, like the SDLP, was absolutely opposed to the use of violence. The sense of nationalist alienation following the hunger strikes was felt very strongly by the Dublin Government. There was a deep-seated feeling that Northern nationalists had political problems which were not being addressed, they were not getting a fair deal, and that the Irish Government needed to help them in getting a fair deal.

The East–West strand does not seem to have been analysed or discussed to the same extent as the North–South strand does it?

What happened between 1982 and 1985 has not been much discussed, especially in terms of the changing relationship between the Dublin Government and the nationalists in Northern Ireland.

Can you elaborate?

During the 1970s the Irish Government, for information and for policy-making purposes about Northern Ireland, relied almost exclusively on discussions with the SDLP, and particularly with John Hume. There was a feeling in Dublin at the time that Northern nationalists were divided into two groups, those who supported the SDLP and those who supported the Provisional IRA. However, there were people in Northern Ireland, like Father Dennis Faul and Father Raymond Murray, who were very vocal in their criticism of institutions like the Royal Ulster Constabulary (RUC), the Ulster Defence Regiment (UDR) and the Prison Service and who had very little contact with the Irish Government. They were not Provisional IRA supporters but weren't necessarily SDLP supporters either; there were others who held ideas close to those of the republicans, particularly in the Irish-American community, with whom the Irish Government had little contact. The FitzGerald Government, and especially Peter Barry, the Foreign Minister, encouraged wider and increased contact with people in Northern Ireland. There was a conscious attempt made to widen understanding in Dublin of the problems faced by people in the North and then seek to resolve those problems through contact with the British. If a particular person or family was being harassed by the RUC or the security forces the details would be passed on to us by the SDLP, or by other reliable people, which would then be raised at ministerial or official level in order to try to resolve them. Over a period of time it became much easier for us to look at what was feasible and what wasn't feasible, what complaints might have legitimacy and what complaints might have less legitimacy. It also became obvious to the people in the British Embassy that many of these issues that we were bringing to them could be resolved in political terms within Northern Ireland and that had never really been tried in that way before.

When was that?

Starting at the end of 1982. We were trying to talk to as many people as possible in Northern Ireland, excluding people actively involved in terrorism, to try and understand what their problems were and find solutions to those problems, whether they be educational or about employment or housing, and this was a background context that enabled a build-up of trust and confidence between nationalists from the North and the Irish Government. The Irish Government was seriously interested in the condition of nationalists and Catholics, and if satisfied they had a legitimate grievance, would seek to resolve that grievance. That also was an essential part of the 1985 Anglo-Irish Agreement and it forms a very big part of what we were actually doing in the Maryfield Secretariat. We talked a lot to unionists too, and I had regular contact with a DUP councillor, with the agreement of Dr Paisley. We were meeting a lot of solicitors and barristers. To take an example, there were ten senior judges but only two of them were Catholic. The Irish Government was keen to try to get balance into the administration of justice in Northern Ireland to ensure that nationalists and Catholics got a fair representation within a society which was largely unionist controlled and administered by the British. The Taoiseach raised this issue with Mrs Thatcher because it was of concern to nationalists in the legal system, and over time it was resolved.

Were you talking to anybody in the IRA at that point?

No.

So the aim was very much build up the moderates?

Yes. There was absolutely no conscious contact as far as I am aware between the FitzGerald Government and the Provisional IRA.

Was the strategic goal of building up contacts used to try and ease the situation between the nationalists and the Catholics and defuse any legitimacy in the armed struggle?

There was a great concern in Dublin that the political advances made by Sinn Fein had the potential to significantly destabilise not only Northern Ireland, but the rest of Ireland and there is no doubt that dealing with alienation was an essential aim of government policy – to try and neutralise any credibility that might be gained by the use of violence. But it was not entirely or simply that, more what an Irish Government could do to try to resolve the problems faced by the minority in Northern Ireland through dealing with the British Government. That is what was new. I and other travellers would regularly meet with the British Embassy with whole lists of questions that we needed them to answer, that had been raised with us by people in Northern Ireland and which we took to be genuine, because we sifted them. Peter Barry, who was Minister for Foreign Affairs, would meet with his opposite number and these issues would be raised if they had not already been dealt with. I remember the first meeting Peter Barry had with Douglas Hurd, which took place in Dublin. I had told my opposite number in the British Embassy that there was one particular issue that Barry was certainly going to raise and I expected him to tell Hurd. When Barry raised the matter, Hurd was furious and appeared not to have been briefed about it. It was about minority rights as I recall.

What did unionist backlash in the wake of the Anglo-Irish Agreement do for relations between East and West?

I don't think anybody anticipated the degree of the unionist backlash. They made a very silly decision to resign their Westminster seats, because they actually lost a seat in the subsequent by-elections held in January 1986, which Seamus Mallon took. What became very clear very quickly was that the British Civil Service, the Northern Ireland Civil Service, Mrs Thatcher and particularly the RUC intended to uphold the law and uphold the Anglo-Irish Agreement. I think the first important visitor that we had to dinner in Maryfield was Jack Hermon, who was boss of the RUC, and then Tom King came round for dinner. Ken Bloomfield was Head of the Northern Ireland Civil Service and there was a small body called the Central Secretariat in the Northern Ireland Civil Service which was run by Ronnie Spence. It co-ordinated Northern Irish matters across the Northern Ireland Civil Service. Ronnie Spence was instructed to work very closely with us, and I worked very closely with him on issues such as education, cross-border co-operation, etc. and we very quickly built up a close working relationship. We would bring together the Northern Ireland Department of

Enterprise and Irish Department of Enterprise to discuss cross-border economic co-operation, to the mutual benefit of each. It was not about a united Ireland, it was just practical and pragmatic co-operation to mutual benefit. We also dealt with the Prison Service; we were getting many complaints about conditions in the prisons; we sought to ameliorate these conditions so things would get easier. So it was practical work we were doing all the time, and the British and Northern Irish civil servants worked in a pragmatic way too. I think the unionists began to realise very quickly that the Agreement was not for turning. It cannot have been an easy decision for the British to keep the unionists out of the negotiation of the Anglo-Irish Agreement, but it was a very specific decision. We honestly thought that the unionists were better briefed than they were. The SDLP and some other nationalists in Northern Ireland were certainly briefed.

To what extent were unionists able to exert influence at that time?

They were largely powerless. They were astonished that Mrs Thatcher had actually agreed to the Anglo-Irish Agreement with the Irish Government. They never thought they would see the Irish Government involved in Northern Ireland in that way, and there is no question whatsoever that they felt they had been sold out. I don't think there was any question about Northern Ireland remaining part of the United Kingdom, the Agreement accepted that constitutional change could only take place with the agreement of a majority in Northern Ireland, but the British Government had decided that majoritarian unionist rule was no longer acceptable and that in the absence of devolution the Irish Government could put forward proposals on behalf of the minority in Northern Ireland.

Did they try to pull the Anglo-Irish Agreement apart?

Oh absolutely.

How?

If you remember, there was a legal challenge by the unionist McGimpsey brothers in the South to try to prove that the Anglo-Irish Agreement was unconstitutional in the Irish sense and that the Irish Government had violated its own Constitution. There was also an attempt made by Peter Robinson to come across the border and he spent the night in an Irish cell for his pains. On top of that Molyneaux, and Ulster Unionists, as well as Paisley and the DUP, resigned their Westminster seats. The by-elections were held in January of 1986 where, as said, the unionists lost a seat to Seamus Mallon, who kept that seat until he resigned from Parliament in 2007. There was no doubt that around one in two of all male adult unionists took to the street on that Saturday in December to protest against the Agreement, and it was a huge demonstration. There was also the march from Derry to the Maryfield Secretariat in January. Michael Lillis and I were inside, terrified. Many other manifestations happened during the months which followed.

Was your perception that it was going to collapse?

We never thought it was going to be easy. I think that the determination of Mrs Thatcher was something quite extraordinary, as was the determination of Jack Hermon, the leader of the RUC. Thatcher had made up her mind, but she hadn't come to it easily. Some of her best friends, like Ian Gow, didn't like it at all, and in her ghosted biography which was written years later she wonders whether she should have signed the Agreement, although she did stand by it. There is absolutely no question, once she had signed it, that she stood by it. The RUC also stood by it and many of its members were attacked in their own communities. There were some eight hundred to a thousand RUC men who had to leave their homes because of pressure from within their own communities when they stood up to defend the Anglo-Irish Agreement. The following April, after the Agreement was signed, there was a big demonstration in Portadown and there was a loyalist shot dead with a plastic bullet. The fact that Mrs Thatcher and also Jack Hermon stood firm in spite of this massive resistance by unionists was a great credit to both of them. Nor should we forget that though they may not have liked it, the Northern Ireland Civil Service also proved loyal to that decision. While we did not think it would collapse there was no certainty it would work, and it took much effort to ensure it delivered what it was mainly designed to do, to improve the lot of nationalists in Northern Ireland and create better security co-operation.

What period?

We went into Maryfield on Sunday 8 December 1985 and maintained a twenty-four-hour, 365-day presence from then onwards. The main team were usually there from Monday to Friday and there was a weekend team that used to go in from Friday to Monday. I was there as deputy of the main team for nearly two years from December 1985 until August 1987, until I went to New York as Consul General.

Are you of the mind that the Irish laid the foundation of what was to come from the Anglo-Irish Agreement?

The 1985 Agreement was a major step on the way to the present structures. The British had accepted that majoritarian unionist rule would not work and that in the absence of devolution the Irish Government could make proposals on behalf of the nationalists and could interact with the British Government on non-devolved matters through the Anglo-Irish Conference and the Anglo-Irish Secretariat established in Maryfield. The relationship of the Dublin Government with Northern nationalists and the efforts being made by the Government on their behalf represented a major change in policy. When I got to New York in 1987 I was treated by many Irish-Americans, particularly by those who were more 'green', in a different way from my predecessor because many of them felt that previous Irish Governments had not done enough for Irish nationalists. While some of them were clearly Sinn Fein supporters, they accepted that Garret FitzGerald had made an attempt to engage the British for the advantage of nationalists within Northern Ireland, and there was an acceptance that a really serious attempt had been made to deal with their problems.

What kind of problems did dealing with the British bring?

A recurring question in Irish nationalism and its relationship with the North is the issue of engagement with the British and unionists: do you best advance your interests by standing on a soap box, disengaged from negotiation and saying this is what the world should be, or do you best advance your interests through engagement and in the back of your mind think about the art of the possible? Traditionally, Irish nationalism, especially Sinn Fein and Fianna Fail, were disengaged. Put simply, the argument was that partition was wrong and that it was up to the British to persuade unionists. This attitude had clearly failed. Charlie Haughey did try to seriously engage with the British in 1979 and 1980 but it went awry for a number of reasons. Nevertheless, during the 1983 to 1985 period, because of the negotiations between Dublin and London, and because the British now accepted that the Irish Government had a role to play in putting forward nationalists' demands, it was widely accepted that progress had been made. What was achieved was not Irish unity, but it was a definite advance.

How important was pragmatism, given the different outlooks of those involved?

There were some on the Irish side, including within the Department of Foreign Affairs, who were not involved in Anglo-Irish or Northern Irish issues, and who might have shared the old unitary principles of de Valera, who didn't agree with engagement with the British and who had doubts about the Agreement. Both Fianna Fail and Sinn Fein rejected the Agreement, in the case of the former changing their view afterwards. There were equally on the British side some who were deeply committed to unionism as distinct from the Union. The New Ireland Forum from 1983 to 1984 in effect redefined Irish nationalism. This enabled the Irish Government to engage in the negotiations which led to the Anglo-Irish Agreement, where it is clearly stated that there will be no change in the constitution and status of Northern Ireland without the consent of a majority there. There was an acceptance that that majority was not available. So, to answer your question, pragmatism was an important element in that both Governments had moved on from their traditional outlook, in the case of the Irish to partition, and in the case of the British to majoritarian unionist rule in Northern Ireland.

Is it the case that for FitzGerald nationalism was more about people than land?

I don't know. Probably. John Hume is central to the changes which have taken place, be it in the North or the South. For Hume, nationalism was certainly more about people than land. Hume fundamentally felt that the Anglo-Irish Agreement provided an opportunity for the republicans to maintain their dream and to fight for their dream in a legitimate political way, rather than through the use of violence. Republican followers must also have asked themselves why more than 200,000 unionists took to the street in protest against the Anglo-Irish Agreement in 1985. Why did unionists dislike it so much, and why did they continue to dislike it? Because they correctly concluded that the Agreement represented a major advance for nationalists. The symbolism of Maryfield was huge, since it personified the Irish Government presence in Northern Ireland assisting the British Government to administer the place. If I remember correctly one of the last demands made by David Trimble before he signed up to the Good Friday Agreement 1998 was the closure of Maryfield.

Do you think the perception or one of the reasons that Adams didn't want to move at that time was because nationalism, as the SDLP saw it, hadn't really been absorbed into the republican psychology?

Somebody asked me a question recently, a 'what if' question. That question was what would Adams and Sinn Fein have done if Charles Haughey and Fianna Fail had supported the Agreement in 1985? Would it have led to an earlier ceasefire by the Provisional IRA? Who knows? I suspect that there were many in Fianna Fail who remained wedded to old-style nationalism, just as in Sinn Fein many believed in the methods of violence.

Did Haughey come close to supporting it?

He certainly supported it from 1987. The then British Cabinet Secretary, Robert Armstrong, was sent over by Mrs Thatcher just after the Irish Government changed in 1987 to ascertain Mr Haughey's position on the Agreement. Mr Haughey made it quite clear that he would support it. You do have to remember that at the time of the Agreement, and for a good while after, the percentage of votes cast for Sinn Fein in Northern Ireland was considerably less than that achieved by the SDLP. It was between ten per cent and thirteen per cent for Sinn Fein, while the SDLP share was around eighteen to twenty per cent. I share the view that it was not easy for Martin McGuinness and Gerry Adams to turn a very determined, experienced terrorist movement into a democratic force, and it is probably unrealistic to think that they could have achieved that in the 1985 to 1987 period, even if they had wanted to do so.

Was the Irish view that Hume was the man to provide the leverage to do that?

There were very considerable differences within the SDLP about Hume's talks with Sinn Fein. Seamus Mallon had very significant differences with Hume about the talks with Sinn Fein. The received wisdom was that Hume was prepared to sacrifice his party for peace if he could persuade Sinn Fein that they could pursue their vision for a united Ireland through the structures of the Anglo-Irish Agreement, which allowed them to advance that aim in a political way. I know that is true because Hume told me so in 1993 when I was staying with him in Donegal. He was at that time engaged in talks with Sinn Fein, and for his troubles was being demonised in the newspapers in Dublin for meeting Gerry Adams. Hume told me that Mallon was very unhappy with those talks.

It is said that Sinn Fein were keen to develop a pan-nationalist front. Did the Irish see it that way?

I don't think it was possible to put together a pan-nationalist front while the Provisional IRA was still prepared to use violence. Don't under-estimate how deep the antipathy of the vast majority of people in Ireland is to that violence. It was not understood in London and it was not understood by the unionists, but we were deeply opposed to the use of violence. From November–December 1985 Haughey very publicly opposed the Agreement, and presumably republican supporters of Sinn Fein were also opposed to it. Haughey sent Brian Lenihan to Washington to try and persuade Irish-Americans, who were up until then supportive of the Irish Government, to come to his point of view. That tactic failed, and both the US Government and the Four Horsemen supported the Irish Government. Haughey realised very quickly that he wasn't on to a winner, and if you examine his actions very carefully you will see that he very quickly stops all that negativism about the Agreement. One reason, of course, was that it became clear that there was overwhelming support in the Republic for the Agreement. Another reason why a pan-nationalist front was impossible in the mid-1980s is that the number of people in the South who in any way agreed with republican violence was fairly small. Most felt that the State was being threatened by the republicans, likewise in Northern Ireland a clear majority of nationalists were SDLP supporters who were opposed to Provisional IRA violence.

Did you find the British civil servants suspicious of you, or obstructive?

There was a trust, not necessarily that we always agreed, but there was a trust and a respect built up between the two Governments, be it politicians, or civil servants, as a result of the Anglo-Irish Agreement which was frankly unthinkable before, and that's where I think the real importance of the Anglo-Irish Agreement lies. It created solutions to problems faced by nationalists because British and Irish civil servants and politicians had worked together to resolve problems. We both began to realise that the other side didn't have horns on their heads and that there were solutions that we could find together. However, there certainly were civil servants in the Northern Ireland Office, especially at the higher levels, who did not like the Agreement and who probably tried to slow things down. And, of course, there were people in the British Government who were less than fully supportive.

And even in that time the British had dropped any reservation about the Irish having an executive role, a harmonising role, is that so?

I have no doubt the decision to allow the Irish Government to become involved in Northern Ireland was only taken after much deliberation by the Prime Minister. It was discussed by the British Cabinet and it is probable that many in the Cabinet were of the same mind as Jim Prior, who wrote that the approach from the Irish Government represented a historic opportunity which should not be missed. Though there have been ups and downs no British Government since has denied the legitimate interest of the Irish Government in what happens in Northern Ireland.

It seems hard to believe that the hunger strikes didn't affect Thatcher in some way. Do you think that influenced her approach to the Anglo-Irish Agreement?

She knew things could not continue as they were. Geoffrey Howe later told me that he played a big role in helping her along. He said, 'You know, she's English, she doesn't understand the Celts. I'm Welsh, I do,' and there's a sense in which that was true. She was quintessentially English.

What would be that difference of understanding?

It's very difficult to put a finger on it. There's no doubt that for a very long period the vast bulk of the English establishment was Protestant and deeply prejudicial against the Irish, and not only Irish Catholics. That anti-Irish and anti-Catholic feeling was very deep, and it was palpable when I worked in the Embassy from 1977 to 1982, but it had largely disappeared in the almost twenty years I was away and there was very little trace of it when I returned to London in 2001. I remember trying to explain to Harri Holkeri, the former Finnish Prime Minister, before he went to Northern Ireland in the mid-1990s to work with Senator Mitchell, that he needed to understand the depth of that anti-Catholic feeling. Because of his own country's history, I said to him that the differences in Northern Ireland were the last vestige of the Thirty Years' War, which was largely Protestant versus Catholic. The English did not understand that. They seemed to have no concept of their historical mistreatment of the Irish and Irish Catholics. We did.

How important do you think the European context has been for the East–West relationship?

Both the UK and Ireland joined the then EEC, later the EU, in 1973. It is since that period, within the European envelope, the British–Irish relationship has improved so profoundly. We have to remember that Ireland is not a NATO member, and since 1948 not a Commonwealth member. So there was no forum in which Irish and British ministers met regularly. Diplomats met at the UN and in bilateral missions, but that was it. That changed once we joined the EEC. Ministers and civil servants, trade unionists and civil society met regularly in Brussels and elsewhere; they came to know one another, to work together; respect and confidence followed. Additionally, it enabled ministers, and especially the Taoiseach and the Prime Minister, to hold bilateral meetings in the margins of Council meetings etc. I am in no doubt that joint membership of the EU was a hugely beneficial element in the improved East–West relationship. Furthermore, the Commission and the EU were very helpful in Northern Ireland. As MEPs, John Hume and Dr Paisley worked well together in the European Parliament. The Commission Office in Belfast, especially under Geoffrey Martin in the 1980s, played an important role in getting people to work for common goals. The EU has also provided large sums of money for projects in Northern Ireland connected to the peace process and for cross-border projects.

Did you have a number of important meetings in the Irish Embassy when you were there as Ambassador?

In London, yes.

Can you elaborate on what happened there?

The first formal meeting between the Irish Government and the DUP took place in the Embassy.

When was that?

I think it was 2005. Dr Paisley came along with all his MPs and the Taoiseach came along with an equivalent number of ministers. There were three or four Irish officials and two or three DUP officials. It was all choreographed in advance.

Was it confidential?

The meeting itself wasn't held in public, but it was public knowledge that it would take place. Dr Paisley said he would have no objection to meeting the Taoiseach of a foreign country in his Embassy in England. We didn't have any objection either. The DUP delegation used my office, where they could discuss and talk in advance. The meeting took place around the dining table; Dr Paisley and his delegation on the one side of the table with the Irish delegation facing them on the opposite side. Before we went into the dining room I asked him if he would like to sign my visitors' book, which he and his delegation did. He put a little notation in it, a biblical reference. The Taoiseach opened the meeting saying while he did not always agree with Dr Paisley he had always greatly respected Dr Paisley's work for his constituents. Dr Paisley thanked him and then told him a story about a Catholic who had come up to one of his clinics and asked him to do something for him. Dr Paisley said of course he would do that. He asked the man who had advised him to seek the help of the leader of the DUP, to which the man replied that it was his parish priest who had suggested it. Dr Paisley then told him to go back and tell the parish priest he is a wise old man! Thus the meeting got off to a good start; it lasted over an hour. In response to a question from the Taoiseach, Dr Paisley said that he would not say anything to the press waiting outside that he had not said inside. He was as good as his word. So, in a way, the fact that the atmosphere between the two leaders was good at their first political meeting was the beginning of what became a mutually trusting relationship. After the DUP delegation had left we looked up the reference in the Bible in my flat, which happened to be in Irish, but the significance of the reference left by Dr Paisley remained obscure. Minister Tom Kitt phoned his wife, who gave him the quotation from an English-language Catholic Bible; we were still in the dark. It was only the following day when we got our hands on an authorised King James' version of the Bible that Dr Paisley's reference made sense. 'For you are an Ambassador of the Lord', it said, which showed you the sense of humour that he had.

Were there subsequent meetings?

Yes, but not in the Embassy.

Did you meet republicans there?

Yes, although by the time I arrived in 2001 Sinn Fein were deep into the negotiations to give effect to the Belfast Agreement, so the meetings were mainly working meetings. The talks could be difficult at times, and at one stage the DUP were in the House of Commons and Sinn Fein in the Irish Embassy. It was shuttle diplomacy, with the negotiators going from the Commons to Number 10 and to the Embassy. This was during a period when we were trying to get the DUP involved. I remember going to see the Sinn Fein delegation, who were in the library in the Embassy, to say we needed something more from them. When I went into the room there were at least three of them fast asleep. Martin McGuinness had pulled two chairs together and was asleep on them, and there was another sleeping on the table on his back.

Describe your role as Ambassador a bit more?

The Ambassador is the accredited representative of one state to another and work undertaken by the Ambassador is very varied. In general terms, the Ambassador tries to advance the interests of his or her country and seeks to build up relations between the two states to the benefit of both. For the purposes of this interview I will limit my remarks to the role played by the Embassy in the negotiations on Northern Ireland, and the bilateral relationship between the two countries, of which two central elements were EU policy and building up a relationship with the British establishment. The fundamental negotiation, when I was the London Ambassador, to implement the Belfast Agreement, which was a framework agreement as you will recall, was led by Number 10 and the Department of the Taoiseach. There was a four-man negotiating team, as there had been when I was in Dublin, consisting of a Secretary General in the Department of the Taoiseach, a Secretary General in the Department of Justice, a Second Secretary General in charge of the Anglo-Irish Division in the Department of Foreign Affairs and the Taoiseach's political advisor, Martin Mansergh. When the negotiations took place in London, which was more likely than not, the Ambassador, be it my predecessor or myself, was always present at those meetings. I certainly was active on the Northern Irish issue, as were my predecessor and my successor. We would engage continuously with the British administration on British–Irish matters and on Northern Ireland. The primary negotiation was that small negotiating group but the Ambassador was only a member of that group when the negotiations took place in Britain.

What sort of discussions, or conversations, or meetings, took place in the Embassy or in London that you were part of?

Let me distinguish between the negotiations between the two teams and the individual work of the Ambassador. The Ambassador was certainly a major channel for passing information between the two countries. I met regularly with Jonathan Powell or whoever it was who was handling Irish matters in Number 10. The latter included very high fliers within the British system. Among those in Number 10 with whom I worked on Irish and EU matters were two future British Ambassadors in Washington, two with the United Nations in New York, one to the Vatican, and one who later became head of MI6. It is a measure of how seriously the Blair administration took the Irish issue that civil servants of this capacity were assigned to deal with it. If we had a particular problem I might go and talk to Number 10 about that, or, if they were having a problem, they would come to me and I would pass it on.

What kind of problems?

There were many issues which required solutions acceptable to both Governments and to the parties in Northern Ireland. We have to remember there was a continuous negotiation from the Good Friday Agreement in 1998, through the St Andrews Agreement in 2006, until eventually the devolution of policing and justice some years later. The London Ambassador was central to contacts between the different groups, particularly with the British. I would do breakfast practically every day of the week in the Embassy in London, generally one-to-one, as well as lunches and a lot of dinners. There were formal negotiation meetings in London every two or three weeks. I would usually meet someone on the British side a couple of days in advance for breakfast and we'd discuss what issues they were going to raise in the meeting. I would report to Dublin so our people could prepare in advance. This was in relation to meetings on Northern Ireland, but I prepared for EU Councils and other EU meetings in a similar way.

Can you recall vital meetings during that period?

Among the more important high-level meetings involving the Governments and the parties during my time were the meetings in Weston Park, when agreement on the future of policing in Northern Ireland was agreed, the Leeds Castle meeting and that at St Andrews, when the DUP came on board. I wasn't necessarily involved in all of the key meetings, nor indeed was the Irish Government or the British Government. Meetings took place in different formats. Bilateral meetings with Sinn Fein would often only involve the Irish Government; on the other hand, bilaterals with the unionists might be only with the British Government. Let me give you an example coming towards the end of St Andrews. There had been all sorts of talks going on the penultimate night, with Michael McDowell and others talking to different groups and people to get a feel for things and to see what might be feasible. The night before the end we were a bit despondent on the Irish side because we thought Dr Paisley might not do the deal. Blair and his team met Paisley and his team quite early on the last morning, and after about an hour one of the British came out and said Dr Paisley was looking for three things, one of which was support for the North West 200. The British hadn't a clue what that was about, but we knew; it is the most important motor-bike race in Ireland and it takes place in Dr Paisley's constituency. We were told he was looking for some support for that race. The obvious conclusion was that he was on board for an agreement. 'It's all over. It's done,' we concluded because he was looking for the few little sweeteners at the end of the negotiations. There were similar negotiations involving the Irish side. For example, in Weston Park the Irish side played a big role, which was critically important because the SDLP said they would support the new Police Service of Northern Ireland, and this was the first time that nationalist politicians had given their support to any police service in Northern

Ireland since 1921. Seamus Mallon eventually said okay we'll go for it. Those sorts of meetings took place all the time in different formats. You asked about the Embassy. There was one occasion which was quite difficult where the DUP had not come on board because of serious problems with Sinn Fein. The Irish negotiating group was in Dublin and the DUP were in Westminster in Tony Blair's rooms, and if I remember correctly, the Trimble unionists were in Number 10 while Sinn Fein were in the Embassy. There was shuttle diplomacy going on. We were shuttling between the three. The Irish Government wasn't dealing directly with the DUP. Jonathan Powell and his staff did that, but the British would come to the Embassy and talk to the Sinn Fein or we would bring the Sinn Fein people down to Number 10 and out again. It was quite an astonishing negotiation and it was quite fluid, if intense. Different moments present different problems and a different approach. The format or context for that approach was also indicative of those differences.

During that period when you were London Ambassador the Robert McCartney murder and Northern Bank robbery took place. What were the reactions to that?

I was present when Tony Blair and Bertie Ahern discussed these matters and when other things were discussed, such as the police raids on Sinn Fein in Stormont. The British used to say earlier on in the negotiations that they were harder on Sinn Fein than we were, but there was a certain period after the bank robbery and the McCartney murder that they thought we were harder on Sinn Fein than they were. Bertie Ahern got very annoyed with the British at that stage, who were perhaps a bit more determined than we were to get an agreement at any cost.

Did you think it was going to collapse at any point?

There were many times when we thought it was going to collapse. It was not an easy negotiation, but I have never seen two leaders, Tony Blair and Bertie Ahern, take so much abuse and yet maintain patience and determination throughout. It would never have been achieved without those two men, who had total trust in each other. Bertie would say to Tony you'd better go off and talk to the DUP and see if you can do this, and Blair would say to us can you go and talk to Sinn Fein and suggest that? Those two men drove this process forward. There would be no peace without them.

When you met republicans, how did they differ in their negotiation skills, broadly speaking, in comparison to, say, the DUP?

Most of the negotiations with the DUP would have been conducted by the British. The thing that you experienced with Sinn Fein all the time was the extent to which they were prepared and were unified. They had a team with prepared positions and would sometimes come in at the end of the negotiations with a list of thirty-nine or more things that they wanted. There were times when it was hard to know whether they were serious or not, but from the negotiating point of view they were very good. The skill of negotiation is to listen very carefully to what people say, try to understand what they want and move towards a compromise. You need to understand where that compromise can be and the extent to which those involved can compromise, or not. The two Governments wouldn't always reach the same conclusion but would have to decide whether it was for real or not. Republicans were very impressive negotiators. They were very cool and level headed, whereas sometimes the unionists could be very abrupt and even downright rude. In contrast, Sinn Fein were always polite.

Would you say that Sinn Fein really were the key influence in determining the pace of the process?

No, I think the core elements were the two Governments and the key influence was Bertie Ahern and Tony Blair. We wouldn't be where we are now without those two men, and they drove the Agreement.

How?

They just pushed people into corners until they got a deal.

What is your view of republicans?

They were extremely skilful, but, as said, they would bring in a whole load of issues at the last minute. We had a very difficult negotiation with the British over policing, and then eventually we got to Weston Park and got a deal which the SDLP were able to support. Around about the same time in Weston Park, when Brian Cowen tried to persuade Sinn Fein to sign up to policing, they came in with a long list of demands that had emerged from a (largely academic) study on policing. There would have been twenty or forty different things and they said they couldn't sign up for policing unless they got all of these. It took quite a while, maybe two more years, before they signed up for policing, but what eventually emerged was not in any way significantly different from what the SDLP had achieved at Weston Park.

Did they do this on a regular basis?

Yes. It's just the way they operate. They would have huge lists of things, all of which came out of a consultation of which I wasn't aware. It was very oblique, these lists had to be ticked off in their eyes. It did slow things down, but it did mean that from their point of view they made a lot of progress.

Why was policing so difficult?

Who had the Provisional IRA been fighting for the past thirty years? Three hundred policemen had been killed by them. Policing was at the very centre of the nationalist and republican difficulty with the Northern Ireland administration; the RUC were perceived as a political rather than community police force. If you talk to any nationalist they will tell you horrific stories of RUC actions, particularly early in the Troubles, and a number of policemen were involved in murder. It was not easy for the Sinn Fein, nor indeed for the SDLP, to agree to policing of any kind, but to agree to serve on boards at a district level, a very local level, to agree to serve on the Policing Board in Belfast and to oversee a police force which was not the RUC, but which would involve members who were formerly in the RUC, was exceedingly difficult for them.

Did controlling the pace in that way undermine the credibility of the process?

There were stages when people became very impatient, especially as with the McCartney killing and the bank robbery. The Irish view was that you could not have had that bank robbery without the agreement of the Sinn Fein leadership, so there was a deep feeling of betrayal and it lasted for a very long time.

What was their response to it?

The Sinn Fein leadership denied any connection with either the McCartney murder or the bank robbery. Nobody believed them, but they denied it.

Did the Irish consider walking away at that point?

You'd have to ask Bertie Ahern, but at the end of the day the two Governments could not walk away, they had to keep on going until they got the institutions up and running. And, of course, that gave those with the greatest demands, like the DUP and Sinn Fein, an advantage.

What about the difference between formal negotiations and informal negotiations? Is a conversation over a cup of tea to assess personality important?

I was doing that all the time in Northern Ireland from 1982 to 1985 and an enormous amount of informal contact and dialogue took place in 'The Bunker' at Maryfield. Informal contacts are an essential part of diplomacy.

It must have been more difficult to probe the personalities and the psychologies of republicans when essentially the whole team worked as one person?

The essence of negotiation is to use all of the chats and talks to build trust and confidence and then make a decision or make a judgement as to what can be done, how far you can go and where the red lines are.

Jonathan Powell says in the book Great Hatred, Little Room *that he thought Sinn Fein over-negotiated and could have made a deal five years previously. Do you agree?*

When they made the big moves they had to bring everybody with them. Adams used to say he didn't want to be a Michael Collins, or an Eamon de Valera. I think there are times when what he was saying was truthful. They were very cautious. They probably could have made a deal earlier, but the number of dissidents might have been much greater.

Many see Sinn Fein as being skilful in negotiations. What does that mean though?

They always hoped to get something additional to the achievements of the SDLP, who were their electoral rivals. Take policing. I happened to be the civil servant with oversight of the negotiations on policing in 2000–1 until the SDLP signed up at Weston Park. Very much against the wishes of the Dublin Government, Mandelson had reneged on promises about policing reform that he had made to Seamus Mallon and to the Dublin Government. He made political judgements to which we were deeply opposed, as was Mallon, who was the lead man on policing for the SDLP. Eventually we got to Weston Park, where negotiations were about policing and the implementation of the Patten Report. Blair agreed to implement the Patten Report in full. At the end of those negotiations Mallon said the new policing arrangements were acceptable and he used a phrase he had used in 1985: 'A camel is a horse designed by a committee and I know the difference between a horse and a camel. This is a horse.' Brian Cowen tried really hard to persuade Sinn Fein to sign up because that was such an important step forward. What was interesting was that the SDLP were convinced that the deal that they and the Irish Government had done with the British on policing would work, but Sinn Fein still wouldn't sign up. Was it because they couldn't sign up or was it because they were looking for another slice so as to be able to say we've got one up on the SDLP? Who's to know?

Or was it because they read that in relation to decommissioning?

Who knows, but the DUP did the same thing. The DUP always tried to get another slice of what the Ulster Unionists hadn't got. So, for example, they claimed that the St Andrews Agreement was a new one, but in actual fact it's fundamentally the Good Friday Agreement with a few changes.

To what extent was the peace process designed to draw the extremists into the middle ground?

In the 1980s the Irish Government tried to find a political solution in Northern Ireland which nationalists could support. We were trying to get reforms in policing and the Prison Service to produce a place that would be less cold for Catholics. There is no doubt that there was great concern then about the manner in which Sinn Fein had become a political movement on the back of the hunger strikes. I don't think that Government foresaw a situation in which Sinn Fein would become the largest of the nationalist parties. Similarly, I don't think anyone envisaged the DUP becoming the dominant party on the unionist side either. In fact, Sinn Fein and the DUP only became the dominant parties in 2005.

Was there any attempt to communicate with Sinn Fein?

Not to my knowledge. I would be astonished had there been any contact between the Irish Government and Sinn Fein of any meaningful kind before the collapse of the Fine Gael government in 1987.

Were you picking up soundings through the Catholic Church?

In the period before the Anglo-Irish Agreement the Department of Foreign Affairs, including myself, had contacts with clergy of all denominations. I personally didn't have contacts after I went into Maryfield, with one or two exceptions. There was also contact with people like Father Denis Faul and Father Raymond

Murray, who were deeply critical of actions of the security forces, and with prison chaplains.

Were you picking up indirect contacts through the media or from republican wings at the time?

We did pick up information from other sources about the republicans and the loyalist paramilitaries. But I was strictly forbidden to talk to republicans in the period before I went into Maryfield. I could talk to anyone as long they were not paramilitaries. I did have a lot of contact through the chaplains indirectly with prisoners, and I dealt an enormous amount with prison issues and, on occasion, with the families of prisoners, but never met with the prisoners themselves. I also had a lot of contact with solicitors and barristers, including those who defended paramilitaries, including Paddy McGrory.

Are you of the mind that the British put a lot of stall by text, bits of paper, and that for the Irish talking is more important?

I don't know. During the negotiation of the Anglo-Irish Agreement we could tell the British a great deal about the unionists that they didn't know, and the reason was because they hadn't been talking to them or listening to them in Westminster. Talking and listening is critical in any negotiation. You have to understand what the others want and where the deal is available, otherwise you're just talking to yourselves.

In a situation like this, can risks be equitable or is it really the Governments that have got to take the biggest risks?

In the negotiations to implement the Belfast Agreement, when Sinn Fein thought they weren't getting what they wanted, they used to say it was up to the Governments to force the unionists to give in. But, they did seem to realise that the other side also had to take risks, especially when they achieved the position of Deputy First Minister in the Northern Ireland Executive. I thought it was very significant that when Peter Robinson was in personal difficulties that Martin McGuinness gave him his full support. Risk taking is essential. Politics is always a compromise.

There's something important about human relationships in all this as well, then?

Yes, this is where talking is so important. When Dr Paisley accepted Bertie Ahern's invitation to the opening of the site of the Battle of the Boyne, Dr Paisley said he was beginning to trust Mr Adams. That's why talking and meeting are so important. It can affect relationships.

Was the starting point for the East–West relationship the Anglo-Irish Agreement?

Between 1974 and 1979 Dublin felt very strongly that the Labour Government had let them down, and when Callaghan appointed Roy Mason as the Secretary of State for Northern Ireland he in essence told him to put a lid on things and there were no developments at all. It was a time when they tried to depoliticise what was going on in the Maze and we ended up with the hunger strikes, which was a disaster and created Sinn Fein as a political entity. What the Irish Government tried to do once Garret FitzGerald came into power in 1983 was to try to build up a working relationship with the British and out of that came the Anglo-Irish Agreement. An Anglo-Irish Ministerial Conference, which met regularly, was established, as was the Joint Secretariat in Maryfield. Thus, permanent communications were established between the two Governments and they were working all the time together to try to resolve problems. However, we should not under-estimate the risk undertaken by the Irish Government in signing up to the Anglo-Irish Agreement. Its success depended on the willingness of the nationalists to engage with the Irish Government and on the willingness of the British Government to initiate change to resolve the problems so raised.

Is it the case that you kept an extensive list of things that happened?

We developed a thing called 'The log' to record issues, both individual matters and generic themes raised either by ourselves or the British and to monitor progress on the issues raised. Many of the issues were raised in anticipation of discussion at the Ministerial Conference. By the end of January, within seven weeks of the establishment of the Joint Secretariat, the Irish side had raised about forty different issues. Among the specific matters were an incident of alleged harassment by the UDR, a prison sentence review, and a shooting by the UDR where the soldiers were immediately stood down from operational duties. Among the generic issues were cross-border roads, the Emergency Provisions Act, the use of flags and emblems, the Irish language, public appointments, the Newry–Dundalk road, Northern Ireland electoral matters, a code of conduct for the police and advice to be given to new British Army regiments. I should mention two specific matters. The first is Navan

Fort, an important historical monument of not only Irish but European significance. Quarrying was taking place around the site and in spite of objections made by, among others, Cardinal O Fiaich, both the local council and the Department of the Environment had permitted it to continue. The Minister responsible was Richard Needham. We asked him into dinner, discussed the matter at length, and Michael gave him a copy of Thomas Kinsella's translation of the Tain, which is centred on Navan Fort. The result was that Needham took a ministerial decision to stop the quarrying and preserve the site, beside which a visitors' centre has since been constructed. The second is Divis Flats and two other tower blocks in Belfast and Derry. We made a request that they be demolished, and so it happened. The result was that the nationalist community began to have confidence in the capacity of the Irish Government to deliver on their behalf.

Could you then argue that the success of the East–West relationship emerged precisely because the Northern Ireland Office was excluded from the Anglo-Irish Agreement?

Not after November 1985. The Anglo-Irish Agreement represented a very big step forward by the British, leading to the inclusion of the Irish Government in the government of Northern Ireland. On the British side they felt that they could not have achieved this had they involved the Northern Ireland Office and Northern Irish civil servants at the outset. This was a very conscious decision taken on by the British negotiators in Number 10 to keep this to themselves and the Foreign Office at the beginning, and certainly, I've heard Northern Irish and Northern Ireland Office civil servants say that they shouldn't have been kept out.

Do the Irish go about negotiations differently to the British?

The British system is more inclined to do things on paper, but the art of persuasion is not simply an Irish art. There were many occasions when Tony Blair, Jonathan Powell and others were exceedingly persuasive and very determined to make sure that people were persuaded.

What makes somebody persuasive in that situation?

I think you're talking about trust, confidence and respect. You are talking about a capacity to listen and the possibility of listening very carefully and judging what's feasible and then doing what's feasible. None of this was predetermined. What came out at the end was not envisaged from the very beginning. People listened very carefully and tried to the greatest extent possible to provide what people said they required. There was a build-up of trust from doing that.

Do you think that just absorbing humiliation, to some extent, was actually an important part of that process because it was proof of how determined Ahern and Blair were to take and overcome that?

Absolutely. I've been with both Blair and Ahern sitting in the room taking it from David Trimble or Gerry Adams. They took it for ten years but were absolutely determined to bring about a power-sharing government in Northern Ireland which all could support. We wouldn't be where we are but for their persistence and determination.

Are you of the view that social networks are an important part of the negotiation process?

You've got to build up a relationship in which opposites can find common ground. You've got to find something that both sides can support, and that wasn't easy. And I don't think, by the way, that it was particularly easy for the SDLP or for David Trimble to bring their followers along either. It was certainly not easy for Adams and McGuinness to bring along all of their followers, but they practically got the whole lot to come with them.

Would the seeds of the peace process have taken such root without American involvement in the situation?

I don't think the American role was as important in the period up to the Anglo-Irish Agreement as it was from the 1990s on. There was an occasion in late 1984 during the negotiation of the Anglo-Irish Agreement when we had the 'Out, out, out' of Mrs Thatcher. President Reagan met Thatcher the following January and he raised the matter with her. Reagan said he regarded both FitzGerald and Thatcher as his friends and because of that he emphasised how important it was for him that each be friendly to the other. After the Agreement the Americans were helpful in providing considerable resources for the International Fund for Ireland, which was intended to try and put money into areas that had been bereft of investment on both sides of the community divide. But Reagan didn't play the really important role that came later with Bill Clinton and Bush. Clinton would press Adams and Trimble, and Bush was very good at pushing Dr Paisley, but direct presidential involvement really didn't exist at the time of the Anglo-Irish Agreement. It came later.

Was Bush good in pushing Paisley?

He'd pick up the telephone. It's quite astonishing that successive American presidents, if they were asked to talk to these people by either the Taoiseach in Dublin or the Prime Minister in London, would invariably do so. There were a number of occasions when President Bush spoke directly to Dr Paisley encouraging him to keep going.

Did the Americans look at this problem differently from the British and the Irish? Is their way of thinking about Northern Ireland, and indeed negotiation, different from the British/Irish perspective?

In a general way, the Americans always think that there are solutions to problems and that problems are there to be resolved. This resonated with the Irish-American lobby, which is a powerful influence in the United States that has tended to be supportive of Irish nationalism. On the other hand, there is also a big element of Irish-America which is of Protestant Irish origin, although the unionists were much slower to take advantage of that lobby than were Irish nationalists. There was also a smallish but fairly powerful element which harps back to the old Fenian and republican tradition that is very much in favour of Irish unity, and some of that element was financially supportive of, and indeed also gave weapons to, the Provisional IRA.

To what extent in a process like this is it made up as you go along?

There's a good deal of that.

To put it another way, to what extent was the spontaneous part of the process?

The Belfast Agreement was a framework agreement which has a lot of principles built in. But how to ensure it is implemented into legislation? How do you translate those principles into boots on the ground? All of that can take a long time working out and you have to listen to people. You may have started out wanting to move dead straight ahead, but you may end up a few degrees to the left or to the right in order to ensure that you're taking everybody with you. There wasn't an exact sense in everybody's head in 1998 of where exactly they would be ten years later.

How much of it is symbolic and down to the way the parties communicate?

First it's a political negotiation with politicians, so the politicians have to feel that they can sell it to their followers. It's perhaps a little bit easier for John Hume and Seamus Mallon to be able to do this than it might be for Gerry Adams and Martin McGuinness, but they have to feel that they can sell it to their supporters. A lot of the negotiation was with Trimble and Mallon, and much of that was based on 'I just can't sell that. I can't do that. I can't go that far and if I do go that far I won't be able to carry my people with me.' Trimble had to suspend the institutions a few times or pull out. I have great respect for his tremendous courage, but I don't think he's a particularly astute politician. It's all a question of being able to sell what you've agreed to your followers, and if you can't bring them with you then you're in trouble. It took Dr Paisley a very long time, but once he learned that Sinn Fein was going to support the police he moved.

Was there ever any double-dealing going on, or were the British generally true to their word?

I was surprised to find out a few years ago that the British were actually talking to the Provisionals when Michael Lillis and I were in Maryfield in the mid-1980s, but I never saw any double-dealing with the Blair team.

The Queen's visit was symbolically hugely important. How do you view such symbolism, and is it as important as it appears to be?

Absolutely. I think symbolism can be hugely important and can lead to changes of perception. The Ambassador can have an effect here. Let me give you a personal example. I wanted to recognise the contribution of Irish people in the British Army, and Dublin agreed. In 2002 I went to Windsor Castle for the eightieth anniversary of the laying up of the colours of the Irish regiments. Never before had this been done and I recognised the part played by Irish people, both nationalist and unionist, in the British Forces. I ended the speech with a quotation from Bertie Ahern, who had done something similar a few years previously in Bandon. I later went and gave a lecture in Sandhurst, and I laid a wreath at the Cenotaph in April 2004 for the Irish soldiers in the Anzac armies. When a stone was laid, I think in 2003, in Westminster Abbey beside the stone to the Unknown Soldier, to honour all of those who had received the Victoria or George Cross, I was asked by the British if could I provide somebody in national dress or uniform, so we had an Irish Army officer with an Irish tricolour march all the way up Westminster Abbey in the presence of the Queen and Prince Philip, with all the brass of the British Army present, to put the tricolour on the altar. That was a huge step.

Who made that decision?

I proposed it and Dublin agreed. But the British made the decision to invite me. In 2005 I attended on Remembrance Sunday at the Cenotaph, not to lay a wreath because only Commonwealth High Commissioners laid wreaths, but to pay respect; this was before Dr Paisley agreed to participate at St Andrews. There was a little reception afterwards in the Foreign Office for the people who were in attendance and Paisley put his arm around my shoulder and said 'Mr Ambassador, you're now my Ambassador'. So gestures can be very important and circumstances created in which both sides can work together and trust built up.

Was that covered in the media?

None of it was covered except the event in Windsor Castle. But the British knew.

What does that tell you about the involvement of the Irish today?

Well, to see how far things have come just look at the fact that in 2014 the then Irish Ambassador became the first to lay a wreath on Remembrance Sunday.

Do you recall clearly the moment when the deal was done with Paisley?

The really emotional bit was when we all met at the end. It was early afternoon and people had to go but Sinn Fein kept us waiting. I think it was the Paisleys' wedding anniversary and the Taoiseach had decided to present them with a beautiful wooden bowl made out of a tree that had fallen at the site of the Battle of the Boyne. You should have seen the response of Dr Paisley and his wife. There was huge emotion. These are the sort of thoughtful gestures which do make a difference.

Is that because all the loose ends at that point had been tied up?

That helped. I was present at Hillsborough in November 1985 for the signing of the Anglo-Irish Agreement and the raw emotion was astonishing. The feelings we had on the returning airplane were very emotional. When we arrived at Dublin Airport the whole Cabinet was lined up to greet us. That is what happens when things come to a successful end. It brings considerable relief and emotion.

One person you haven't mentioned is Gordon Brown. What was he like?

When it was quite clear that Gordon Brown was going to replace Blair I talked to Dublin and said it was essential that we make contact with him because the relationship between Number 10 and the Taoiseach was critical for the future of Northern Ireland. Gordon was very difficult to get to. He didn't like diplomats, even his own diplomats never mind others, so I talked to Des Browne, who at this time was Secretary of State for Defence and who I had come to know well from his role in Northern Ireland. I told him we really needed to get to Gordon Brown before he became leader to ensure a good future relationship. He said he would try to get him to come to the Embassy for dinner to meet Irish ministers, including Brian Cowen who was Taoiseach in waiting. It took quite a long while to organise, but we got it organised and there were just the five of us at dinner. Besides the two British ministers and myself there were Dermot Ahern, the Irish Foreign Minister and Brian Cowen, the Finance Minister. At the outset Dermot Ahern talked soccer with Gordon Brown for half an hour, recalling goals scored thirty years earlier, and the whole atmosphere relaxed. Over dinner Brian Cowen argued for an economic dividend to be made available should the DUP and Sinn Fein agree to share power. He was very persuasive, and Gordon Brown agreed that there should be an economic dividend for the peace process. As a result, meetings took place in the Embassy involving civil servants from the British Treasury, the Irish Finance Department, the Northern Ireland Finance Department and others to agree a financial package for Northern Ireland which would be made available in the event of a deal. Incidentally, I had asked the Taoiseach to explain to Blair in advance what I was trying to do. I was told that Blair was quite agreeable but that I was not to call Brown 'Prime Minister'!

Did Brown have a grasp of the detail?

He was very clever. He had gone to Northern Ireland before he came to the Embassy, specifically to be briefed, and he was briefed not only by the police, the civil servants and the politicians, but also by the intelligence people. He did it so that he would know what he was talking about when he came to the Embassy.

Brown was coming into a situation where Blair had been successful, so were you concerned that he might be less engaged or interested?

Gordon Brown had shown no interest in Northern Ireland, but in my view it was absolutely essential that the Taoiseach and the Prime Minister keep close on Northern Ireland. I have felt for a long time that it will take several generations for the people of Northern Ireland to become reconciled. Des Browne agreed with me. We knew Gordon Brown was going to become Prime Minister, so it was vital to build a relationship with the next Irish Taoiseach. At the end of the day you have to work with whoever is elected, but this is also about the importance of establishing personal relationships in advance. I came across Des Browne when he was a Junior Minister in Northern Ireland and we used to have dinner regularly, I'm very fond of him and I liked him. Then he became Secretary of State for Defence and there was an issue about a pardon for the British soldiers who had been shot at dawn in the First World War, allegedly for desertion. A number of Irish soldiers had been shot, roughly half and half nationalist and unionist. Dermot Ahern was very interested in this and was in favour of a pardon for these people, but it had proved very difficult and John Reid when Secretary of State for Defence wasn't prepared to move, saying he couldn't do it. Dr Paisley was also very interested. I engaged with Des Browne and with a former Minister of the Army, Philip Tuowig, and the result was, every single one of them was pardoned. Des Browne signed all the certificates. I think the Irish interest in this was a significant factor. Over the years a common ground between London and Dublin has been built, as well as a determination to try and resolve the Northern Ireland problem together with the politicians there. I hope to God it lasts for at least another twenty or thirty years because that's how long it's going to take. The North remains in a very delicate, very fragile state.

5

Foundations and principles of a peace process: an interview with Sean O hUiginn

Graham Spencer: *How far back was it when you started to pick up signs that a peace process could be emerging?*

Sean O hUiginn: It would have been in the late 1980s. The Hume–Adams dialogue, as reflected in the exchanges between the SDLP and Sinn Fein published in 1988, gave a very significant pointer to something new. The traditional republican view derived a supposed authority from a doctrine as arcane as that of the hidden Imam, which would have been comical except that some people felt justified in killing in its name. The 1988 papers were a clear departure from the magical thinking of traditional republican fatwas. There was an acceptance that the desired alliance with other strands of nationalism, almost all vehemently opposed to political violence in Northern Ireland, required a meaningful debate with them. Sinn Fein may have under-estimated the distance they themselves would have to travel to achieve any such alliance, but the acceptance that their positions had to be justified rationally rather than simply asserted dogmatically was a significant change in the right direction. Of course, there was a very long road still to travel, and many major obstacles to overcome. One such obstacle was the near-universal disbelief that the republican movement could ever be capable of the transition to genuinely democratic politics. Their entire record seemed to prove otherwise, since they derived a mystical authority from Irish history which they believed overrode and indeed rendered invalid the existing democratic structures on the island. The traditional republican leadership saw conventional politics, except for demonstrative or propaganda purposes, as distractions from their core mission, so the scepticism about change in these long-standing postures was eminently understandable. Others who accepted there was a change in republican rhetoric felt it reflected at most some devious change of tactics. I felt personally at the time that the possibility that it was genuinely a new departure should not be dismissed out of hand, but rather carefully tested. I had great respect for John Hume's political instincts and felt we owed it to him and his political record to explore carefully and in all good faith a new development which he saw as one of great potential.

The campaign of violence had been intolerably costly in terms of human suffering and material and economic damage. To crush it decisively by military means would require very drastic emergency measures, and no student of Irish history could overlook the possibility that these could backfire very badly, leaving our democratic system badly tarnished and the advocates of violence strengthened. The prospect of securing a voluntary end to violence was therefore at an enormous premium, and the risk of compromising the democratic values of our society in a careful exploration of that option would almost certainly be far less at the end of the day than betting everything on military repression. Moreover, I never felt that the risks of dialogue were as acute or one sided as the opponents of the peace process made them out to be. The republicans were putting in jeopardy a core element on their side also, namely the unexamined myths which rallied young people to their violent campaign.

The myths had proved their potency in that respect, even if at the cost of limiting the influence of the movement in respect of constructive potential. The myths would tend to shrivel in the light of day when exposed to wider examination. Even if people who came out of the tunnel went back in, they would do so with a wider perspective than that of their original isolation. There are copious records of the negotiations which will eventually emerge, but I am utterly confident there will not be a single line showing any Irish Government representative wavering for even a second on the precondition of a total cessation of violence. Some elements in the movement may have harboured notions of occasional violence to influence the democratic processes, but the more astute accepted the Government position that this was not viable. This was not primarily because of the obvious moral considerations – in my experience such discussions always ended in 'whataboutery' – but for the pragmatic reason that no responsible democratic politician could afford association with a group capable of suddenly tainting them with some brutal atrocity.

Can you tell me what you thought when you very first saw the Hume-Adams document?

It would be wrong to imagine the Hume-Adams document as a kind of tablet of stone brought down from the mountain. It was rather a floating drafting exercise where many hands refined a text to arrive at a result that might reflect a generally acceptable compromise. We had heard reports in the late 1980s that the republican leadership was attempting to reach out to other elements in the nationalist community. This had been tried before, but on the basis of the old shibboleths, and if this was another such attempt it could be safely dismissed as of no consequence. John Hume's judgement and the tone of the 1988 papers suggested that this time the Sinn Fein overtures might be grounded in a better appraisal of political realities, and so it eventually proved. The document had its origins in discussions between Gerry Adams and Father Alec Reid. Father Reid was passionate about the need to end the suffering caused by the 'armed struggle' and felt the way to do this was to create a viable political alternative to it. He thought this could best be achieved by uniting all the resources of nationalism behind a common programme, which obviously had to be an exclusively democratic and peaceful one to have any prospect of winning general acceptance. In the course of subsequent discussions, the draft morphed from a common nationalist platform to the more ambitious and operational form of a draft declaration by the two Governments which would open the way for a complete cessation of IRA violence and comprehensive negotiations including Sinn Fein. The Irish Government's involvement in these discussions was initially at a remove, largely between Dr Martin Mansergh (technically a Fianna Fail operative rather than a formal Government representative) and Father Reid, and later between John Hume and Government ministers and civil servants. When in 1993 the process was judged sufficiently advanced, texts were discussed between Dermot Nally and myself and British officials led by Sir Robin Butler, usually with Sir John Chilcot and Sir Quentin Thomas. Our work was reviewed at intervals between the Taoiseach and Tanaiste and their British counterparts. This process culminated in a very fraught summit in Dublin in December 1993.The British had sought to discard the earlier work and proceed on a basis which would have rebuffed any prospect of a wider peace settlement. Happily, wiser counsels prevailed, leading to the Downing Street Declaration shortly afterwards. Because, as I said, there never was a talismanic text carved in stone, but rather a multi-layered process of collective drafting, I can recall no moment of epiphany when I saw the text for the first time. My operational engagement with it began very soon after I took charge of the Anglo-Irish Division in the Department of Foreign Affairs in 1992.

What about the nature of the text itself? Was it necessarily oblique at that point? Did it need major refurbishment or did you think it was structurally a solid foundation?

There were a lot of very solid elements in it. One of the most valuable, in my view, was its ingenious treatment of the Irish right to self-determination. The right to self-determination for Ireland is a defining belief of the republican movement, and indeed of Irish nationalism in general. The document affirmed that right, but registered also the indubitable fact that Irish people were divided as to its application. This might seem mere casuistry, but it was in fact a most creative deconstruction of the Irish conundrum. It was coupled with the assurance that the British would accept whatever application of self-determination was collectively agreed by the Irish people. (This was a polite way of saying they would no longer pursue the old imperial agenda, with all its baleful hostility to Irish separatism.) The obstacles to Irish unity were therefore not on the level of British doctrine, or even London throwing its great weight on the unionist side of the scales, but in the existence of a unionist community with an assertive sense of identity very different to Irish nationalism. Achieving the goal of unity was therefore a process of political persuasion among Irish people. This approach had the great merit of corresponding to the facts on the ground rather than to abstractions which disregarded them. We know from Irish history the damage these abstract formulas can inflict, so this reformulation did a great service to the peace process. As far as I know it originated with John Hume, and certainly I have always associated it with him.

What about the concept of self-determination? Did Sinn Fein want to know a lot more about what that potentially meant?

Every party had some red lines; issues that we knew were potential deal-breakers for them. If the unionists were asked to sign up to some dilution of their bedrock principle of majority consent for a change of sovereignty in Northern Ireland they would simply have left the table. Similarly, if republicans had felt that a draft rejected their principle of the Irish right to self-determination they would have left the table. So a way had to be found to accommodate these realities. I don't think the republicans had engaged in elaborate refinements of the theory of self-determination. For most of them, the involvement of the British State in Ireland was, as Wolfe Tone had put it, 'The never-failing source of all our ills' and 'Brits Out' was the correspondingly comprehensive cure. Many took the simplistic view that since Northern Ireland had been cut off from the rest of the island by an arbitrary stroke of the British pen, another stroke of the British pen was all that was needed to undo that and restore the status quo ante. This view conveniently ignored the realities of unionism and assumed these were certain to vanish when unplugged from the sustaining current of British support. It also avoided the legal implications flowing from the separate existence of Northern Ireland over four or five generations. So there were undoubtedly some simplistic aspects to the republican concept of self-determination. Nevertheless, they could not have engaged in the peace process without a British acceptance of Irish self-determination as the outside envelope, so to speak. However, within that envelope the winning of unionist consent was a requirement valid on the level of theory, as well as very obviously in real life. The text sought to integrate these two indispensable requirements in a single framework.

Were you responsible for drafting the Downing Street Declaration and Frameworks Document?

I had some role in the drafting, but these documents had a complex genesis with inputs from many hands. The Downing Street Declaration, for example, contained elements from Father Reid and his republican contacts, from Hume and Adams, from Irish and British officials, from loyalists mediated through eminent clergymen, and from earlier canonical Irish or British texts. I recall work with Martin Mansergh and Quentin Thomas in arriving at the admittedly knotty text that proved serviceable on the more challenging constitutional and related issues. Reading the text now I would be at a loss to say which element came from whom, any more than I imagine a team of stonemasons could remember which hand had placed which stone in the finished wall. On the Frameworks Document, Quentin Thomas and I chaired our respective teams of officials and meshed their inputs, so our roles in respect of that document were more clearly profiled.

What about the narrative structure of the Declaration? Is there a formula for such a document, for example, the preamble, the key principles and so on?

The conventional format for intergovernmental agreements is a preamble, setting out the context and motivation of the exercise, followed by operational paragraphs enshrining the substance of the new agreement. The Downing Street Declaration blends these two elements. It has some of the characteristics of a joint manifesto between the two Governments, aimed at bridging existing divergences between London and Dublin with new joint understandings and a proclamation of common purpose. No less importantly, it stresses the high cost and futility of violence and offers the prospect of a viable and meaningful political alternative within which paramilitaries could pursue their aims by peaceful and democratic means, once violence had been ended.

In light of the chronology, Sinn Fein had got rid of abstentionism in 1986, then in 1988 they are in dialogue with the SDLP, so the momentum was towards some sense of serious political engagement. Was that crucial to starting work on the Downing Street Declaration?

The entire exercise was aimed at testing, with best endeavour and the utmost good faith, the proposition that the republican movement was prepared to abandon violence if offered a meaningful political framework to pursue their aims on a peaceful and democratic basis. It responded to hopes that that could now be the case. It would have been pointless, or worse, if they were bent on pursuing the old strategy of making the British so weary of Northern Ireland that their Government would simply cut Northern Ireland adrift. There was a certain shallowness or volatility in British public attitudes to Northern Ireland which fostered both hopes and fears that such a tactic might prove effective. Burke's observation that the chief British ambition in regard to Ireland was to hear no more about it remains as sadly pertinent to our era as it was to his. I personally always felt such a drastic lurch in British policy was unlikely. The appearance of capitulation to terrorism would be toxic for any British Government, nor was any likely to regard the risk of destabilising the whole of Ireland as a mere bagatelle. I think the more perceptive strategists on the republican side had also begun to understand the limitations of what the armed struggle could achieve. Building a political escape route from violence made sense only if people were willing to take it, obviously on unambiguously democratic terms.

When you put the text of the Declaration together did the Irish version go out first to the British? Did you get a head start on that?

There are contexts, mostly in multilateral negotiations such as the UN, where an early draft can confer significant advantage by defining the framework to which others then react. This was not really a factor in these bilateral negotiations, leaving aside occasional tactical leaks aimed at swaying public opinion rather than the other Government directly. The British posture up to the time Tony Blair assumed office could best be described as one of semi-indulgent scepticism. They were willing to listen, but the burdens of advocacy and proof were placed firmly on Irish shoulders. This was an adroit tactical stance, since it cast the goals of peace and stability as Irish demands to which they might make concessions, rather than as goals equally if not even more incumbent on the British themselves. It also probably reflected divided counsels within the British system, which no doubt contained currents reluctant to accept any end to violence other than a Waterloo moment of annihilation of the terrorists, however costly and elusive that pursuit might prove in practice.

Can you talk to me about the problem or danger of putting too much into a document which presumably, early on, has to stay ambiguous?

I accept the document will never feature in any anthology of majestic prose but I would defend it against the charge of ambiguity, at least as regards most meanings of that word. It was an attempt to contain contradictory goals of nationalism and unionism within a single conceptual framework, and governed by agreed ground rules. What was uncertain, or ambiguous if you want to call it that, was not the meaning of the words, which I think is actually clear, but the context in which they would be applied, whether a politically divided or united island. The ambiguity people see is not that the words can be resolved into contradictory meanings, but because they can be applied equally to two radically different scenarios.

If you look at those documents the language appears close to neutral. I am assuming that was the aim?

Yes, exactly. It would have served no useful purpose if one side or the other felt the text was hopelessly tilted against them or amounted to a repudiation of their core values.

When you draft a piece of text are you imagining Adams talking to Molyneaux or Trimble? Who is the audience?

Only a master playwright could do justice to that dialogue; maybe a half-page of Beckett's monosyllables, or perhaps Friel's technique of long parallel monologues? The question touches, though, on a very serious point. Finding agreement on the basic requirements of London and Dublin as such would have been a relatively straightforward matter, and probably have been written on the back of the proverbial beer-mat. Our goal was, however, to embrace all the constituencies with a role in the problem, and therefore in its solution. That required altogether more complex equations, and people sometimes confused the two purposes. I sometimes used the analogy that the position of each protagonist was like a black sheet of cardboard with irregular holes marking their potential openness to other groups. When you superposed the sheets and shone a light through them all, the jagged area where the light came through all of them defined the area of potential agreement, which you could then seek to enlarge. The British sometimes acted as if we were creating these complications, rather than merely reflecting them, and if we could be persuaded to drop them they would vanish from the agenda. I never regret our insistence that the solution had to be expanded to meet the real dimensions of the problem, rather than pretending the problem could be shrunk to fit the solutions which we would find it most convenient to offer.

Was your reference for framing text the key principles?

Coming from an Irish State which experienced a bloody civil war caused, or at least justified, by reference to rival texts and formulas, we were fully alive to the importance of issues of principle. If we got them wrong the entire negotiating process would almost certainly founder. It was a success that has been rather under-appreciated that this dimension was managed without poking or arousing the various dangerous doctrinal guard dogs which might have wrecked the process. I was amused and gratified that the various parcels of principle which we had wrapped up at that point were passed respectfully down the various stages of negotiation and eventually incorporated into the Good Friday Agreement without anyone seeking to challenge or reopen them. This left the politicians free to concentrate on the practical issues, and not drown in treacherous doctrinal swamps.

Were you ever taken by surprise in the way people reacted to text?

Not really.

Did you think that words like 'harmonisation' in the Frameworks Document would be explosive for unionists?

Modern unionist leaders have all had the same intractable problem. Northern Ireland had been created to ensure their political control in the maximum area of Ireland where it could be achieved. They had tweaked matters further to reinforce this and to ensure a comprehensive domination of the nationalist inhabitants. The initial situation could scarcely be bettered from their point of view, and that was the root of the difficulty. The changes required by the various cultural, economic and social changes affecting Northern Ireland all appeared to their community as degradations, compared to the initial endemic state of total and unfettered unionist control, which they regarded as the norm. Further change could only mean further erosion of unionist power, so Dr Paisley and Mr Molyneaux, in their very different styles, saw resistance to change as the best strategy and immobility as the best attainable outcome. The only justification for change which could be sold to their followers was as the lesser evil compared to some other option. This naturally fostered the temptation to present proposals for change in just such terms. As to words like harmonisation, since unionists were logical that in their zero-sum perspective all change was to their detriment, I think it would have been foolish to believe they could be managed by euphemism. I recall a time when the late Mo Mowlam said the status quo was not an option and produced a storm of unionist outrage at such an abominable heresy. It is right to be tactful in the use of language, but also realistic about the extent to which this can disguise unwelcome realities.

Why was the Frameworks Document sorted between the two Governments and not with other groups and parties?

A more consultative approach would have amounted to something like multi-party talks. This exercise was supposed to provide a framework to give a focus for discussion in such talks, not to pre-empt them. If you tried to involve others in consultations you would be in essentially a kind of serial multi-party talks, and you would probably never have got anything like a coherent initial framework.

Did a principle like the 'totality of relationships' end up becoming a quagmire?

I was in Saudi Arabia, diligently supporting our dairy industries, when the controversy about 'the totality of relationships' emerged. It was a term of art, if you like, which was intended to say that all dimensions of the British–Irish relationship were under reference or to be looked at. Mrs Thatcher understandably just nodded it through on this assumption. It only became explosive when it was presented, quite unjustifiably in my view, as code for a willingness to put Irish unity on the agenda.

Do red lines mean core principles?

Yes, the things that would be deal-breakers if you violated them.

One British official referred to that as 'zones of convergence', which was the shrinking territory where you had to try and land?

It is a different perspective on the same concept. As I said, the process was so complex because we had to take account of positions that could not be subsumed readily into the positions of either Government. We were naturally alert to red lines on the green side of the equation, and the British on the orange, but in fact there was little dispute as to what constituted these red lines. For example, the principle of consent would have been an Irish red line also, if it had ever been under threat.

Was the pace slow, could you make quick progress and did it move from one to the other?

There was no uniform pattern or rhythm. The pace was determined in the main by political calendars. Work naturally intensified when meetings involving the Taoiseach and Tanaiste were in prospect. Other times it went at a more deliberate pace, to allow for internal consultations by the different participants. This was important for Sinn Fein also. The process was also very delicate for them. Unprepared developments or surprises which could 'frighten the horses' in their constituency carried dangers for them, and at the extreme could be 'very bad for their health' as one colleague drily phrased it. I do not recall any 'hothouse' negotiations on the Sunningdale or St Andrews model in my time.

Quentin Thomas on the British side said you need a piece of paper on the table or else people will talk forever, so in that sense is the text more important than formal communication and does it develop trust more than the informal, or does it cause complications around trust?

Texts are always important in such negotiations and were particularly so in this case, since it involved both new players and hitherto uncharted territory. Quentin Thomas was right. Without a text to anchor points of agreement you risk having a never-ending minuet in the negotiating phase and afterwards polemics and recriminations as to what was or was not agreed. Of course, there is also a dimension to such negotiations which will not be captured in texts, such as, for example, the degree of trust, or indeed mistrust, contempt or hatred protagonists may feel for each other. The spirit of negotiation can have a malign or benign effect, but I cannot think of any instance where the warm glow of simple goodwill was a substitute for a concrete agreement. I think the informal positive effects can be maximised, or indeed the negative minimised, when sheltered by a written understanding giving a clear point of reference and protecting the vital interests of the parties. I also think the media tend to exaggerate the impact of these informal personal factors. Countries have interests rather than friendships. Recently released papers show the British and Irish systems much exercised by the operatic side of the relationship between Mrs Thatcher and Mr Haughey. At this distance, it is hard to see where the fascination or repulsion expressed in their respective sets of blue eyes changed anything very much.

Is there a distinction between a senior civil servant that writes a piece of text and a prime minister or a secretary of state who might be reading it in terms of political impact for themselves and others?

There is a clear distinction between their respective roles. In the traditional system in which I worked I thought it ironic that each possessed what the other most craved; permanence for the politician, public gratification of the ego for the civil servant. A good civil servant will tailor the draft to the politician's known attitudes and politics, which requires the skill to recognise and interpret these things. I remember as a young diplomat being asked to brief a journalist from the *Reader's Digest*, which professed to have no political stance or interest. At the end of a most exhaustive and well-informed grilling on Irish politics I expressed my surprise that the representative of a magazine which avoided politics could ask so many shrewd political questions. His reply was 'How can we avoid politics if we don't know what they are?' That comment has always stayed with me. The good civil servant avoids partisanship not through ignorance of politics, but by knowing what they are and a lively awareness of the sometimes subtle distinction between what is agreed policy, validated through due democratic process, and what is partisan or polemical, a matter of electoral politics, in short.

Jonathan Powell and others have spoken about constructive ambiguity, but was there a negative ambiguity? Can you remember when ambiguity set things back?

Not specifically. I would take issue, as I said earlier, with the word 'ambiguity' if it implies 'meaningless' or 'holding contradictory meanings simultaneously'. I think a close scrutiny of the texts shows this is rarely the case. The texts were potentially applicable to two very different scenarios of Northern Ireland under British or under Irish sovereignty, but that is a different matter.

There were many difficulties, but none that I remember was caused by difficulty in construing the import of the texts. The obstacles corresponded rather to Machiavelli's famous analysis of the difficulties and dangers of introducing a new order of things, which has to deal with both the resentment of those who feel the loss of the old and the incredulity with which people regard the potential benefits of the new. The settlement of the 1920s was more a stand-off than a settlement, and that led each protagonist to develop mechanisms of denial. One can now discern more clearly each rationalisation, the way each protagonist suppressed one or more aspects of the collective situation to defend their own position against inconvenient truths. It was comfortable to regard people in Northern Ireland as hopelessly addicted to sectarianism, rather than as people who had been bequeathed that legacy, which individuals could only ignore at their social, and sometimes even physical, risk. It was comforting for the British to present themselves as the adults driven to distraction by the tribalism of their charges, as the neutral arbiters, hapless victims even, of this terrible situation without analysing their own role as the most important influence by far in creating and sustaining it. One of the important contributions Albert Reynolds made was that he defined the 'terms of a trade' for co-operation between Dublin and London in a more realistic way, not as a process which had always to be within the British comfort zone. Taking people out of their comfort zones of denial will almost always require a degree of confrontation. It was a regrettable but necessary preliminary to finding the deeper level of agreement which finally prevailed.

On ambiguity, is it a generalisation to say that Sinn Fein were more comfortable with that than the unionists, and were the unionists more literal or forensic in their analysis of words?

Unionists have a highly complacent notion of the virtue of their own plain-speaking, but I found it is something where they place firmly the biblical category of it being more blessed to give than to receive. Their admiration for plain-speaking evaporates very quickly when the bracing qualities of home truths are directed towards themselves, and they show no mean ability to deploy all the tricks of the rhetoric of outrage to discourage such tendencies on the part of others. It is true that republicans have a long tradition of political debate centred on text, starting with de Valera's famous Document Number Two and including, in Mark Durkan's memorable quip, many 'textually transmitted diseases' over the years. The Presbyterian tradition is, however, no less meticulous with regard to text, even if the context is religious rather than overtly political. In short, I regard these distinctions as amusing topics for the pub or dinner table, but of no real analytical, still less predictive, value.

How do you determine where a common point of terrain might be?

By experience really. I go back to the analogy of the cardboard sheets with openings in them. You had to know what might be negotiable or not in each case, and where possible openings to others' demands might lie. You did not waste time on demands which would never be met; for example, discarding the principle of consent was unthinkable for either Government, so you worked with that reality as a given. There was the occasional borderline issue, for example, the notion of the British becoming persuaders for Irish unity. You could take the view that would be greeted in practice as a British declaration of withdrawal, with all its turbulent, unpredictable effects, or, alternatively, that it could be presented as a long-term aspiration, making clear that persuasion meant an undiminished right for unionists not to be persuaded. We put it in good faith to the British, as it was in the Hume–Adams draft, but did not greatly challenge their rejection of it, presumably reflecting their judgement that its real impact would be closer to the worst-case hypothesis.

But when you write text are you thinking of blocking exits too?

You refer, I assume, to an earlier conversation when I recalled how we supplemented the family protein, when I was a boy, by the cruel practice of sending terriers or ferrets into rabbit warrens. To put meat in the pot you didn't need to know everything that happened underground, but only have a clear picture of all the hidden exits the rabbits would eventually choose from. There was always only a limited number of them. Our system could never rival the British capacity to monitor what happened deep underground. On the other hand, a good mental map of the exits, and an instinct for which option was likely to be chosen, was also a serviceable guide for engaging in negotiations, and sometimes maybe even gave a clearer strategic perspective on future developments.

What about the redrafting process? Can you recall a text which moved substantially from an initial draft, or was it always within predictable limits?

All of the texts I can recall went through a painstaking process of refinement. It is also true that the parameters within which these changes occurred remained predictable. This was because each time you mapped accurately the forces in play you came up with much of the same areas where a compromise could or could not be found. Since both Governments were concerned with stability, and wanted evolutionary rather than cataclysmic change, the texts, however much amended, were usually within the same outside envelope. There is a congruency, therefore, to the successive models for compromise.

If there is a contentious issue, how important is it where you place it in the text? Do you surround it by 'feel good' language? Do you flag it up early in the text or try to disguise it?

Basically, it is hard to fool negotiators with rhetorical flourishes. Collectively they tend to home in unerringly on the real import of the text, trampling all the flower-beds you might have planted around it. The only process I know where you can succeed by stealth is in the US Congress. There, astonishingly, a legislator can smuggle into a bill of maybe a thousand pages a few extraneous clauses bringing some unrelated pork barrel to a particular district. In the case of Northern Ireland negotiations, the many seasoned politicians at the table were particularly unlikely to be taken in by presentational ruses, and indeed certain to make that brutally clear.

To what extent do you think the success of the process was dependent on pieces of paper, compared to dialogue in a room?

A successful negotiation will usually be some combination of the two. Text is important for all the reasons I gave earlier. The wrong language can hinder progress, and if it conflicts fundamentally with one or other core position, can drive that party from the table. An agreed text can also be a comfort blanket, enabling parties to branch out further in their dialogue, for example to derive corollaries from what has been written down to produce new practical arrangements.

Can you remember when text became a wrecking mechanism?

Well, the famous 'Washington Three' text would be a prime example. I suppose it was less a problem of text as such and more one of the substance underlying the text, but definitely a wrecking mechanism. Every child who bakes a cupcake learns that you must not only have exactly the right ingredients, but also mix them in exactly the right order. Decommissioning was indeed an essential ingredient, but it was deliberately demanded out of sequence to create a test the republicans could not pass. The explanation most current at the time, rightly or wrongly, was that Mr Major's political leash had been shortened by his patron, Lord Cranborne, and the decommissioning roadblock had been rolled on stage to disguise his incapacity to pursue the peace process further. (It is, by the way, if true, an illustration of the singular continuity of English political power structures, since Lord Cranborne would have exerted his influence from some of the same houses, and for all I know seated in the same chairs, from which his great ancestor Lord Burghley helped manage the Tudor conquest of Ireland.) The decision to degrade the important and strategic goal of decommissioning to serve as a tactical blocking mechanism, or even a wrecking ball for the whole process, was a sobering reminder that the British attitudes to the peace process were complex, comprising distinctly indifferent and negative strands also.

So the tensions were not so much about the actual meaning of the text or the principles but, from your point of view, it was about a process that was much more amenable to a required outcome?

There had been a tendency on all sides to create comfort zones to protect against vulnerabilities derived from the loose ends of the 1920s arrangements. This was not always by blanking out the outside world. Mainly it was asserting convenient theory to suppress inconvenient realities. The British pretended that Northern Ireland was as British as Finchley, and that Dublin's role in it was on a par to that of Bulgaria. The Irish Constitution treated Northern Ireland as a phantom phenomenon which should not be dignified with even a mention. Unionists vehemently resented any suggestion that a permanent monopoly of power exercised by a community of just over half the population over another community just a couple of percentage points smaller might be either wrong or unsustainable. Republicans saw the unionist community as victims of a false consciousness promoted by the British, and once violence persuaded the British to switch off the sustaining current, harmony and a happy ending would ensue. I spoke earlier of the British self-projection as the well-meaning adult, haplessly trying to bring delinquents to reason. The notion that the situation just happened, rather than being created and sustained by a long chain of active and passive British political decisions, was of great use in deflecting British responsibilities. I see the entire process as one of taking all the protagonists as much as possible out of these states of denial. That means abandoning some or all of a familiar comfort zone, and pressure to do so can easily be regarded as simple hostility. People now tend to see the harmonious partnership between Tony Blair and Bertie Ahern as the norm or default state. Without in any way diminishing the part played by the enormous dedication and talent of the two leaders, they were also building on the work which had been done by their predecessors, on occasion necessarily in a more confrontational way, to bring parties to see their patterns of denial for what they were.

How would you describe the differences between the two Governments in the struggle over text to reach a common outcome?

There is an enormous disproportion between the resources and reach of the two Governments and their respective systems. The British psychology is, inevitably, greatly influenced by that awareness. The British have also an immemorial tradition of statecraft, and a very pervasive security apparatus to go with it, which has never been broken or reset by war or revolution, as happened in most European countries.

All these factors required a certain vigilance in negotiations with them. I recall that just before the summit of December 1993 the British signalled that they wished to jettison the text elaborated over many months in the official contacts led by Dermot Nally and Sir Robin Butler and replace it with anodyne wording which would have undermined rather than advanced the search for peace. It had also emerged that in spite of John Major's famous declaration that contact with paramilitaries would turn his stomach, he had sustained without any sign of gastric distress protracted contacts with the republicans, all carefully concealed from the Irish Government. Albert Reynolds had made clear in informal remarks in advance of the summit that if the British changed the basis on which both Governments had been negotiating he would simply walk away. I recall the full panoply of British ministers solemnly intoning that this remark was so damaging to relationships that everything else paled in comparison. The low quality of the humbug served up to us was sometimes unflattering.

Was there a tendency for Albert Reynolds to think in terms of the deal, the final goal, rather than process?

Yes. It was both a strength and weakness of his. The British can be very adept at drowning adversaries in process, and Albert's near-total immunity to that technique served him well in the negotiations. Of course, you can also argue it was a great weakness in other respects, and contributed to the ending of his political career. His practical focus on the bottom line gave him a realistic sense also that British credibility on Northern Ireland was greatly enhanced when they had the support of Dublin, and vice versa. He did not use that factor crudely, but felt it was reasonable to ask that London should take account of Dublin's views as to what would or would not work, all the more so as we were not making irredentist demands but promoting goals of peace and stability which should have been theirs also. He also had a keen sense of when he was being given the run-around, and was prone to dismiss such attempts in pungent short order.

To what extent was the Irish position influenced by a need not just to work well with the British but to maintain a degree of distance and so not be accused of being sops to British demands or being absorbed into what was ostensibly a British process?

It was important for us in any case to maintain our independent perspective, and also important for us in the sense you suggest. Sinn Fein were very aware of the imbalance between the power of London and Dublin, and it would have greatly diminished whatever influence we might hope to have with them if they saw us as merely British puppets. The same factor also gave great weight to the US role, as supplying a counterweight to the imbalance arising from the preponderance of the British influence.

Can you give me a sketch of how you saw Sinn Fein as political figures and how they operated? Were they strategic and tactful or did they rely on you to steer them?

The Sinn Fein leadership, in common indeed with most of the key politicians in Northern Ireland, had emerged from the crucible of the Troubles. That sort of selection process brings able leaders to the fore. In terms of ability the Sinn Fein people we dealt were far ahead of earlier leaders one reads about. At the same time the campaign of violence had left them very isolated. I remember vividly their first entrance to the Forum in Dublin Castle. The other participants were milling around in a waiting room, and when the Sinn Fein delegation came in it was as if a lepers' bell had been rung. The other people literally fell back against the walls, away from them. They did have a lot to learn about how conventional politics operate and the kind of interactions with others which would be productive or otherwise. The learning process was complicated by the fact that they were too wary to take much guidance in this respect, and of course their relations with almost all other parties started from a point of mutual hostility and distrust. They were able people and quick studiers, and soon proved adept. Their American contacts helped in this respect, as I think did their contacts with the Irish Government, although they might challenge that view.

Was engagement a big fear for them?

Yes, their engagement was a fraught exercise for them, and for very good reasons. Getting off the tiger's back, in terms of the campaign of violence, was manifestly a dangerous exercise where a serious mistake could indeed 'be very bad for your health'. There were also less drastic risks, that if the peace outreach clearly amounted to failure they would be excoriated in republican mythology, always an important consideration. Moreover, the whole idea of a peaceful strategy would be discredited into the future.

Did they use the 'process going wrong' or 'we have to go back and consult' argument as a negotiating tactic?

We all accepted these were real considerations for them, even if exploited tactically on occasion. You could misjudge the situation by presuming that Sinn Fein and the

IRA were the same thing, and equally so by assuming they were completely separate and different. It was a complex relationship which contained overlaps, but also demarcations which were observed with some punctilio. Sinn Fein heavyweights such as Adams and McGuinness were never hapless hostages of their presumed wild men, but they were constrained by the need to bring on board influential people not necessarily sitting at the table. Moreover, their ambition to bring the great bulk of their movement with them made sense to everyone, and the degree of success they achieved in that respect, while not total, was very impressive.

Initially Sinn Fein was calling for a date of British withdrawal. Did you think this is a non-starter or worth pursuing?

An abrupt British withdrawal would have a convulsive impact on the whole island. I think Iraq stands as an awful warning of the dangers of fatuously assuming a best-case scenario instead of planning for the worst one. The furthest the text that we presented went in that direction was that the British would be persuaders for Irish unity, but we were not really surprised that they rejected that, defining their role more neutrally as persuaders for agreement. It could perhaps have been managed on the basis of careful reassurances to the unionist community, but it was equally possible that the unionists might have taken the wish for the deed, and the situation would veer out of control. I think there is an ever-growing realisation now that the only worthwhile unity, and incidentally the only form of unity likely to be endorsed by the population in two referendums, is one that the bulk of the unionists feels is of value for them also.

When you first met Adams and McGuinness what did you make of them? How did they come across?

First of all, I did not meet them until 1994. Contacts prior to the IRA ceasefire were not permitted for civil servants, but were conducted through intermediaries or Dr Martin Mansergh in his Fianna Fail role. When I did get to know them I found them very intelligent and effective advocates of their cause. They were personally always courteous and affable. Their wariness about the Government, which is bred in the bone in the republican tradition, was rarely allowed to intrude. They were complex individuals, with no doubt complex pasts, but that factor also qualified them to bring violence to a voluntary close if the negotiations were successful. They were very different in individual character and temperament. I was intrigued by the way they corresponded broadly to the contrasting personalities and skill-sets we associate, rightly or wrongly, with de Valera and Collins. I thought it was greatly to the credit of both men that there was never any hint of the jealousy or rivalry that had such damaging consequences for the whole island in the earlier instance.

When you met republicans what did you think of them as negotiators, and what they were saying to you?

As negotiators Sinn Fein were diligent, shrewd and wary. They kept copious records and would home in on any weakness or contradiction they discerned in the Government position. They had doctrinaire moments, what I thought of privately as the 'LP passages', where they rehearsed at length the verities of the republican position. I never knew whether this was as education for us, for the benefit of those reading the record, or for some other purpose. One could also sense uncertainty on occasion, reflecting the fact that their learning curves were still incomplete on the views of other protagonists and what could or could not prove acceptable to them. Their tradition contained a significant strand for which the political process with its inevitable compromises was simply a betrayal of the sacred armed struggle, so they had no accepted precedents they could rely on in this new territory.

Were they trying to get you to help them to decide what to do, or do you think they had already made those decisions themselves?

That is difficult to say. Their demeanour was absolutely never that of pupil, but I think the dialogue with us nevertheless helped them find or refine their bearings as they emerged from the original bubble of political isolation caused by the violence.

You talk about the theology of the movement, which seems very apt, but that implies the religious cult-like nature of the organisation, and that very different scenario about what is negotiable and so movable, and what isn't. Presumably this was a conundrum that you were constantly trying to work out?

Well, theology is a loose use of that word, but doctrine was very important. Something which denied the Irish right to self-determination would have driven them from the table. The Downing Street Declaration contains such dense language not because officials were incapable of writing simple texts, but because they had to embrace and reconcile complex values, self-determination being a very important one.

When Canary Wharf happened did you see that as part of the negotiating strategy?

I saw Canary Wharf as a huge setback. I had been in Washington, accompanying Dick Spring to a meeting with Tony Lake aimed at getting political negotiations finally underway. The bomb happened while we were in the plane on the way back. It was a horrible reversion to the bad old ways. It destroyed not just the victims, but also much of the confidence which had been growing around the peace process. In spite of the enormous damage, however, I did not regard it as the end of the road.

Why not?

The Sinn Fein leadership were serious people, and took themselves very seriously. They would never resign themselves to entering the annals of their movement in the role of the Grand Old Duke of York. If Canary Wharf had ended the process their political epitaph would be as fools who had just led their followers up and down the hill. So I took for granted they would devote their energies to getting the peace process back on the rails, even if in the now much more difficult conditions of their own making.

Did you hear rumblings before that the ceasefire was going to break down?

There was enormous and palpable frustration at the delay in proceeding to political negotiations as had been promised. This is not of course to mitigate in any way the crime and folly of what had been done, which recharged the toxic legacy of distrust. Part of the difficulty was that Prime Minister Major was at that stage hostage to 'the bastards', as he called them, in his party, who reflected a distinct current of hostility to the premise of the peace process. Whatever he might have personally hoped to achieve on Ireland in the last phase of his premiership, he simply lacked the capacity to do it.

The British met Martin McGuinness within a couple of weeks of the bomb. Did it accelerate things, and was there a lot of rushing around behind the scenes at that point?

The Irish Government felt that the republican movement had put themselves beyond the pale once again through the Canary Wharf bomb and that on their side there should not be contact with Sinn Fein. At the same time people had invested considerable hope in the peace process at that stage and mostly wanted the process relaunched through a restoration of the ceasefire. I was optimistic that that could eventually be achieved, not from any hidden knowledge I had, but from analysis of the dynamics within the movement, on the lines I said.

Was Canary Wharf an indication of how republicans sought to control the pace of the process?

I believe the slow pace of negotiations was due to many factors, including some originating with the British, particularly in the last phase of Major's Government. I think it just happened that way, rather than being due to any Sinn Fein optical needs. The latter certainly had a cautious and deliberate negotiating style, but that was justified for reasons everyone understood. It is an interesting speculation whether matters could have been speeded up, or brought to a head, as George Mitchell eventually did at the end. I think it could have been fast-forwarded a bit, but probably not by all that much. 'Ripeness is all' is a maxim applying to politics as well as in Shakespearean tragedy.

Is it about allowing people to exhaust their concerns verbally so they can't come back later and say they were denied an opportunity to talk?

It was obvious in all kinds of ways that the Sinn Fein leadership were determined not to become detached from their followers. The history of republicanism is punctuated by episodes of leaders trying to adjust to political realities, only to be displaced by new leaders reasserting the ancient verities, namely that repeating the formulas of the War of Independence would end partition, never mind that they had failed in this respect even at the time.

Would you say republicans were more prone to compromise than unionists, or vice versa?

There are many ways in which the unionist and republican positions are 'asymmetrical'. On the level of theory, the republicans can define their doctrines as they see fit. Unionists, as the name suggests, are constrained by the logic of the Union. There is a limit to the extent they can credibly espouse policies in drastic contradiction to the terms of membership of the UK. On the level of psychology, the unionists are pessimistic about their long-term prospects. Every concession seems a loss that can never be retrieved. Republicans feel that the influence of the majority on the island, presumed to be nationalist, will eventually prevail in one form or another. That enables them to take a more flexible attitude to change than unionists feel they can afford. The unionist tendency to react to the erosion of their original dominance by brandishing even more fiercely the now hollow symbols of the old supremacy is off-putting to outsiders and adds to their problems. There is a danger also that views about the future can become self-fulfilling prophecies. These factors have to be included in any assessment of their relative willingness to compromise, which I fear is not in overabundant supply in either case.

Is that a reflection of the static defensive position of unionism as opposed to the more dynamic position of republicanism? Where republicans could see how a position might or might not buttress the journey towards a final point, but for unionists it was always going to be loss every step of the way?

Static and dynamic would be another way of describing it. In the zero-sum mentality which the creation of Northern Ireland both reflected and fostered, unionist opposition to change was logical rather than perverse, and unionist leaders reflected that. It was not a sustainable long-term strategy, given the inexorable process of change around them. Perhaps not enough unionists read Lampedusa, with his famous insight in *The Leopard* that it was necessary for things to change in order for them to stay the same.

People have said that Sinn Fein would write everything down and log it all, whereas the unionists were more likely to not do that and disagree in front of everyone. Is that a picture which bears scrutiny?

Sinn Fein were part of a coherent system, with elaborate reporting systems. The unionists were more divided into different streams, including outliers and mavericks, whose vanity or convictions kept them separate. I suppose that led to a degree of incoherence on detail. Many, particularly in the Ulster Unionist Party, were good, robust individual politicians, not cogs in a well-oiled machine. On the subject of notes, the records of the British and of Sinn Fein will be far more comprehensive than any others. The limited resources of the Irish Government had to be concentrated on doing the business, sometimes at the cost of comprehensively recording it, and we will no doubt pay the price in future histories.

You could obviously not give good news to the unionists, so what argument did you make to them about the advantages of movement?

Well, I tried to espouse their much-prized virtue of plain-speaking but found, as I said earlier, that they regarded it as for export only! I thought the most respectful attitude was to spell out plainly the kind of compromise that might work to the benefit of the whole community, without assuming they could be fooled by lathers of soft soap. In the last analysis, though, the offer was long-term gain for short-term pain, and that is one of the hardest sells in all political contexts. They disliked the message and hoped that shooting the messenger would make it go away. By 1997, thanks mainly to the work of Albert Reynolds and Dick Spring, the rail-lines for a solution had been laid down. The train, though static, had not been allowed to roll down the embankment. The coincidence of new Governments in Dublin and London opened the prospect of negotiations with genuine momentum. It was not difficult to anticipate that unionists might suggest my removal would be a useful earnest of goodwill from the new Taoiseach. However unfair I might feel that unionist views of me were in the real order of things, I felt the process was much more important than my susceptibilities, and that Mr Ahern was likely to take the same view if the issue arose. The opportunity to go to Washington as Ambassador forestalled the danger I could become an issue in the negotiations. It also meant I could still contribute something to Northern Ireland, even if in the marketing rather than in the production department, so to speak.

Do you think that partly explains the British insistence on the IRA ceasefire being permanent?

Well, I felt the permanence issue was a bit absurd. The IRA were never to be trusted, but if they uttered the word 'permanent', that could safely be relied on. Moreover, the utmost sincerity in pledging permanence and good faith in pursuing it did not guarantee it would be delivered without fail. It was a question that could only be answered with authority by a historian in the future.

The issue was a device to buy time and slow down momentum. It was a relatively harmless way of doing so, compared to the infamous Washington Three. Much of the effort that should have been devoted to negotiation was in fact consumed by just climbing out of the hole dug by the latter precondition in the two years after.

Were you shocked when Washington Three was presented?

Yes, I was. It put an unmistakeable question mark over the real British priorities.

What was the reaction amongst the Irish camp about dealing with that?

The Taoiseach, John Bruton, was in Washington celebrating St Patrick's Day. He endorsed the British stance publicly and without reservation. He was no doubt projecting on others his own transparency and honesty of purpose and did not pause to question whether there might have been ulterior purpose behind the urgency suddenly ascribed to the decommissioning issue. It was very effective as a braking mechanism. All right-thinking people agreed the IRA should never have had weapons in the first place, and that they had to be given up as part of the peace process, so what could be wrong with demanding that they do so upfront in the proceedings? The whole art of the process, as Mr Reynolds and Mr Spring understood, was to find a way of persuading the paramilitaries to end violence voluntarily. This was greatly preferable to the alternative option of pursuing an end to violence through a very drastic escalation of emergency measures and repression. The peace process required firmness on essential principles, but pragmatic flexibility on aspects that did not jeopardise such principles. Decommissioning was indeed essential as part of the process. When the arms were not being used, the upfront timing demanded was not an issue of principle, merely a plausible test that Adams could not pass. Eventually, you can argue, some good came of the contrivance, since the attempts to find a way out of it brought Senator George Mitchell onto the stage, to the lasting benefit of the overall process.

Do you think that one of the reasons that Washington Three was thrown into the works was because the British were losing purchase or direction? What could be the logic at that moment of putting those conditions in?

I think the Irish attitude was that the end of violence would be so transforming that it took precedence over other matters; other of course, than the integrity of the democratic process itself. I suspect the British saw things in much more relative terms, qualifying any commitment by reference to their retaining the initiative and maintaining control, always hugely important for them. I think they may also have given thought to the political impact of Sinn Fein, once freed of the hobble of violence, whereas the Irish historical experience would have been that the electorate imposes its own discipline. There was a complexity to the British attitude, and they had also to deal with the 'Blimps', who resented the notion that a satisfactory end to violence could be on any basis other than demonstrative and crushing defeat and for whom the satisfaction of the repressive process outweighed any concerns it might prove counter-productive, as so often in Irish history.

Where you surprised to hear that the British were meeting the IRA?

Not hugely surprised, because I have great respect for British statecraft, and some sense of how ruthless and devious that statecraft can be on occasion. Caveat emptor is a maxim that it is wise to take into the negotiating chamber. I should make clear that I am talking here about the collective impact of the machine, and not about the British officials I dealt with. These were in almost every case very impressive and also very upright individuals, well able to assert or defend the British Government's policy effectively without recourse to any form of personal subterfuge. I can think of only one individual who corresponded to the less uplifting bureaucratic stereotypes, and I was suspect at the origin of various Alan Partridge-style negotiating wheezes guaranteed to bring the Irish to their senses. Because of his access to Major they had an impact entirely disproportionate to their merit.

Do you think that Adams and McGuinness were thinking about decommissioning from some way back?

I do not recollect Sinn Fein having ever challenged across the table our view that decommissioning was essential as part of the process, and we would have reacted very strongly if they had. Rightly or wrongly, I always assumed they saw the sense of decommissioning for their own reasons. We were not dealing with pikes in the thatch, or Fenian muskets in the attic, but a lethal arsenal, including Semtex from Libya. They could hardly have been oblivious to the possibility that this might fall disastrously into the hands of their dissident enemies, so I felt that at the end of the process this would be dealt with as a common objective. The IRA, as the name suggests, saw itself as an army, and for armies to disarm other than as part of a peace settlement implies surrender. Washington Three gave the issue a symbolism wholly at odds with the goal of actually achieving it and was a very clear signal that the British were giving priority to delaying tactics at the expense of the professed objective. Sinn Fein may indeed have drawn some advantage from decommissioning being made into a fetish and therefore enhanced as a bargaining chip, probably beyond their initial expectations.

Did you think the process would collapse at that point?

The republicans had been explicitly led to expect political negotiations about three months after a ceasefire, and we were very concerned about the delay which had intervened. Washington Three showed the delay was not an accident. The British were bent on deflecting pressure for negotiations by insisting on decommissioning at a time and in a context where all informed observers, including their own security experts, knew Adams could simply not deliver. I recall a diplomatic occasion when I was making conversation with the Ambassador of a country with some experience of terrorism. He remarked to me 'The thing is, you cannot cheat terrorists.' I thought it a very profound maxim. He did not mean of course that such people were too clever to be deceived. It was rather that for the most part people resort to terrorism because they believed prevailing systems were irretrievably corrupt and deceitful. Cheating them just reinforced that view and deepened their conviction that their atrocious methods were thereby justified. The IRA campaign of violence had been justified by the assumed bad faith of British statecraft, and the belief that violence was the only way to deal with this. I obviously hoped the strain on the process would not lead to its collapse, but felt it a very great pity that the old toxic views were being refurbished. It was not just for moral reasons, but also for pragmatic ones, that I felt honesty was indeed the best policy in this particular process.

Would you take decommissioning as symbolism, which republicans saw as surrender?

Treating decommissioning as a symbolic issue, rather than as a practical housekeeping measure that was indispensable as part of an overall agreement, ensured the most difficult context possible for its actual achievement. It would have been very odd if that rather obvious fact had never occurred to those who took this course, and whose real goals must have been different.

Did anyone ask what parity of esteem meant and what you meant by it?

I often invoked Batt Masterson, of OK Corral fame, on this issue. He observed the rich and poor get an equal amount of ice, but while the poor get it in winter, the rich get it in summer. Parity of esteem was a term of art borrowed from the Fair Employment agenda to signify a proactive and meaningful equal treatment, rather than the technical equality of Batt's analysis.

What about drawing the extreme parties into a process at the expense of moderate parties? Was that a concern?

The idea of building a compromise through the presumed 'moderates' had everything to recommend it. It recognised and would reward the people who had never resorted to violence. Moderates would be more amenable to compromise with other moderates and together they could isolate the extremes. The only drawback was that it had never worked, in spite of the many variants which were tried. It had never worked for the simple and depressing reason that the moderates on each side were much more afraid of their own extremes than they were trusting of their fellow moderates on the other side. The many failed attempts to apply this approach was why I personally was receptive to Hume's suggestion of a different strategy.

You have mentioned before about fast-forwarding a process and the need to get to a position quickly, but for the British, as indeed for Sinn Fein, was prevarication also important for enabling counter-balance, check, counter-balance etc., to wring out as many risks as possible?

This presentational aspect was taken very seriously. Albert Reynolds, in particular, was hugely conscious of the constraints on Major and tried hard to minimise presentational difficulties for him, so the process could be sold to his recalcitrant Tory party. In view of the negative optics for Major of appearing to respond to a Sinn Fein text Reynolds stressed the governmental aspects of its provenance. He sought to remove Gerry Adams' fingerprints from the draft, which necessarily meant removing Hume's also. Hume found this difficult to understand, and it gave rise to considerable tension, and indeed something of a backlash against Reynolds from within his own party. Of course, it later transpired the British were talking secretly to the republicans all along, so Reynolds' efforts to protect Major from such a dastardly imputation were moot, even if they demonstrated on his part a laudable if unreciprocated solidarity with his partner in negotiations.

How important were the Americans in the peace process?

The American role in the peace process was hugely significant on several levels, indeed I believe indispensable for its success. There is a very long back story to the American influence on Anglo-Irish relations. Ever since the Victorians found to their consternation that their Irish nightmare had escaped the confines of the island and was gaining influence in the United States, this has been a factor in the meticulous, not to say obsessive, attention the British system has paid to the American relationship. From an Irish point of view that has been very helpful at many junctures of our history, both in moderating some of the more extreme impulses of British policy on Ireland and in overcoming their default setting of neglect of the problem. For the most part, however, British influence in the US was sufficiently strong to ensure that Irish-American sentiment did not translate into any policy leverage, notably through a convention, jealously guarded by the State Department, that British policy on Northern Ireland was an internal matter, on which the US deferred to its close ally without comment. The modern US engagement with the issue dates back to 1977, when the efforts of brilliantly effective Irish diplomats, notably Sean Donlon and Michael Lillis, the growing influence of John Hume and the concern of Irish-American political heavy-weights, collectively dubbed 'The Four Horsemen', combined to organise a statement on Northern Ireland by President Jimmy Carter. This was significant, not so much for its relatively anodyne content as for breaking the stifling convention of US official silence on Northern Ireland, to the lasting benefit of the search for progress. An unacknowledged truth of British statecraft is that they view policy on Ireland primarily through the prism of control, and only secondarily by reference to the other needs of the situation. This priority explains their consistent pushback against the US role, even in the scrupulously sensitive and well-informed guise it had under President Clinton. US officials were baffled by this, not understanding that for the British control and retaining the initiative trumped pragmatic requirements for progress.

As to the overall American impact, the best illustration I can give is an occasion when I asked our key official dealing with Fair Employment issues to substitute at a security-related meeting for our usual expert, who could not attend. When I debriefed her afterwards she was almost in shock at what she saw as the dismissive attitude of the British officials to the points she raised. She had assumed that the spirit of genuine co-operation she had experienced in the Fair Employment negotiations was the norm. I explained that the contrast which shocked her had a simple explanation: close American monitoring of discrimination in employment meant that the British genuinely worked for agreement with us. In areas not subject to such American scrutiny, the imbalance of power and perhaps atavistic attitudes shaped the British demeanour. That illustrates the pervasive importance of the US role. Margaret Thatcher said of the Anglo-Irish Agreement that 'the Americans made me do it', acknowledging the impetus given by President Reagan to this landmark agreement between the two Governments (I might add that the International Fund for Ireland which flowed from the Agreement played a role not sufficiently appreciated in promoting reconciliation and cross-community co-operation at grassroots level). The impact of the outreach of President Clinton and his administration cannot be over-estimated, both in terms of laying the foundations for the Agreement and bringing it over the line. Senator Mitchell extracted the two Governments out of the hole they had dug for themselves on prior decommissioning and chaired the subsequent talks with peerless skill and patience, which look even more remarkable in the hindsight of twenty years. Ambassador Kennedy Smith set the gold standard for a US envoy, and was tireless in making US pressure for peace palpable on the ground in Ireland. The stars were truly in alignment for once.

So would the outcome of the peace process have been any different without American involvement?

Both the shadow and the substance of US involvement played a vital role. By shadow I mean the awareness of actual or potential US interest. I mentioned earlier its benign influence on British policy. It also had a positive impact on the paramilitaries. They were conscious of the disparity of power between Dublin and London. There was a strand in their thinking which rationalised terrorist atrocities as a response or sanction to assumed British bad faith. It was very helpful for those opposed to violence to point to the US shadow as a democratic or diplomatic factor which would give the British pause, should they ever be tempted, as the paramilitaries feared, to react in bad faith to the end to violence. The substance was of course the stellar talents put with unstinting generosity in the service of peace by President Clinton and key players in Congress and significant figures from civil society. Both traditions in Ireland share a pride in what their kinsfolk contributed to the United States. It was very gratifying in that perspective to see how many willing hands reached across the Atlantic to help the island overcome the nightmare of violence, to build the foundations of peace and bring agreement over the line. The progress made would be unthinkable without them.

Were you looking outside to other conflict situations to help you consider this problem?

I have been asked from time to time to talk about peace processes and I often quote Tolstoy's famous opening to *Anna Karenina*, about all happy families being alike but each unhappy family being unhappy in its own way. I apply that, perhaps a little flippantly, to peace-making, which deals with the reality that most unhappy political situations are unhappy in their own way. You can deduce some basic maxims that apply to all situations, but only on a level of generality that is not of great practical value. Tony Blair's autobiography has a chapter which makes a valiant effort to list them. In practice there is no alternative to exploring all the quirks and dimensions of the individual conflict and designing a solution that is tailored to measure. We did do studies of other conflicts which might have lessons for Northern Ireland, but found Tolstoy's rule also applied in reverse.

What were your main worries or misgivings as regards the process?

There were bound to be many in any such radically new policy shift. Attempting to bring the republicans into democratic politics seemed downright wrong, or at best irresponsibly quixotic, to many people of goodwill on our own side. It is easy to understand their reservations. One was aware that if the peace process failed, the recriminations and indeed career repercussions for those most deeply associated with it would have been severe. There were also worries about the good faith or the capacity of other protagonists. I never believed that the republican change of direction could be just a cynical tactical feint. People rarely put basic core values into play for tactical gambits. One could not rule out the danger they could fail in all good faith, or, if under pressure, seek to combine political dialogue and terror, as happened at Canary Wharf and in some less conspicuous ways. There was also a permanent concern the process could draw us into postures which compromised fundamental values, although I feel in hindsight that we avoided that successfully. The British attitude to the process was complex and frequently difficult to decode. Often it seemed to correspond to the old adage 'Thou shalt not kill/ but shalt not strive/ officiously to keep alive'. Washington Three showed at the very least a cavalier attitude to putting the process in jeopardy.

The bizarre tabloid story that Martha Pope, Senator Mitchell's able Chief of Staff, was having an affair with Sinn Fein's Gerry Kelly could only have been promoted to force Senator Mitchell's withdrawal, and would have succeeded had not Martha been able to show it up as a complete fabrication. Someone in the British system saw the Senator as a threat, rather than the invaluable resource he proved to be. Such discrepancies between British professions of support and actual practice were very unsettling. There were also philosophical concerns. We were advancing a model which entrenched classification of people as unionist or nationalist, rather than seeking to escape from these categories. This dilemma had already arisen in the context of earlier work on Fair Employment, one of the significant advances we achieved under the Anglo-Irish Agreement. We had concluded that since social attitudes treated the unionist/nationalist classification as paramount in real life, it was better to recognise that reality in law, entrenching it for the purpose of moderating its impact. I thought that same approach would also do more good than harm in the political sphere and that the provisions for political structures eventually enshrined in the Good Friday Agreement were justified on that basis. There was also the weakness inherent in an Assembly deprived in practice of the advantages of alternating roles of government and opposition on the classical lines. Again we opted for what seemed the lesser evil. Our concerns were somewhat mitigated by provisions that these things could be changed by agreement, once politicians felt the conditions they were meant to address had disappeared. So, there were many internal perplexities and doubts, but we felt the prize of peace was so great and the goal of political agreement so important that we concentrated our public focus on that potential and on the positive aspects generally.

6

Back-channels and the possibilities of movement: an interview with Martin Mansergh

Graham Spencer: *Where do you think the origins of the peace process actually lay?*

Martin Mansergh: Well, this is a contentious matter. My view would be fairly close to the Sinn Fein view on this. Some people would say it goes back to the prisons in the mid-1970s, others to the hunger strikes, and the SDLP would tell you it goes back to the Anglo-Irish Agreement, but my view is it happened in the aftermath of the Anglo-Irish Agreement. I wouldn't be giving the Agreement exaggerated credit for this, because it was an exclusive initiative, whereas the peace process was in principle inclusive, but I think the origins of it were in the 1986 to 1987 period. I suppose the first phase in 1988 was exploration of the possibility of an alternative, which I would date to August 1986, when Father Reid first met Charlie Haughey as leader of Fianna Fail in opposition.

Can you tell me about when you were asked to meet Sinn Fein in 1988 and the context that surrounded that?

I'll give you the context as I knew it then, and how I know it now, because they are a bit different. I was with Charlie Haughey, who was Taoiseach at the time, and he asked me if would I meet Father Alec Reid and, as far as I recall, he explained, as a bit of the background, that the SDLP were meeting with Sinn Fein and he wanted to complement this with a secret Fianna Fail delegation to meet with Sinn Fein. From that I would have met Father Reid, and arrangements were made to go to the Redemptorist Monastery in Dundalk with Dermot Ahern, who was a newly elected deputy from the previous year, and Richie Healey, a party official who was one of the party's honorary treasurers from County Meath. I was involved in two meetings at Dundalk, the first on 2 May and the second on 24 June. If you go back to the previous year of September 1987, Charlie Haughey was contemplating directly meeting Hume and Adams himself, but various dramatic events in the autumn of 1987 made that impossible. There was an intercepted importation of arms from Libya that autumn, the kidnapping of a dentist and a subsequent rampage through the countryside by 'the border fox', and, worst of all, the Enniskillen bomb on Remembrance Sunday that killed eleven people. Earlier in the year we had also had Loughgall, where eight IRA men had been shot dead. The net point in September 1987 is that Haughey was seriously considering not renewing the Extradition Act, which had been passed by the outgoing FitzGerald Government in December 1986 and was renewable on an annual basis. Again, I think his attitude was that so many things happened in the autumn of 1987 that this also became quite impossible. So he moved from Plan A, when he might have been directly involved, to Plan B, where all that would be involved would be a low-level delegation.

Did he give you a brief on what he wanted you to do, or was it about going along to see what Sinn Fein had to say?

Essentially the latter, but I would have to say that is an instruction that is impossible to follow if you are to have a constructive conversation with anybody. You have to interact, so, while I was given the instruction just to listen, I'm afraid I did a great deal more than that. You have to remember that this was taking place in a context where the political orthodoxy, and I am putting it crudely, at its most brutal and the mantra of 'You don't talk to terrorists', was very strong. Garret FitzGerald would have been the leading proponent of this. He was very critical from the early 1970s of meeting the republican movement, on the grounds that you would only encourage them to think they are winning. The orthodoxy has completely changed in the last twenty years. Nowadays the orthodoxy is that it's always good to talk to terrorists, but then it was the opposite, and this had political implications because Charlie Haughey had a lot of baggage, and if it had come out that he was in dialogue there would probably have been a political furore. I suspect one of the reasons I was selected to do this was because of my background, where I might have been less easily portrayed to the public as a 'crypto-Provo', shall we say. The two discussions we had in 1988 were what you might call exploratory. There was no formal agenda. In a sense they were parallel to talks and exchanges of papers going on in the public domain between the SDLP and Sinn Fein. Our second meeting did take place after the SDLP–Sinn Fein dialogue had broken down. I think what Sinn Fein was trying to do at the time was to break out of the extreme political isolation that they were in, especially after the Enniskillen bomb.

Do you remember the initial conversation about Reid?

What I remember Haughey saying was that he would like me to meet Father Reid and then explaining why. It was to do with the SDLP having started to publicly meet with Sinn Fein and was put in that context as a kind of flanking move or initiative, but was to remain strictly confidential. I can't remember as to whether he mentioned on that first occasion if I would be going with Dermot Ahern and Richie Healey, but he did say that Father Reid would ring me, which he did, and we would meet up. Reid then explained what the purpose was and what his own thinking was, and he gave me two or three of the papers that he had been working on at that time, setting out principles, putting the emphasis on self-determination and so on.

Were you the main contact after those Dundalk meetings to fill Haughey in on what was happening?

No. I can't tell you what other conversations he had, but my relationship with him was very much a one-to-one relationship, so when I talked to him it would have been on my own. Each of us was in a different position. His attitude was you are there just to listen. But, as I said, that was an instruction I completely ignored, because you can't have any kind of sensible dialogue just sitting there and taking it in. That takes you nowhere. Having said that, I wasn't at all clear how much he wanted to know. He didn't question me very much, and I didn't go into a lot of detail, and I certainly put nothing in writing.

You said you spoke to Reid on the phone. Did you meet him alone before you met Sinn Fein?

Oh yes, and probably more than once.

In Ed Moloney's book on the IRA there is the 10,000-word letter that Reid wrote and passed to Tim Pat Coogan, who then passed it to Haughey. That letter is interesting because it talks about 'the alternative method'?

I think that would have been around 1986 to 1987.

Who was at those first two meetings in 1988 from Sinn Fein?

I think in both cases it was Adams, Mitchel McLaughlin and Pat Doherty.

And was it Adams who did most of the talking?

Yes.

What did he say to you?

Well, it was more what we said to him. We would have made the point that violence was unacceptable as a route forward, to which his retort would be 'If you had British troops on the streets of Dundalk what would you do?' I put forward the argument that nationalism was strongest when it was politically united, as in the 'new departure' of 1878 between the Irish Parliamentary Party, the Land League and the Fenians, but that it was divided over the use of violence, which weakened nationalism in the North, between North and South and indeed in Irish-America.

Do you think that is what Adams was hoping you were going to say?

I've no idea. I do remember one other point, and this was where I would not have taken the same line as John Hume. His thesis was that following the Anglo-Irish Agreement the British were politically neutral with regard to the future of Northern Ireland, and I made it clear that I didn't agree with that, because you have to distinguish between the rules of the game and what you are actually trying to achieve in the game. I have never believed that, notwithstanding particular things that might have been said by particular people, and especially some interlocutors with Sinn Fein from the British side. Just saying it's bound to come to a united Ireland sooner or later is not something to which anyone could be held or made accountable for, and these things were sometimes said to senior civil servants on our side back in the early 1980s. I regarded them as valueless. Unless something is part of an agreement, it is just speculative, and that would have been an area where I would have differed from John Hume in my analysis. You could say maybe I wanted to show that I was a realist, and this would be true even of Sinn Fein, where there might be things they would prefer to be told because of wishful thinking, but I always took the view, and in subsequent dialogue, that you need to be realistic and not to engage in anything which in the medium term will undermine your credibility.

You say the meetings were exploratory, which is an interesting term, but what were they and you looking for?

I suppose what we were going there for was to assess, given the political disaster of Enniskillen, the situation to see if there was any worthwhile prospect of them disengaging.

Did they talk about Enniskillen?

No. But I think I would have come to the conclusion, certainly by the end of the second meeting, that it seemed they did want to move towards another strategy, even if they were not talking about any time soon. I would have been of the view that the political risks of carrying on were simply too great. You can only defend what you are doing if there is some prospect of success, and although the odds were always against winning the war, there was still some possibility that things might lead to peace. It may be at that time that Adams had a long-term strategy, but the trouble then was that we would have been much too exposed to productive and progressive engagement and that if this got out we would be in trouble, although I doubted that they would leak it. If it had become public in 1988, then that would have simply exploded it. Once things started to creep into the public domain, just before the Downing Street Declaration, the context and the circumstances were different.

When you went for the second meeting, what were you looking for that was different from the first meeting?

Nothing, it was simply a follow-through. I also believe Dermot Ahern had a third meeting unknown to myself, possibly in September, but the difference for me was that, even though I was actually working in the Taoiseach's Office, I could say I was working for the party, which was different from those who were in the Government.

The point you raise about who you were representing in those talks raises an interesting question in terms of distinction between an informal and a formal contact. How would you have seen yourself at this stage?

Back-channel discussions are by their nature informal.

What vital purpose does the back-channel serve?

It was never the case that another political or religious sermon would get the IRA campaign to stop. You can say what you like from a distance, but eventually you have to persuade an organisation like that that there is an alternative, that there is an interest to pursue. If you fast-forward a bit to when dialogue was used indirectly, in the autumn of 1991 some work was being done on an embryonic joint declaration between Taoiseach and Prime Minister, and, over months, communications went backwards and forwards through Father Alec Reid. In the autumn of 1992 it got to the stage where that could go no further without a direct meeting. Albert Reynolds and I agreed at that point in time that we could go no further without some direct contact.

Do you think Reid was influential on them?

At a certain stage, yes. From their point of view he was a trusted intermediary, and he could go backwards and forwards if necessary several times in a week in a way that they couldn't. Remember, before the first ceasefire all their leading people would have been under fairly strong surveillance about where they were going and who they were meeting, so they needed a runner like Father Reid not just to carry bits of paper across from one source to another but to pick up what people were saying. He was, apart from anything else, representative, in an unofficial rather than official manner, of the Church. He did have the blessing of Cardinal O Fiaich, who died in 1990, but Cardinal Daly was a good deal cooler, to the extent that he knew what Father Reid was doing at all, but I suppose Father Reid's involvement gave a more ethical dimension to what was going on, or underlined that there was an ethical dimension to what was going on.

Do you mean ethical dimension demonstrable by his presence as a representative of the Church?

The ethical dimension came from the objective, and his objective was very clearly to find an alternative to conflict and stop people getting killed. It's not necessary to explain the ethics of that. He had a strong conviction, and this goes back to the 1980s, that if the Church didn't do more or try harder, then it would look bad in the eyes of history. There was a wide Irish perception that support for peace was coming from the Church or individuals within the Church, but for those like Reid engagement was about moral purpose, even though Paisley tried to assimilate the Catholic Church to the Provos. The Church was a potential safeguard in defending and explaining the purpose of back-channel talks to public opinion, but against that it could have provided Paisley with the opportunity to depict the Provos and the Church as hand in glove. One should also acknowledge that you can accept what the Church says, but you can do something different. You can have a set of beliefs, but mental reservations too.

Is it the case that after the second meeting in 1988 you did not see republicans again until 1992?

Yes.

Was there any call from Sinn Fein to meet you again in that period?

No, there wasn't.

Was there anything that obstructed that?

Well, remember in 1988 the SDLP had ended talks. We had done the same, and in defensible terms what we were doing was in support of that. There is a theory, which one can speculate on, that Haughey was the lead player in this, and he was pushing forward Hume because he couldn't do it himself. At that particular time, Sinn Fein might have taken the view that Father Reid's efforts were not going anywhere. There were a couple of times around 1990 when the Redemptorists did a review as to whether the work of Father Reid was worth carrying on. One event which I and the Government was not involved in, although other parties were, was the Duisburg meeting in 1989, where Father Reid provided a view on where he thought the Provos might be coming from. When that meeting became public it was repudiated by Hume and others, showing the sensitivity of the issue.

When you met them again in 1992, what happened?

It was different from 1992 because most of that time I was meeting Martin McGuinness, whom I had not met in 1988. Martin was nearly always accompanied by Aidan MacAteer, but from time to time one or other in the leadership circle would come along instead, probably just to observe what was going on. Martin always had a second person with him.

Was this at Dundalk again?

Yes.

Was it just you?

Me and Father Reid.

So what changed by 1992, as far as what they were saying was concerned?

Well the point is, we were by now working on a text which in principle could provide the basis for them shifting from violence to a peace strategy.

What role did you play in helping them with that text?

What happened initially was I was called in late one evening in the autumn of 1991, and it was just Charlie Haughey and John Hume there. Haughey handed me a text that John Hume had to a degree worked on. I don't know the exact origin of it, but once it was handed to me I worked on it a bit further. I don't think John Hume entirely liked the results, but after further work another text was produced, and at that point it went through Father Reid to the Provos.

When did you meet McGuinness in 1992?

That was in October, but remember there were some exchanges first, and the reason the meeting happened was because of the feeling that they couldn't get any further with this project unless there was direct contact. I think on their part this was based on the view that if we didn't trust them sufficiently to meet face-to-face then this would not be going anywhere.

Was McGuinness saying anything different from what Adams had been saying in 1988?

I suppose the difference is that we had something in principle to work on. The meetings always took the same form, which was in two parts. It was usually tea-time, around five or six o'clock in the evening, and it was in the recreation room in the monastery and the meetings lasted about two hours. The first hour might be about what one might call 'general political discussion', which meant pretty well anything of relevance by way of background. It might be about Europe, or the domestic political situation, or about whether the Government was going to last, or it could be events in the North and so on. Then it would move to a focus on a text and arguing through different textual points. Sometimes there would be letters or communications for me to take back to Albert Reynolds, sometimes from Sinn Fein and sometimes purporting to come from the IRA.

How did you conduct the conversation with them about what self-determination meant?

After the meetings in 1988 there weren't direct meetings until October 1992, but they then took place at four- to six-week intervals through to the ceasefire in August 1994, with the exception of the autumn of 1993. Now the whole question of consent and self-determination came much more into focus when there was a draft to work on. I'm not certain that they came up with much, if at all, in the 1988 conversations. Those were exploratory meetings, and there were no texts or documents that anybody was working on. There may have been between the SDLP and Sinn Fein, but there wasn't between Sinn Fein and Fianna Fail.

So in those conversations was the substance, for them, about pushing for a nationalist consensus and getting the Irish involved in that consensus?

That didn't crystallise until later. I think it was more a question of them explaining why they were doing what they were doing, but perhaps referencing the need for a credible political alternative. Not going into any detail on the content of that, but also discussion of ideological questions like whether Britain was neutral or not. The idea of the nationalist consensus also in part came from me. I'm not saying that Father Reid was not pushing that, but remember he was not present at those early meetings, he was outside.

What were your thoughts about a nationalist consensus terrifying the unionists?

It was to be a democratic, non-violent development. You see, what Sinn Fein would have liked was what the unionists sometimes called a 'pan-nationalist front', where you had a nationalist consensus while the IRA campaign was going on. But that was totally out of the question. You could only have a nationalist consensus if violence was taken out of the equation. Now obviously, if violence is taken out of the equation then that becomes less threatening, providing the unionists believed the Major Government reassurance given to them that the quid pro quo for a ceasefire had not been a British secret deal. It was perfectly clear from the content of the Downing Street Declaration that that wasn't what they were about. I think for a few days after 31 August 1994 unionists might have worried that there indeed was a secret deal. The British were absolutely emphatic that there was not, and so were we. The furthest the British went was in their clarifications, which were made public. They had clarified to some degree what their intentions would be if there was a ceasefire, and that was necessary but not the same as a secret deal.

But what about their argument for British withdrawal? Was that seen as unrealistic?

I don't think that was pressed very much with us. The discussions in the 1980s were fairly general and not like the discussions in the 1990s. Their priority in 1988 was trying to break out of the total political and diplomatic isolation they were in post-Enniskillen. But in the context of the discussions they wanted a time limit put on the exercise of self-determination. I think they were probably looking by negotiation for something that could look or could be presented to their followers as a substitute, or equivalent, for a time limit for withdrawal. Now a time limit for an exercise in concurrent self-determination is obviously very different from a time limit for withdrawal, but the British in negotiations on the Downing Street Declaration were very clear that they didn't want anything that even hinted at a time limit, for the sort of reasons you are stating. Anything like that would obviously have been misrepresented, particularly by the DUP, that this is British surrender etc. I was pressed quite hard by a journalist who came to see me in or around April/May 1994, which was a few months after the Declaration, who would have been close to Sinn Fein and lived in West Belfast, and it rapidly became clear that this journalist was coming not to interview me or get a background briefing from me, but as an emissary. I had known the person for some years previous to that, but this person clearly had wanted to transmit a message, which was that more was needed. I think that the more that was needed was probably to do with the time limit on the exercise. You see, they were coming under fire. If you look at people like Anthony McIntyre, a purely political dissident but ferocious critic of Sinn Fein, he said they should not have given up without getting some time limit, even if it was a hundred years hence. This was totally unrealistic and the argument doesn't stand up, but obviously they were looking for something which would enable them to put the best possible face on it to their members and their supporters, and to give the impression that they had kept the faith and not abandoned their positions. I'm not convinced that they were necessarily looking for anything of substance. It was more about looking for what might improve, from their point of view, the perception. The journalist concerned was well informed about the situation and was clearly there to try and lobby for a bit more.

So, in your view how did they get through the withdrawal problem with their own people?

I think it was done not just in that period but from the late 1980s with a gradual shift of emphasis from withdrawal to self-determination, and then, of course, they would have seen self-determination in a thirty-two-county context. Our position was very clear, which was that that was not compatible with the terms of the Anglo-Irish Agreement, and, even though Fianna Fail might have voted against the Agreement in opposition, we were bound by it as a successor Government. Countries are bound by agreements, regardless of who the Government is, and so I think bringing in self-determination was important in all sorts of ways. The principle of consent is simply

Northern Ireland self-determination, concurrent self-determination is the island as a whole, albeit in two parts. I think essentially they were looking not so much for any sort of explicit statement for a commitment to withdraw, but something that vaguely hinted in that direction.

The basis of a lot of the SDLP dialogue with Sinn Fein was to try and convince them that the British were neutral, is that so?

Again, I am afraid I took a different view on that, and I don't believe that the British were neutral before or today. I never bought that argument. You might have the odd voice when talking to us saying something different, but my view was that the British wanted to hold on to Northern Ireland, and I have always argued that Northern Ireland is the outer bulwark of the Union. The union that really matters from the British point of view is the one with Scotland, with Wales less at risk, because that is so integrated into England anyway. I think a thirty-two-county Ireland, particularly one that is doing politically and economically quite well, would have bolstered the case for Scottish independence. Before the economic crash at the beginning of 2008 the Scottish nationalists mentioned Ireland a lot of the time, but since then they rarely, if ever, mention it. They mention Scandinavian countries which are roughly the same latitude and a similar size such as Sweden, Norway etc., and they obviously prefer being inside the EU rather than outside. People would say it was the end of the Cold War that really made the difference and enabled Brooke to make his statement. By the time you got to the mid-1980s the idea that Ireland had any serious strategic importance in the fag-end years of the Cold War was getting increasingly threadbare.

There is also a note to Father Reid from no later than 1987 privately indicating that the British would be prepared to say that they didn't have a selfish strategic or economic interest. In other words, they were moving towards that before Brooke made his statement publicly. It has been said that Tom King said it somewhere, but nobody seems to be able to find it, if he did say it. It may be that the Hume thesis that the Anglo-Irish Agreement made the *situation* neutral is right, but are you seriously telling me that the Thatcher Government was neutral about Northern Ireland remaining part of the UK?

Jim Callaghan, long out of office, once said privately to Reynolds the British would only be too glad if you took it off us, but that could have been said half in joke; and now and again in the early 1980s senior civil servants had mooted this. Whether Sinn Fein believed it then or now, those sorts of things are absolutely meaningless because they are part of an agreement you can't hold anyone subsequently to. They might have said such things speculatively in a conversation, but such comments are absolutely unbankable assurances. Father Reid was quite friendly with Desmond Boal, who was a QC very close to Paisley, and, although we are talking about an earlier period, Boal said to him if the violence stops we can talk, but as long as there is violence we can't. Now in the 1970s Paisley and Boal would have flirted briefly with an independent Ulster scenario, which by the 1990s had lost all economic credibility, let alone any political credibility. But when the ceasefire did eventually come, Reid tried to make contact with Boal, and needless to say was quite unsuccessful.

When did the argument about British neutrality start to subside, because it did?

Maybe you could say it partly did to establish our credibility. I was making clear that we were not simply a clone or an echo of the SDLP. The SDLP had their positions, and in broad terms we may be allied to them, but that does not mean that we think identically to them, and for a long time the SDLP, and particularly the Hume side of the SDLP, flirted with what you might call post-nationalism and regionalism, and for a while he was a European federalist. That was quite prevalent thinking at that time. I think post-dialogue with Sinn Fein Hume gradually moved to a more nationalist position. I am not saying his view was the same as Mallon's, who was a nationalist politician, but certainly for a period Hume flirted with what you might call a kind of European-coloured post-nationalism. On the neutrality issue, I would have been of the view that this was a hopelessly rosy-eyed or rose-tinted view of the British position. I would imagine Sinn Fein was probably fairly sceptical of the notion that the British were and are neutral. It would have been difficult to convince them of that under Thatcher as well. But it's not just under Thatcher, because Patrick Mayhew, who was Secretary of State for a lot of the Major period, was a self-declared unionist, as was Major. If you study the Frameworks Document there is a whole lot of language there which attempts to bind Britain as close as possible to a sort of constitutional neutrality, but this was definitely aspirational. One of the first things Blair said in office was that the Union would remain in the lifetime of the youngest among you. In the negotiations on the Downing Street Declaration we would have pressed them to pick up on the Brooke statement of no selfish strategic or economic interest by asking why that did not include the word 'political', and that really tells you everything you want to know. Self-evidently they didn't have a selfish economic interest with five to ten billion a year being pumped into Northern Ireland.

Did you meet Sinn Fein with the SDLP present?

No.

Why not, given that Hume–Adams were engaged in dialogue?

Well there was no request to do so. Hume saw himself as the intermediary, shall we say. I remember John Chilcot said, although it was later, that the Hume–Adams dialogue was the reason why the British entered into dialogue with Sinn Fein around 1990. The British Government needed to check out what John Hume was telling them, so did the Irish Government, and Sinn Fein or the republican movement certainly needed to check out what John Hume was telling them, so the different players wanted to be in direct contact with each other rather than just via John Hume.

To what extent did the Downing Street Declaration differ from the initial Hume–Adams text?

The initial Hume–Adams text, so-called, was at the outer limit of what we could accept in terms of remaining consistent with the Anglo-Irish Agreement. The curious thing is that Sinn Fein's great fear was that the British might say 'snap', which would create considerable difficulty because they had not fully prepared the ground in their own movement, and even in the context of 1992 to 1994 they didn't want to be rushed. Albert Reynolds had wanted to hand this draft over to the British because we had got as far as we were going to get with McGuinness, and Reynolds wanted to move to the next stage. Albert would be like a businessman in that he wanted things to happen quickly more than most heads of Government, and perhaps he took an orange light from Father Reid as a green light. But then Adams and company were very unhappy that this had been handed over to the British supposedly with their approval, when they hadn't actually been asked for it or given it. Now the British for some months did not really want to touch it, and I think Mayhew and the Northern Ireland Office didn't want to go along with it, but gave priority to getting the talks process between the constitutional parties revived. At that time there was an 'under the radar' peace process, and there was a talks process with nothing actually happening, but it was there above the surface and Mayhew seemed to want to go along with that. Albert was absolutely determined to build a peace process, and did not have much interest in the talks process. Remember, they had been suspended since 1992, and he didn't see the talks as leading anywhere. He thought this back-channel initiative was a much more hopeful line to pursue.

Was this before the Downing Street Declaration?

Yes, I am talking about the six months of June to December 1993. You see there was a tremendous battle to get the British to go down this road, and Albert made it clear that he was going to do it. There was a Plan B on the Irish side, which was, if the British wouldn't go along with this and provide a statement of principles, then the Irish Government, John Hume and the SDLP and Sinn Fein would produce their own statement of principles. The problem with that is that you might spend years negotiating with the British to get them to accept what was in this, so it was very definitely a less preferable alternative. If you remember, there was a meeting in Brussels on the margins of the European Council at the end of October and Reynolds and Major had a bilateral meeting with literally no one else present, and they both went away with different impressions of what had been agreed. Major thought he had persuaded Albert to drop this initiative, because the British couldn't touch anything that had Hume's and Adams' prints on it, and also you have to see that Hume was linked and allied to the Labour opposition at Westminster, so he wasn't seen as a friend of Major at all. Albert, on the other hand, took the view that the British would agree to pursue this, provided it was clearly distanced from Hume and Adams, and it took about a fortnight before it was clear that there were diametrically opposed understandings. Albert then got in a bit of trouble at home for distancing himself too much from Hume. The British came to Dublin Castle in December and had produced an alternative, more orange version of the text, and Albert's response was that if this was on the table then the summit was over, and he forced the British to withdraw their alternative to what we had been working on. I would have played some role in elaborating the document presented to the British, this along with Archbishop Eames, who was respected by Major. Albert took Eames into his confidence and in fact commissioned three paragraphs, which I think are seven to nine, of the Declaration, which were more about unionist mood music. I was the editor-in-chief of the Declaration on the Irish side, and those paragraphs were incorporated into the draft with minimal alteration. Then, on television one night, I saw the Reverend Roy Magee, who sat in on some of the Combined Loyalist Military Command (CLMC) meetings, and I said to Albert I should go and meet him. Magee then provided a set of principles which the CLMC was prepared to accept, and they were incorporated at the end of paragraph five of the Declaration. The only change we made was where they listed various forms of discrimination. We added in gender, but that was the only change we made to it.

What about the clarification that Sinn Fein asked for with regard to the Declaration?

They were, if you like, covering their tracks, and it was more about clarification in order to support building confidence. We entered into this rather more enthusiastically, but even the British were eventually persuaded in May 1994 to provide a reply to some twenty questions. Albert had no hang-ups about clarification, we could clarify as much as you want, but I think clarification from the republican movement's side was more about can we get a bit more from this. You see, I think they were looking for something else, and you raise the question of withdrawal, but that something was really about what could be presented as a commitment, however distant, and the British wouldn't have been prepared to do that. They often made the point they were prepared to be persuaders for an agreement, but not prepared to be persuaders for a united Ireland. So there were the confidence-building measures like the American visa, and that caused major rifts all round, and the lifting of the broadcasting restrictions and a few things like that, but they only formally rejected the Downing Street Declaration at their Ard Fheis at Letterkenny at the end of July.

Did you know they were going to reject it?

Yes, by 18 July, and I remember warning the British too, although I could not say much. I warned them not to be too rebarbative in their response.

What was your reaction?

I paid no attention to what happened at Letterkenny. You had got to the point by July of a coalition of partners and others, including the media, who had decided this is not going to fly and that they were only interested in dragging things out. Albert sent a missive to them, which I personally gave to Martin McGuinness on 18 July, saying that if there is not a decision by the end of the holidays other arrangements would have to be made. Albert also put it a bit more colourfully than that, saying he was the only person left believing in the possibility that there would be a ceasefire. That is not quite true, because I would have shared that view, but when I took it to them they had clearly recognised that that point had been reached, and to that extent they did not need the letter. Suddenly the discussions moved into a different mode, where we needed to work out the arrangements of what was going to happen and when this would be done. It was never explicitly stated on their part, the ceasefire, but Father Reid came to me in early August and asked me to write down what language would need to be in the ceasefire statement.

So within a month of rejecting the Downing Street Declaration they called a ceasefire?

Yes, but what you have to remember, and this is absolutely crucial, is that they needed to be in command of the narrative all the time. If they allowed the media for a moment to think they might be on the point of a ceasefire then the pressure of the media on their doorsteps would have been unbearable. Part of the aim of the Letterkenny thing was to throw everybody off the scent. I did know that was precisely what was happening, but I remember having a rather difficult meeting with Seamus Mallon in Newry when, even though I knew what was going to happen, I couldn't tell him. In fact, I couldn't tell my colleagues either, because, as Albert Reynolds understood very early on, if there were any indiscretion, all bets would be off. He knew he had to exercise a tight hold on what he could say. I did not discuss these matters with anybody except Albert himself.

Did Sinn Fein test that confidentiality?

Obviously it was in many respects far more fraught for them. They were always in between one meeting and the next, usually every four to six weeks, and you could absolutely take it that every communication that they got they would think of as a package, turning it upside down and pulling it this way and that. They had to be absolutely satisfied that there wasn't a booby trap somewhere in the middle of it, and, of course, they move through the means of collective leadership. This is not a one-man republican movement. It was more of a politburo, set-up, where only two or three would have been publicly known and others would not have been publicly known, or very little. I am sure that they checked me out in all sorts of ways that I am unaware of, but I exercised discipline on myself to give no grounds for complaint or breach of faith.

Did they use you to clarify their position for them, because the British said this was the case?

Every now and again, and this would not only be at this phase but later, when post-ceasefire officials would meet them too. More than once they might come with requests for ideas or suggestions about how to move things forward. I think occasionally they did want their interlocutors to do some of their thinking for them, or at least to lay out the options for them. What you say there tallies with experience, particularly further on. I would have had one or two meetings at the Redemptorist Monastery in Orwell Road, Dublin, where Adams would have been present with McGuinness, and I do remember one time before the first ceasefire Adams pointing at the person with him and saying to me 'It's not me you need to persuade, it's him.'

Isn't it an advantage for them in that it allows them to control the pace by saying they had to go away and talk to others?

That happened particularly in the more open phases of negotiation. I remember one time in Hillsborough prior to September 1997, when the split occurred with the Real IRA, which made one realise that this couldn't all be play-acting. The key thing for Adams was that he wanted to bring the vast bulk of the movement with him. As we know, de Valera in 1926 split off and formed Fianna Fail and he brought the bulk of the IRA with him. He didn't bring all of them but most, and I think Adams was trying to do better than de Valera had done in 1926.

Were you dealing with the same people from Sinn Fein?

I didn't meet Mitchel McLaughlin and Pat Doherty again until 1994, after the ceasefires, so they were not directly involved in the second round, so to speak.

Is consistency in a process with the same faces turning up in the same kind of way important? Are surprises problematic?

Sure, no surprises are best, and I think that was part of the use of meeting, where there is a tour of the horizon, a general discussion of what's going on and not just about domestic politics but European politics. They would, I suspect, have had a limited familiarity (although they obviously had their own networks with other liberation movements) with the way governments think and operate, so I suspect the discussions were quite useful in the way I was marking cards on what people were likely to do and what was likely to happen. I'm not saying I always got it right, because I didn't, but at least my assessments were offered in good faith, and I didn't say things purely for the purpose of getting them further along the road. I felt that credibility and trust mattered much more in the long run.

Was context more important to them than detail? Was the symbolic stuff, the visa, the broadcasting ban etc. more important for them to sell to their troops than bits of paper with words that could have meant a number of things?

They had a lot of interest in detail. If you fast-forward to the Good Friday Agreement, the night before it was concluded they came with a list of seventy-plus points that needed to be addressed, and they had plenty of resources in terms of folks working in the background on this, that or the other. Obviously, they did have an eye for the big political picture, but they also had an eye for detail too.

It has been said that symbolism entailed them talking late into the night, with statements often saying 'as of midnight', because the perception of them being hard and tough negotiators was important?

There was always a tension, and very understandably, between the maximalist claims that they had once made and what they were going to end up with, so they were always trying to improve what they could end up with.

How do you think they could sell rejecting the Downing Street Declaration, while also getting agreement for a ceasefire from their people?

Remember that the Downing Street Declaration had moved way beyond the document that they had only half agreed to back in June 1993. So to that extent, and since they had not been involved in negotiating the further stages, they did not feel bound by it. If you like, that was a stand on principle, but it didn't alter a pragmatic decision to call a halt to violence. Some parts of the Declaration were key, such as the late addition that if they stopped for good they would then be entitled to take part in politics on the same basis as everyone else. That pledge has been fulfilled and they made, some would argue, an almost brilliant transition from paramilitarism to politics that has not happened successfully in virtually any comparable situation around the world where, if you like, the paramilitaries haven't won. Obviously, the ANC in South Africa won, but the Provos didn't win in the sense that the ANC did.

The question is, how did they do that? There has to be something in the psychology which has enabled the shift, apart from tight leadership?

Obviously there was the prolonged stalemate, but they were perfectly prepared to carry on in other circumstances. I can remember being told by Father Reid, when it looked as if Albert was going out of office after his first Term in 1992 and John Bruton was about to become Taoiseach, that Sinn Fein were saying that they might have to put this in a drawer for another four years.

Do you think Enniskillen led to a major internal re-examination of the republican movement, and was that part of this picture?

I think so, but I would not put it solely down to Enniskillen. The thing about the Anglo-Irish Agreement is that it did fulfil Garret FitzGerald's and John Hume's principal aim of stopping the Sinn Fein Northern electoral gallop. FitzGerald was terrified of Sinn Fein becoming a majority in the North while the IRA campaign was still continuing, because they could then claim they had some sort of mandate from the nationalist community for carrying on IRA violence. That was his motivation even beyond devolution for the Anglo-Irish Agreement. Now whether Thatcher was persuaded of the importance of this, or at best only half, doesn't really matter, the fact was it was concluded, and maybe her civil servants were more persuaded than she was, but you see Sinn Fein had an abysmal general election in 1987 in the South, where they got 1.2 per cent of the popular vote. Effectively, the growth in Sinn Fein support off the back of the hunger strike, where Bobby Sands was elected to Westminster and two more hunger-strikers to the Dail, was halted. But I recall Adams saying publicly a month of two after Enniskillen something along the lines of if there were another Enniskillen he wasn't sure that he could go on supporting the IRA campaign. Further, the public reaction led both the SDLP, ourselves and Father Reid to look at this and see if they were considering the intention to stop, and certainly the vibes we were getting were that in the fullness of time yes, but you can also see that we would have been in a very weak position if we had been exposed having discussions with people who could be plausibly represented as having no intention of stopping.

Did you make an assessment early on that this was an endgame?

Well, if you are going back to 1988 my attitude, which was why I kept meeting Father Reid, was that yes, this may lead to something in due course, and so, by staying in contact, it meant someone would be around if and when the situation changed and became more hopeful. At the same time, meeting only Father Reid lowered the political risk considerably. But remember, there was a history going back to the early 1970s of many peace efforts and mediations of one sort or another that also had to recognise that the odds were against success, and that was the realistic assessment. It wasn't a case of this being a certainty or likelihood, even until very close to the end. I suppose six weeks towards the end in 1994, from about mid-July on, I realised this was going to happen, but I had to keep it strictly to myself, apart from discussing it with Albert.

In the build-up to the ceasefire were there frantic contacts between you and Sinn Fein?

No. There were perhaps a couple of meetings. There were questions asked like how soon would Albert meet them once a ceasefire is declared? What will be the attitude to prisoners? Now we only gave a very general answer to that, but we did start releasing prisoners pretty soon after the ceasefire, reopening cross-border roads, and then the Forum for Peace and Reconciliation was established. You needed understandings as to what was going to happen so that they knew and could tell their people.

Did they say to you we need visible proof to help us make the case for the political road? Did they talk about a series of symbolic moves and gestures to show the gains for abandoning violence?

They certainly talked about 'putting a package' to their people. That 'package' would be something they would draw up themselves by using elements that we might have supplied them with, but it wasn't a question of us drawing up or putting together the package. Obviously, there were important inputs, and the dialogue they had with the British in the post-breakdown period around December 1993 may have enabled them to draw elements into the 'package'.

Did they try to get from you any information on the British?

Once I remember being asked by Adams before the ceasefire, around June 1994, about whether the British had raised with us the question of arms, to which the answer was no. What's more, in their twenty clarifications they studiously evaded the question. I think they probably sensibly took the view that there was only so much traffic that could be borne at any one time.

Was the exploratory interaction a part of the negotiation process? That is, was it part of a more general picture of building trust, offering clarification and encouraging exploration?

I wouldn't call it negotiation, because that implies something formal, but maybe there was an element of informal negotiation. Something that mustn't be lost sight of is we were trying to bring about peace, but we also wanted a comprehensive political settlement of the question which had been open, to a greater or lesser degree, since the 1920s, and was to do with the option of a united Ireland in the future. There was a strand of unionist thinking which looked at South Tyrone and saw that as evidence that the border should be fixed for all time, regardless of what anybody wanted or felt. We certainly wanted to renew the understanding that went back to the 1920s, that if the two parts of Ireland wanted to come together, then obstacles would not be put in the way of that. In fact, the obstacle to a united Ireland without that meant there would have been no peace, and that was vital.

Did they ask you a lot of questions about the self-determination issue?

I think they had a problem with it, because their ideology would always have been a majority in Ireland as a whole, so it was one of the things they had most difficulty swallowing. The consent principle sounds very unionist, but self-determination sounds much more republican, so the challenge was to bring the two principles into play rather than just the one. The Anglo-Irish Agreement would have been purely based on one, consent, which equals self-determination in Northern Ireland, but that's all. The point is, we wanted to move beyond something the British never explicitly recognised in the 1921 period, when they sought to present the establishment of the Irish Free State as almost a grace-and-favour concession and not based on recognition of any new principle of international law. Of course, the Good Friday Agreement and the voting on it were effectively a first expression of concurrent self-determination, with both parts voting on it and both parts agreeing to it. To be fair to Father Reid, he had grasped the point early on that the important thing is to get the self-determination principle agreed. Now, there might be a different result of self-determination in the two jurisdictions, but at least that principle was in action and meant, in effect, that any change in a constitutional settlement, as contained in the Agreement, was one we would have to be involved in.

When did you meet them prior to the ceasefire being called in 1994?

I had a second meeting two or three days before the ceasefire, but I knew it was coming some weeks before. Though not stated explicitly, I knew the language.

What happened from the IRA ceasefire of 1994 to the ending of that ceasefire with Canary Wharf?

I was certainly aware that things were getting difficult. By the autumn of 1995 there was the impasse over decommissioning. Remember, also, that we were in opposition at the time and, although we were staying in touch with the situation and with the parties, we were not in power. I was working with Bertie Ahern, and he was leader of the opposition. We were meeting the SDLP, Sinn Fein and Alliance as well as one or two smaller groups in the Forum for Peace and Reconciliation, which met regularly and was trying to finalise a report which ended up not being finished because there was stand-off between Sinn Fein and the rest. I don't remember the precise details of what the issue was, but, notwithstanding the fragility of the situation, Canary Wharf came as something of a shock to me. I happened to be in the south of England at a conference which was about the EU. This was on 8 February, and there were a lot of senior people from the Northern Ireland Office there, as well as Northern politicians. About two hours after the conference had started, the news came through, and anyone closely involved disappeared. As I was in opposition, that didn't arise for me, but I certainly remember being deeply shocked at the time. It wasn't as if I was entirely oblivious to the danger, though, but it happened so abruptly and without notice.

I remember being told after, although I have not been able to verify this, that towards the end of February John Major was preparing to meet Gerry Adams. When I got back, I met a couple of Sinn Fein people, and there was one who lived quite close to me who was part of the Forum for Peace and Reconciliation delegation who told me they were just not winning the arguments internally. With the benefit of hindsight, I think the purpose of the breakdown of the ceasefire was two-fold: first, it was obviously a shot across the bows of the British Government and sending out the message you can't just kick us around anyway you like, but also, and I think more importantly, it was an attempt to keep the movement united. Now, as we know, in September 1997 it split with the people who were to go on to form the Real IRA, and presumably it was an attempt to keep others on board in the face of dissent. What one didn't know on that Friday night was whether this was a complete breakdown of the ceasefire and return to war or whether it was something short of that. Bertie Ahern had a meeting with Sinn Fein in Dublin Castle, because the Bruton Government had cut off all contact, but being in opposition the decision was taken that we would maintain contact with Sinn Fein, and there was a meeting with a fairly full delegation on both sides. There were pretty tough words spoken on both sides too.

Did Sinn Fein try to put some of the blame at the feet of the Irish Government for not putting more pressure on the British to move?

I think the Sinn Fein attitude to Bruton went through three phases. The first, when the Reynolds Government fell, was horror, because this upset all their calculations. Then, a bit more reflectively, they would have met Bruton in the early sessions of the meeting for the Forum for Peace and Reconciliation, so they got to know him a little before he became Taoiseach. Their second reaction was coming to the realisation that they would need to work with any Irish Government, so they would give them the benefit of the doubt. But I think their confidence was badly shaken when in March

1995 Bruton backed Mayhew's Washington Three condition. Now under pressure from Spring and Foreign Affairs he did pull back from that, but in a sense a fair bit of damage was done on that front. Then, in the early autumn, Hume put in a request that Bruton would meet him and Adams together, which Bruton turned down on the grounds that this would upset unionists. I think that was taken badly by Sinn Fein, as one of the premises was that well, at least you would have something approaching a democratic nationalist consensus. That was their thinking at that time, even if it is not what they would think today. And then, paradoxically, though it may seem the Clinton visit on the surface was a big success, the Provos just saw that as Clinton ganging up with two Governments against Sinn Fein, and if anything it stiffened their resolve. It is now said that in or around that time they decided to break the ceasefire. It would appear that even Adams was taken by surprise by the exact timing of what happened. I have heard it said that he thought he had more time to play with.

Do you think that would have caused serious tensions in the Army Council, particularly if a figure like Adams did not know this was going to happen?

I can't really speculate on that, because I simply don't know, but you can assume that there were arguments. But let's look at Major's position. Major was in some respects a much better negotiator than he was politician, and his forte in a way was in negotiation, but arguably he overplayed his hand. I think he was certainly shocked when the ceasefire broke down, as if he hadn't believed they would really do it. The other thing is one or two angry exchanges took place at that time with journalists who would put it to Major that they weren't going to decommission, certainly not at this stage, and he would retort angrily, how do you know that? I think it is a matter for speculation as to whether some tentative thinking was given to the possibility of doing something on that front from the republican side, but it was flatly turned down by the Army Council. One might imagine this, but you see I'm trying to think how otherwise you could explain Major's 'How do you know that?' response. That is sort of hinting that he had intelligence, that it wasn't quite as open and shut a case as thought. Now it doesn't make a lot of difference in the long run, and, as we know from later on, it was difficult enough to bring them to that even well after the Good Friday Agreement. Prior to the first ceasefire the British did not put decommissioning upfront, and when they were asked for clarifications on twenty questions by Sinn Fein I think their replies avoided saying anything that could be construed as a demand. That only came afterwards, and when the Frameworks Document came out, which the unionists rejected, Ken Maginnis was very quick off the mark to insist that instead of unionists accepting the Frameworks Document as a basis for negotiation the IRA should start decommissioning. I think it was a unionist ploy to put off serious negotiation. Remember, this was still the Molyneaux leadership of the Ulster Unionists in November 1995, and during the whole 1990s they were trying to keep as much distance as they could from serious negotiation. Things changed under Trimble, because it looks like he thought the best way to secure the Union was to negotiate an agreement rather than endlessly be on the defensive trying to put things off as the situation deteriorated politically.

When you met them after Canary Wharf did they tell you what was needed to be done in order to get the process back on track?

I met a couple of them, but the party met them as a group. No, but they were giving out the reasons as to why the thing had not worked.

So where was the momentum taking them back to the ceasefire coming from?

I can remember Joe Cahill telling me in Belfast, when we were walking along the Falls Road with Bertie and several others in August 1996: 'I think we'll wait until after the election,' and the election being referred to was the British one. I'm not saying they didn't have any interest in the Irish election, but they would have analysed it that way. Arguably, you can say that Mayhew from about 1995 on was managing the peace process in such a way so as it wouldn't precipitate the premature fall of the Major Government, because it was becoming a minority government at that stage. Of course, they had the example of what happened to Callaghan when he lost the vote of Frank Maguire in 1979. That's not to say that the Tories didn't want further progress, but not if it endangered their continuance in government, so you could argue from the start of negotiations, which of course did not include Sinn Fein, that putting that mechanism in place was about as far as they were able to take it.

To be fair to Bertie Ahern, he stayed in touch with Adams and made strenuous efforts, particularly just before the talks started, which was the end of May–early June 1996, and he tried to persuade Adams to reinstate the ceasefire and go into the talks. Obviously, if that had happened maybe there would not have been too many unionists in attendance, certainly to begin with. So Ahern did not adopt a selfish party position where he used the ceasefire breakdown electorally to help us get back to power the following year. He didn't adopt that attitude, because, apart from anything else, I remember asking one of the Sinn Fein people that I was friendly with what guarantee there was that if a bomb went off it would not cause a large number of casualties. The reply was there is no guarantee whatever. I don't know what their calculations were as to whether the loyalists would go back to war or not. The loyalists played a rather clever game in that they decided not to put themselves in the wrong in the way that the IRA had done, and they were happy to let the British security forces deal with them, even though they kept putting out statements saying if something else happens then all bets are off. It was almost as if they were enticing the Provos to do more, in the hope maybe of bringing the loyalists back in.

When they reinstated the ceasefire, what were the conversations you were picking up?

What you've got to remember is the British election was in May and the Irish election was in June. The Irish election was followed by a three-week interregnum, so the actual change of government did not happen until the end of June. We came back into office on 26 June 1997, so that would have been nearly two months after Blair came in. Now the real issue there with the Provos was would decommissioning be allowed to dominate the negotiations to the exclusion of everything else, or was it going to be parked to one side and allow the rest of the negotiation to happen? There was quite lengthy working on formulae involving the British and the Irish Government, and then they shot two policemen in Lisburn in mid-June about ten days before we came back into office, and I was left for ten days being the only link, because Bruton severed all contact at official level. Bruton had allowed a period after Canary Wharf for his officials, although he didn't meet Sinn Fein himself, to meet them. The day before the Dublin Government changed there was an agreement to meet Sinn Fein between the two Governments. Bruton naturally took the credit for it the day before he left office, and it reasonably satisfactorily dealt with decommissioning by defusing it as a dominating issue, at least as far as the two Governments were concerned.

What defused it?

You will have to look at the details of public statements of that time. The underlying question was whether the unionists were going to be allowed to use decommissioning to prevent any serious talks taking place, or was it simply going to be one issue among others with some kind of soothing formula for unionists? It was the latter. There would have been various assurances sought, the behind-the-scene discussions went on after we formed the Government, and remember, there were also important marches taking place and that was a kind of cross-current which, in the end, wasn't particularly helpful. Mo Mowlam allowed a parade to go down the Garvaghy Road and so on, but the republican movement covered their tracks fairly well. Their second ceasefire came in on about 19 July 1997, and the media weren't expecting it.

But how far before the reinstatement did you know it was coming?

Basically my job in the three weeks after we were back in office was to be the channel to them, because Bertie, in theory, was supposed to stop meeting them once he became Taoiseach. Whether he met them once or twice, I couldn't tell you, but that was the theory. I was doing most of the legwork, shall we say, and I was perfectly clear from the beginning that we were working together for a common objective, which was to restore the ceasefire as quickly as possible, so they would be able to get back into talks by September.

What were you asking of them from the Irish direction?

Basically, I was asking for the reinstatement of the ceasefire, but I didn't have to ask, as we were obviously working to create the conditions that would make that possible.

But presumably they were saying that A, B and C need to happen first?

It was more a question of them looking for reassurances of various kinds. They were keen to reinstate the nationalist consensus, but at this stage their relations with the SDLP had started to deteriorate, and Hume's dominance of the party was beginning to loosen too. The sort of relationship they had with Hume, coming up to the first ceasefire, was not replicated with the SDLP as a whole, and that was a fairly stillborn hope of theirs in 1997. It was not the case that we in the Irish Government were particularly opposed to the idea, but essentially, at that point, the SDLP–Sinn Fein interaction was beginning to diverge to the point where they, as in more recent years, started to fight like cats and dogs.

When the first ceasefire was called, it was celebratory for the optics, but I can't remember what happened around the reinstatement, because they couldn't regenerate the same enthusiasm for that. Was it a more muted affair?

Yes it was, but don't forget they were reinstating a ceasefire from a resumption of violence, which, as far as one could see, had been only half-restarted. It wasn't firing on all cylinders, and it never went back to how it was pre-August 1994. It was more sporadic, but those things had their dangers, and once you start using those methods you could have unwanted consequences.

Presumably when the first ceasefire was called they could depict that as emerging on the basis of strength. The second one could not be presented as such. Perhaps it was seen as more of a conciliatory gesture towards the two incoming Governments?

They always studiously avoided, as far as they were concerned, any appearance of a move under pressure, but the focus would have been less on gain or loss and more on getting into talks. Blair was essentially to take the view that six weeks was enough, and once we got into September the quarantine period was over. Now, of course, the Democratic Unionist Party and Robert McCartney left the talks as Sinn Fein entered, and they didn't come back, but they were there in the talks in July when we arrived.

Did anyone from the Irish side speak to the hard-liners in the IRA such as Brian Keenan?

I met him, but not in any kind of negotiating context, and that was in or around the Good Friday Agreement. I remember him saying to me 'I smell freedom.' But no, we were not meeting the IRA as such. The IRA at that point only held meetings, when strongly requested, out of politeness or not to appear too intransigent, but it was a quite clear tactic from them to insist that the IRA doesn't engage in political negotiation.

Most of your colleagues and the British tell me what good, hard negotiators Sinn Fein were. What do you think that means?

I would have a different view on that, which is that constant hardball negotiation does not always get the best results, and that there is a cost with that. There was also a fundamental contradiction, because when the first ceasefire was put in place the message from people like Adams was we need momentum, but it rapidly got to a stage where they were the people slowing down momentum, because they were very sticky on two issues in particular: decommissioning and policing. Essentially, both of those in one form or another stalled the process for the best part of ten years after the Good Friday Agreement, and hardball negotiation bogs things down. I think they under-estimated the benefits of a more fluid negotiating style.

When you say more fluid what do you mean?

What I mean is a willingness to strike agreements. If you strike agreements, there will always be things that you are dissatisfied with and will leave that to another time.

That would have been the way the social partnership negotiations would have gone. Of course, from time to time hard lines were put down, but at the end of the day the negotiating process happened quite quickly. Now, in defence of Sinn Fein, I would say they were trying to keep their people on board, and they wanted to bring the maximum number with them, and that wasn't easy so they had to stall. In a sense, we would spend a lot of time going round and round the mulberry bush in the implementation phase, and only when they were satisfied that there was nothing more to be extracted would they be prepared to move. Of course, the price of doing that was that you would lose a fair bit of goodwill, which perhaps was fairly considerable at the beginning of the process, and you would lose a lot of that along the way. The other thing is if they set their demands so high, as they did in the mid-1980s, and then what can actually be negotiated falls well below that, then the pressure comes from always trying to use negotiation to close that gap. Whether they always got the best results for themselves and their community I am not so sure.

Do you think they showed enough empathy for the unionists?

They might ask why it was their business to show empathy with the unionists, when the unionists had never shown empathy to them. I think that from time to time where nothing very expensive in terms of gestures was required they have made some movement, as in recent years with, say, McGuinness shaking hands with the Queen and attending a banquet and so on. But in substance that doesn't cost them much, and they may even have gained political support south of the border by doing things like that. Overall, though, the real cost of that was not considerable. They talk about it, and they might verbalise some empathy with unionism, but for much of the time unionism is their political opposition and their job is to checkmate unionism.

When they were dealing with you, did they like bits of paper, or were they wary?

If you are talking about prior to the first ceasefire and the written communications then, they certainly attached value to those, yes. Not to the exclusion of everything else though, because they wanted oral and written communication.

Did they put equal value on both?

I think their view was if these folks in the Irish Government don't trust us enough and they are not even willing to talk to us, well then what is the value of what is written down on paper? They liked to have things as far as possible in black and white and on paper, but all communication, particularly when it involved political risk on behalf of the Government before the ceasefire was an expression of trust.

To what extent was this all choreographed and planned, and to what extent was it being made up as people went along?

Things are always partly made up as they go along, and people can make all sorts of elaborate plans, but, given that you have got other actors who may have ideas of their own, plans only get you so far.

Did they tell you what they wanted, and were they always clear on that?

Usually, but not always clear on how they were going to get there. There was no lack of clarity about what they wanted, but the difficulty was often, how do you get from A to B?

Jonathan Powell talks about the problems Sinn Fein had with long-term planning, because they would often look to the Governments to try and give them a steer?

They would quite often look for ideas from us too, so that would be our experience as well as Jonathan Powell's experience.

Would you say that was an important part of the negotiation process?

No, I am not saying that. Obviously, if you have got demands from one side and demands from the other side, part of the role of the Governments was to try and find ways round a problem and suggest possible avenues which might satisfy both sides. Naturally, they were looking for ingenuity with regard to problems, and I'm sure lots of ideas on different issues at different times were floated amongst them which would have been things they might have felt they were able to use, along with other stuff they could not use at all.

Would you say they were creative thinkers?

If you stand back from it, and I have said this many times, there are many situations around the world where these types of conflict have taken place and where the conflict has not ended with the insurgents winning. In comparison with most of their contemporaries, in most other parts of the world, the republican movement have done extremely well. They have politically extricated themselves from what was at best a long-term stalemate position, and where their underlying position was gradually deteriorating, and where it was becoming less certain that they could have continued indefinitely. Yes, they could have continued for some time after, but if you reach a point, and this is what happened with the Communist regimes in Eastern Europe, where belief in what you are doing gradually ceases, then there is a danger of an implosion which is a morale issue that has nothing to do with the materials or the weaponry, and there was a long-term danger for them that if they didn't come to some kind of negotiated path or settlement, then that could happen to them. I don't, however, buy into the view that the British shouldn't have given in and should have kept hammering away from a security point of view either. I do think they deserve credit for leading their community and, in particular, their own organisation with both political and military elements out of the morass into a place which contains significant possibilities for the future. The future is obviously not predetermined, but at least they have a means open to them they didn't before.

Certain members of Sinn Fein see themselves as socialists and have drawn support from the US at a number of levels, and yet the US is strongly resistant to socialism. How has that relationship and the contradictions of it been sustained?

It's sustained because American supporters, many of whom would be both wealthy and republican in the American sense, see themselves as Irish too. It's an illusion to think that wealthy Irish-Americans are all mostly Democrat supporters, because they're not. They're republicans in both senses of the word. I think they probably discount the rhetoric from Sinn Fein. If you look at it in a realpolitik sort of way, Sinn Fein were not in power either side of the border. North of the border, even though they have been members of the Executive, it has no means, even if it wanted to, for carrying out socialist policies, because they have a budget given to them from Westminster with very few tax powers. They get to distribute public expenditure, and that means you can pull it marginally this way or that way, but they have no control over taxation policy, which is at least as important as expenditure policy, and if you are a socialist this is all about how you redistribute wealth through taxation. The North is looking for the same corporation tax rate as we have in the Republic, and remember most American economic interests would be related to their multinationals. Foreign executives in multinationals don't even pay domestic tax, either British or Irish. They are there for five years and there are special tax rates, so why would they worry about that? Now, where there was a big break was on Colombia when there was a major rift over Sinn Fein, who were seen to be dabbling in America's backyard.

That would have caused serious ructions. Then, of course, 9/11 happened, and that meant that the latitude or the rope that the friends were prepared to extend to Sinn Fein was pulled in very considerably. Post-9/11 they could not be seen to be involved in activities that had terrorist implications, especially not in America's backyard.

Some of the British officials seem to think that the US role was not that significant?

Well, there were officials on the British side who were quite resistant to American involvement and the American view, who would have seen this as 'our' business and where the American job was simply to back that up. It's very clear that the Americans played quite a big role, and to use a phrase from George Canning in the early nineteenth century, who was a British Foreign Secretary after the Napoleonic Wars, the talk was about 'bringing in the new world to redress the balance of the old'. I think the American role was important. The public view that they were best buddies is more complex, and there have been a whole range of different interests on, say, Grenada, the Falklands, nuclear disarmament, and where Reagan pushed Thatcher in the direction of delivering on the Anglo-Irish Agreement after she had fallen out with FitzGerald. There was also the kind of American influence going back to Carter's day, where economic underpinning took shape in the International Fund for Ireland, but when you come to the Clinton era it suddenly becomes different. Up until Bush Senior, it was very much we will support what the British and Irish Governments can agree, and the more they can agree the better, but don't expect us to intervene. I remember Clinton once saying to Bertie that he liked Major, but he detested the Tories, and as you know he granted the visa. You might say apart from the visas he did not do a whole lot, but the point was, if you were coming from a Sinn Fein point of view you want the help of those who are able to push people to make the decisions on the ground. The Americans and Clinton would have been seen early on as sympathetic and not simply pro-British in approach. There would have been jokes in Irish nationalist and republican circles that the State Department was a branch of the British Foreign Office in Washington and rarely if ever went against it, but then you see political influences such as Nancy Soderberg, who wasn't in the State Department, so what the Americans did was give a feeling at the crucial time that there is much more of a level playing field than has been the case hitherto.

What is your perception of the British in how they went about negotiating this process? Were they rigid or pragmatic? Were they less comfortable with the informal, compared to the Irish?

I think you have to divide it into two periods: the Major Government and the Blair Government. In the Major administration you would have been conscious that there were political and ideological lines that couldn't be crossed. Under Blair, it almost went to the opposite extreme, in that you were talking about an ultra-pragmatic situation as particularly exemplified by Jonathan Powell. Now, in some ways that was very helpful from our point of view, because it meant that the Blair Government had few real hang-ups on most subjects. However, Blair would have been personally hesitant to override his security/intelligence advice too much. The other thing is that he wanted to prop up as far as he could a rather shaky David Trimble, because he needed Trimble, certainly in the early stages, for this whole thing to work. He would have had a religious prejudice which was quite strong in the early days in terms of negative feelings vis-à-vis Paisley. When Trimble was no longer there to be propped up, Blair had to work with Paisley, and that was a different matter, but he put off that day for as long as he could.

Are you of the same mind as Powell that Sinn Fein over-negotiated the process and could have got a deal five years earlier?

I think there is a contradiction in their position. As noted, in the immediate aftermath of the ceasefire the message being preached by Adams was, and this is while the Reynolds Government was still in office, what we need is momentum, momentum, momentum. And there was quite a lot of momentum in the early period, when border roads were reopened, the Washington Investment Conference was organised, people were working hard to finish the Frameworks Document, and the Forum for Peace and Reconciliation was running, so there was quite a lot of momentum, but then it started stalling over decommissioning. Arguably, the British Government, under unionist pressure, wanted to slow down the momentum, because it was altogether too fast for the taste of the Ulster Unionists. Their real counter to the Frameworks Document was not rejection but the stipulation that they were not entering into talks until there was some prior decommissioning of weapons, and that held things up for over a year. The main thing that Sinn Fein was interested in during the run-up to their declaration of the second ceasefire was the need for assurances that the talks were not going to be totally dominated by decommissioning, so the decommissioning issue had to be defused and, if you like, put into a siding. Then, post-Agreement, it came out of the siding again, and on both decommissioning and policing Sinn Fein stalled for as long as they possibly could. Now I am of the view on the policing side that they could have moved much earlier, without massive internal revolt or revolution, than they did, but for various reasons it didn't suit them to do so. I think they partly used the policing issue to put off coming to grips with the decommissioning issue, because it was somehow more respectable and defensible, in a public sense, to be having difficulties with policing reform. There was also the whole argument about the Patten Report, which was generally welcomed and broadly accepted, but then Mandelson, who was fairly pro-unionist, diluted it and the British had to return to several negotiations on that. I remember that at Weston Park the SDLP came on board, but it was another five or six years before Sinn Fein did. For a while Sinn Fein nurtured the illusion that provided they stopped attacking British soldiers, policemen, unionist politicians, then they could carry on.

I think Mo Mowlam once called punishment beatings 'internal housekeeping'. They could do that and even sort of carry on their fundraising activities. Remember, there was someone shot in a post office raid in Newry in November 1994, and I think they also thought, perhaps correctly, that the Blair Government wasn't overly hung up on decommissioning. They also thought that the Irish Government was not too hung up either, provided that the weapons stayed silent. Then there was the argument about whether it was a dreadful humiliation or surrender, etc. But essentially the unionists stuck to their position and were clear that they were not going to go into a government without decommissioning, although Trimble allowed himself to be persuaded in December 1999 to go in for a couple of months, provided decommissioning started after that. It was then clear that the republican movement were not going to move on that, so the momentum slowed down very considerably, and it was partly because Sinn Fein were hanging tough and maybe hoping that, at the end of the day, people wouldn't worry too much about decommissioning. But the Democratic Unionists were quite definite weapons had to be decommissioned and that they couldn't work in a government that doesn't support the police.

How good are Sinn Fein at strategy? Are they good strategists or very good ideologues?

I think you can exaggerate the ideologue stuff. Parties often put forward ideological reasons for doing or not doing something, but sometimes ideological arguments are a front, so, to be fair to them, while ideology was important, both historical and philosophical understanding of their position was as important in being able to handle and be interested in their problems. A lot of politicians have no time for ideological arguments, but addressing the ideological arguments in a way was helping Sinn Fein deal with critics in their own ranks. In looking back on it, their ideological conviction was an important part of the armed struggle, and I think in moving to a ceasefire in 1994 ideological arguments were important, but in what has happened subsequently I am less sure that ideology was necessarily the driving force compared with other things. Prisoners were very important, and bringing that constituency with them was vital. As said, they operate like a politburo structure. They like to examine everything and are always looking for potential traps, and they always believed that hardballing was the best means of negotiation. They would adopt hard-line positions and would go round and round until things got frozen. The British would often come back satisfactorily on all points, only for them to adopt a more hard-line position. In general, they were prepared to move, but there were times till mid-July 1994 in particular when they were playing around. But certainly they needed to be satisfied that they had extracted the last drop of what was available by saying the IRA were saying this or that. Clearly, in the later stages decommissioning was their pressure card, but do not under-estimate the various hothouse negotiations in Leeds Castle, Weston Park and Hillsborough, which progressed matters.

How did you notice their thinking changing over the years?

You see, when you are talking about the first phase of the peace process, they were in relative isolation compared to other parties, and just limited contacts at a senior level with the SDLP and with us took place. Once you got into the implementation of the peace process you are talking about a lot of nuts and bolts. The security issues came to the fore, and they found them difficult to deal with or they chose to find them difficult to deal with. Then you had the two Governments with Ahern and Blair, neither of whom were ideologically rigid and both of whom were very pragmatic. Look at the efforts of the Blair Government to deal with the on-the-runs issue as an illustration of that. Now the critics would have said that was totally immoral, that it was appeasement and all the rest of it, but gradually, and partly because of the way they behaved, some of these issues eventually became ones that they had to move on with regards to policing and decommissioning.

Do you think they exaggerated a potential split within the IRA?

Well, anybody in negotiation or diplomacy tends to a degree to play up or exaggerate their difficulties. I don't remember them talking about a split. That was a word they would never use, because that would imply they were not in control of their organisation, so there might have been circumlocutions. They may have said things different to the British compared to what they said to us, or used slightly different tactics. Of course, there was a real split, as we know, in September 1997, when the Real IRA was formed, and there were already one or two small dissident groups in existence, but I suppose we took it for granted that, however you expressed it, whether it was military wing, political wing or whatever, they wanted to be able to bring most of their people with them. You will never get total unanimity, and if something was likely to cause a major split in the organisation they would either stall on it or deny it. As it happened, what the split occurred on was ending the second ceasefire and going into talks. The McKevitt faction clearly thought they should carry on, but there was no split worth talking about, when they eventually accepted policing and decommissioning, that we are aware of. Every now and then there would be individuals, councillors, who would resign, but all of that was pretty well contained, and Sinn Fein, to this day, have not merely held their own but strengthened their position politically, both North and South.

7

Critical minimums and the expectations of change: an interview with Tim O'Connor

Graham Spencer: *You were involved in Northern Ireland from 1986. Can you give me a brief overview of your role and work?*

Tim O'Connor: I had joined the Civil Service in July 1974 as an Executive Officer in the Civil Service and Local Appointments Commission and then I moved across to the Diplomatic Service and the Department of Foreign Affairs in May 1979, entering as a Third Secretary. In my early years in the Department, I was in the Protocol Section, and then I was Private Secretary to the Secretary General (Head of the Office of the Secretary General) from 1980 to 1982. At that point I had my first posting overseas at the Irish Embassy in Bonn, Germany (from 1982 to 1986), until being posted back to Dublin in the summer of 1986, where I was assigned to the Security Section in the Anglo-Irish Division of the Department. This began my involvement with the Northern Ireland process, which has effectively continued to this day, thirty-one years later.

Quickly for the record, the overview of the rest of my career is as follows: I was promoted First Secretary in 1989, while still in the Anglo-Irish Division, and remained there for a further year until my posting to the Irish Embassy Washington (from 1990 to 1994), where I served as the Economic Attaché, while also contributing on the Northern Ireland issue in support of the Ambassador. For the duration of 1992 until the end of my posting in January 1994, I was also the Designated Officer assigned to Mexico (the Irish Embassy in Washington also looked after Mexico in those days) and made several trips to Mexico in that period, organising a series of trade missions from Ireland. In 1993 I was promoted to Counsellor and returned to headquarters in the Department of Foreign Affairs in Dublin in January 1994, where I served in a number of positions over the following years – Anglo-Irish Division again, Deputy Joint Secretary of the Forum for Peace and Reconciliation, Africa Director, Human Rights Director, and then, from 1997 to 1999, Head of the Talks Team involved in the negotiation and immediate aftermath of the Good Friday Agreement. In December 1999 I was promoted Assistant Secretary and posted to Armagh as the inaugural Southern Joint Secretary of the North–South Ministerial Council, where I remained until the summer of 2005, when I was moved to New York to be Consul General of Ireland with the rank of Ambassador. In 2007 I was promoted to Secretary General to the President of Ireland, based in Aras an Uachtarain, where I had the privilege to serve as the Head of the Office of our inspirational President, Mary McAleese (and working closely also with her husband, Martin, who together with the President did such positive work in building bridges with and within Northern Ireland). I took early retirement in 2010, and in late 2016 I was appointed by the Irish Government to be its representative on the Independent Reporting Commission, which under the Fresh Start Agreement of November 2015 is tasked with supporting the ending of paramilitarism in Northern Ireland.

My time working on Northern Ireland began in the summer of 1986, some nine months after the Anglo-Irish Agreement of November 1985, so there was a whole new kind of paradigm in play in terms of Anglo-Irish relations and the Irish Government's involvement in Northern Ireland. The context was that the 1985 Agreement gave the Irish Government a say in the running of Northern Ireland for the first time, so there was a big ramp-up in terms of the resources and capacity that we had to bring to bear. In practical terms that meant the creation of the British–Irish Secretariat in Belfast, which co-ordinated British–Irish relations in respect of Northern Ireland, so there was a whole new structure that had to be supported. There was also an increase in resources in the Department of Foreign Affairs to match that and my assignment came as part of this process when I was a Third Secretary, working across a number of areas such as security and politics. One of my jobs was monitoring the role of the security forces and statistics on casualties of the conflict, and comparing those with previous years. Another role I had was monitoring from public sources the Provisional IRA and Sinn Fein, how that relationship was shifting and developing and what they were saying publicly; so, effectively, I was looking at what was happening inside the republican movement. In addition to those duties, from early 1988 onwards I was on the road once a fortnight for two days in the North, travelling incognito but reaching out to people on the ground and bringing back reports to the Government. In those days Irish Government ministers could not travel North easily and people in the British–Irish Secretariat were confined to their offices and accommodation in Maryfield, just outside Belfast (it was called 'The Bunker'), so we needed other vantage points in terms of what was happening on the ground in the North.

When you say you were talking to people on the ground, who was that?

Ideally it was across the board, but because the unionists were reluctant to talk to us in those days it was mostly engagement with the broad nationalist community. The main bulk of it would have been the SDLP constituency, but also with priests, bishops, teachers and so on. Essentially, people who had a good handle on what was happening on the ground in the communities. We were trying to get a reliable picture of what life was really like on the ground, especially for the nationalist community. At that stage the view, in the light of the Anglo-Irish Agreement, was that we were trying to move towards a political solution. The Agreement itself was not that solution, but an important platform or staging-post towards it, and it was very important symbolically and practically in the eyes of many nationalists.

When you were dealing with Sinn Fein in the talks how did you come to view their approach?

I could see that they were very committed personally to what they were doing and to a 'cause' which went beyond themselves. Their sincerity in that regard was not in doubt. On the other hand, the pathway they had been on had a deeply dark side: violence, armed struggle, non-democratic means or whatever words one wants to use to describe it. I think there was a constant process of trying to come to terms with that and justifying that for themselves. That also involved a tension with constitutional politics, the representatives of which were fundamentally opposed to the use of violence for political means and of the view that such a resort to violence was never justified in the Northern Ireland context. Those two philosophies were essentially in contradiction of each other and the tension between them was there throughout. On the part of constitutional politics, there was a further tension between those who believed on moral grounds that one should never have dealings with those who pursued and believed in armed struggle, and others who were opposed to violence, yes, but were prepared to take a pragmatic approach to the way forward in the interests of peace. To a certain extent, that tension can never be fully resolved and remains intact to this day.

Can you summarise how you viewed republicans in those early stages?

I was the Deputy Secretary for the Forum for Peace and Reconciliation which was set up by the Irish Government in October 1994 after the ceasefire, and the mission for the Forum was to be a place of political engagement and dialogue in the absence of formal negotiations. If you recall, after the Provisional IRA ceasefire in August 1994 the political conditions were such that the British Government under John Major had a wafer-thin majority in Westminster and he was dependent on the votes of the Ulster Unionist Party. This was October 1994 and this was the first time that mainstream Irish politics had become engaged in a comprehensive way with Sinn Fein. In that process we began to encounter how they might operate politically.

Can you tell me about the formation and purpose of the Forum for Peace and Reconciliation?

The opening day of the Forum was 28 October 1994 in Dublin Castle, and it was a seminal day in Irish politics because it was the first time, effectively since the foundation of the Irish State, that Sinn Fein had fully become part of the mainstream of Irish politics. That is effectively what happened on that day. You had an ideological battle going on after the Anglo-Irish Agreement of 1985, with the concept of following an exclusively political path becoming increasingly compelling, and Adams recognised this and that it was also an opportunity to end the isolation of republicanism. Hence we had the Hume–Adams process, which started around 1987 to 1988, which then led to the Hume–Adams statement that in turn fed into a process with the two Governments leading to the Joint Declaration at Downing Street of December 1993.

What was the Forum for Peace and Reconciliation designed to do?

It was a realistic recognition by the Irish Government in the Downing Street Declaration that, because of the electoral politics and the numbers involved, the British, even after a Provisional IRA ceasefire, would not be able to move quickly into negotiations. The whole Sinn Fein rationale was that a ceasefire should be followed immediately by formal negotiations for a settlement, and a tangible demonstration that politics works. The reality was that that was not going to happen anytime quickly, which turned out to be the case. If you remember, from August 1994 full-on negotiations of the kind that Sinn Fein were seeking took another three years to come to pass. So, the Forum was an interim mechanism, a holding space where, ahead of formal negotiations, a serious political engagement could take place involving multiple stakeholders, including Sinn Fein.

There had been the New Ireland Forum before, in 1984. What did that do?

That was a different context and time. The New Ireland Forum of 1983 to 1984 came after the hunger strikes, at a pivotal point in the political life of Ireland. There was a view that constitutional nationalism needed to reclaim the primacy of politics over physical force and that the time had come to redefine nationalism for the modern age. The New Ireland Forum sought to facilitate that. It actually started out trying to be inclusive, because the unionist parties were invited but they did not attend. It eventually became a conversation within nationalism between those who believed in peaceful, democratic politics as the only way forward on the island, led, of course, by the Irish Government. It turned out to be a very important, and indeed pivotal, conversation.

Was that moment influential on Hume's thinking?

Very much so, I would say, because the New Ireland Forum essentially set down the foundations and the underlying concepts for what ultimately became the peace process. The key one was the principle of non-violence and exclusively political means, and getting that enshrined as the new guiding star of Irish nationalism, and that was formulated more concretely in that kind of Forum. The second principle was the principle of consent, although it wasn't called consent at that time. That is, the notion that you couldn't impose a united Ireland against the wishes of the majority in Northern Ireland. That was a new policy position and a very significant shift by nationalism. Before, the ending of partition was seen as a sacred cow of nationalism and not up for negotiation in philosophical terms. Within that philosophy, the unionists were not recognised as having a pivotal say, they were just a minority inside the island of Ireland, which was how they saw themselves. So the overall exercise by the Forum turned out to be a fundamental redefinition of nationalism by constitutional nationalists who were opposed to violence and physical force as a means to win political ends.

Do you recall the time when the Hume–Adams dialogues began and what the reaction was to those dialogues?

The Hume–Adams dialogue was a very tightly driven, private exercise between Gerry Adams and John Hume. Given the complexities and sensitivities involved, there was a lot of speculation about it on the ground, but because it was a very tight personal process you were just hearing snippets of what was being discussed. It was also quite controversial because at that stage we had Section 31 of the Broadcasting Act in play, which meant Sinn Fein voices were banned from the airwaves, and, of course, the Provisional IRA was an outlawed organisation with membership a criminal offence. Moreover, their campaign of violence was continuing during this period. The notion of the senior leader of constitutional nationalism in the North, John Hume, sitting down in conversation with the leader of Sinn Fein while the Provisional IRA were still engaged in ongoing violence was highly controversial. Supporters of John Hume's position pointed to his huge record and status as a peace-maker and that his judgement had to be backed on the basis that he sincerely believed that good could come of the engagement and that these were the risks that had to be taken for peace and to ultimately save lives. Other commentators were less willing to cut him that slack and argued that this was handing Sinn Fein a propaganda victory and undermining the search for a lasting peace. On Gerry Adams' side you could see that the twin-track approach was in play, of sending out signals that the republican movement was seeking to move towards peaceful politics, while at the same time never resiling from the legitimacy of republican physical force. Let's say it was a confusing time, with everybody trying to interpret what was really going on and figure out what the right approach was.

Looking back on it, it was a classic example of John Hume's pioneering vision and courage – the ability to see possibilities into the future that were not yet obvious to most people and having the courage and tenacity to take the risks necessary to move that vision towards reality. As a citizen, and looking back on it all these years later, my admiration for John Hume grows all the time. It was an enormous contribution.

Of course, I cannot mention John Hume without including his deputy at the time, Seamus Mallon. Full disclosure, Seamus and I went on to become close personal friends (which we remain to this day). Seamus brought a different perspective to bear – some would say John had the vision and Seamus had the edge. Certainly Seamus would have had misgivings about anything that would be seen to give succour to Sinn Fein and the Provisional IRA, and indeed would damage the SDLP, such as the Hume–Adams talks. But overall, the power over the years was what Hume and Mallon brought to the table collectively. In many ways they were like brothers; the same (political) family, very different personalities and perspectives, but tied together by a bond of mutual admiration and respect that was unshakeable. History will judge them both as giants of their time, I feel sure, and as an official who got the opportunity to work with them both, I cannot overstate what a privilege that was. I wanted to take an opportunity during this interview to place this strongly on the record and I am glad to have now done so.

Did you undertake formal contact with Sinn Fein to get them to the Forum for Peace and Reconciliation in 1994?

Yes is the short answer. As I have mentioned, the Forum was devised as a kind of substitute space for political dialogue and engagement on the conflict and solutions to it in advance of full negotiations. The Downing Street Declaration prefigured the Forum, but fast-forward eight months to August 1994 and the ceasefire. The minute that ceasefire was declared the Forum concept essentially went live. Very quickly the unionists said there was no basis for comprehensive negotiations any time soon, so, as promised in the Downing Street Declaration, the Irish Government moved to create the Forum. The Taoiseach wrote formally to all the parties inviting them to participate and we, the officials, followed up to discuss the practical arrangements and the kinds of issues the Forum should consider. We knew initially that there would be a Forum but there was no detail about what kind of Forum it would be, what form it would take, what its purpose would be, what precisely it would do, how it would work, what its outcomes would be; none of that was worked out in advance. Essentially, we had to design what that would look like, so the Irish Government side put together proposals for the consideration of the parties. I should add that at an early point I was one of the three senior officials appointed to make the preparations for the Forum, but the Secretary General of the Forum was Wally Kirwan of the Department of the Taoiseach. I was appointed Deputy Secretary and my colleague in the Department of Foreign Affairs, Rory Montgomery, was appointed Assistant Secretary of the Forum. Our task was to advise the Government on the arrangements for the Forum and to undertake outreach to the parties participating in terms of their views and thoughts. The Government appointed Mrs Justice Catherine McGuinness as the Chairperson of the Forum. Born into a Church of Ireland family in Belfast, she had moved to the Republic, married a leading Southern nationalist broadcaster and journalist, Prionsias Mac Aonghasa, and subsequently became a leading member of the Irish judiciary. So, in both personal and professional terms she was ideally placed to play the role required of the Chairperson of the Forum and she did a superb job from day one, proving her appointment an inspired decision.

Like the New Ireland Forum, the unionist parties were all invited but we knew they would not come, and they didn't. However, there were about ten or eleven political parties involved, including all the political parties from the South. The SDLP, the Alliance Party, who were indicating some connection into unionism, the Women's Coalition, the Northern Ireland Labour Party and the Democratic Left all came. The opening day of the Forum was Friday 28 October 1994 and it remained in being until February 1996.

How did you open it? Did you ask the parties to bring a position paper?

We talked things through with them all. First of all, we had to work through how many members there would be in the Forum as a whole. Was it two members per party or was it going to be proportionate, and, if so, proportionate to what? We borrowed from the previous model of delegates and then substitute delegates used by the New Ireland Forum, so you could have a panel and a back-up backbench. It was done proportionately to the strengths of the previous elections, so Fianna Fail had the largest number of delegates and so on.

How often did you meet?

Every Friday, for a full day in Dublin Castle. I think we did a good job in setting out how this was going to work, and we made sure it was an environment that suited the seriousness of the occasion. Dublin Castle is a historic place and it is atmospheric. We gave a bit of thought and spent a bit of money on how we would do the surround of the day, so we started maybe 9.30am and would finish at about 4.00pm.

Do you remember the opening issues that people spoke about?

We got agreement that there would be a formal opening session on 28 October, and that was a really important political moment because that day was exclusively about opening statements by the ten or eleven party leaders, and it was a national event that was televised live from Dublin Castle. Sinn Fein had about ten members in their delegation, so everybody was waiting in the Throne Room in Dublin Castle, waiting for their delegation to arrive and take their place in mainstream Irish politics for the first time since the foundation of the State.

In having the television media there you were enabling unionists to see this without having to be there. What was the purpose of having the media there?

Remember, this was about two months after the Provisional IRA ceasefire, so there was a sense of a new beginning in the air. The Government felt that it was important to keep the momentum of all of that going. The opening day of the Forum was a kind of watershed moment where people could mark the significance of what had happened and the urgent need to grasp the opportunity that represented. At the same time, everybody was conscious that the edifice of peace being built was quite fragile. We had been in a situation of all-out violence and now, finally, we had this moment after the August ceasefire and we wanted to consolidate it. It was really important in every way to consolidate the fragile peace, to send out the right messages and to be able to demonstrate that the political process was working and seen to be working.

Did the British show any interest in this?

They were very interested, yes.

Were they inviting you to ask the parties things?

Not so much, because we knew what they would be thinking anyway. There was a pretty good relationship and understanding of where the British were coming from at that stage and we more or less had a shared understanding about what the core issues were.

Looking at some of the submission papers, Sinn Fein were very much focussing on the British being the cause of the conflict, which you would expect, but was there any pragmatism in their approach?

There was, yes. Remember though, just before the second meeting was scheduled Albert Reynolds was no longer Taoiseach, there had been a political crisis that had nothing to do with the Northern conflict and Fianna Fail were out of power. John Bruton was appointed Taoiseach literally a day before the second meeting of the Forum was due to take place (on 18 November 1994), and frankly we did not know until the last minute whether it would proceed or not. But ultimately, and slightly surreally, the meeting did go ahead and we did get down to business.

We divided the work of the Forum into three areas, or strands, and we designed that in advance. The first strand was about political engagement between the parties themselves. Another strand related to dedicated new research about an emerging peaceful Ireland and considering what the social and economic implications of peace might mean. The third strand related to the Forum as a place of public engagement, enabling submissions from the public and allowing them to come along and meet the Forum in open sessions. That turned out to be a very valuable thing and worked very well. We also had a number of theme days and open sessions on such areas as 'victims of violence', which proved very powerful and insightful.

What difference did it make to have the public in there?

It firstly showed there was a strong interest on the part of the wider public in engaging in the discourse about the conflict and how it could be resolved, and the Forum was very valuable as a place where that could happen. The sessions involving the public and outside stakeholders were among the most powerful moments in the life of the

Forum. We had a chance of peace now affecting everybody, so how were we going to do it? What were the issues? How were we going to capitalise on this moment? What were the obstacles to peace? It was profound and very important for the public too. I should add that RTE TV ran a Forum series, whereby each week during its work there would be a short programme giving the highlights of each session. That was very helpful too, in terms of giving a wider visibility to its work.

Were Sinn Fein wary of the Forum?

No, I wouldn't say wary. I would say they embraced the Forum and the whole experience involved. Frankly, we didn't really know what they would be like, but actually from the outset they were quite pragmatic in their approach. It was decided that an early piece of work among the parties themselves would be to examine what the principles and requirements of a new dispensation might be, and a sub-committee involving representatives of all the parties was set up to undertake this work. We, the Secretariat, put together the first draft of a discussion paper on all this, and that was sent out so parties could respond through their submissions and then debate amongst themselves. This became the context in which the first serious kind of engagement between parties began to happen, as distinct from making statements at each other. Sinn Fein engaged fully and constructively in this exercise, and from that we began to sense we were up and running.

The setting of Dublin Castle was conducive to that kind of engagement and we worked hard at making the surroundings the best they could be in that regard. For instance, lunch each Friday took place around circular tables of ten, which turned out to be a good design in terms of promoting engagement. There were also plenty of nooks and crannies in terms of conversations among smaller groups. Initially Sinn Fein would be sitting with themselves, but gradually they started to break up and sit with others and people began to get to know each other, and then we began to have political engagement back and forth, which proved very important for later on.

When Sinn Fein engaged in formal negotiations later on, had the Forum given them an advantage in that it enabled them to develop or hone their arguments and negotiating skills?

The Forum was, I think, a valuable probing ground for Sinn Fein. After all, the background of many of its members was in a very different arena and very few of them had been involved before in political discourse with other parties. Now they were in a new space, one which involved the give and the take of politics and negotiations with people who didn't share, and indeed opposed, their world-view. There was a learning process going on. What does it mean to sit with other parties? How do you present yourself? How much do you give way and not give way? What are the means by which one negotiates in a multilateral context? How much of it should you be doing around a multilateral table and how much of it should be done bilaterally? If you do things bilaterally with others is that a risk? Who has the skills to be engaged in that? How do you draft documents, and what kind of documents? How do you respond to the drafts of others? On 28 October 1994 we did not know the answers to these questions. We had no inkling of how Sinn Fein would approach all this. In the event, as I say, they turned out to be quite pragmatic in their approach and quickly got into the back and forth of political discourse.

You brought in people like F. W. De Klerk. Why and what did he contribute?

We thought that one of the things that would be good was to bring in some people with a different perspective who would have something to say to the members that could be interesting. That's why we had the public sessions and, for instance, invited victims to address us, because it was important for those voices to be heard directly. Their take and their perspective on that was therapeutic, and very interesting for the politicians (including politicians in the South) to hear that first hand and to engage with directly. But then we also had some outside figures such as economists, and others like Senator George Mitchell and US Secretary of Commerce Ron Brown, who was, sadly, subsequently killed in a plane crash. We also invited the former President of South Africa, F. W. De Klerk, and he was one of the stars actually. He had been through a process a few years before in South Africa and this was 1995, so it was only a few years later, and in a sense he was the unionist perspective from a different context. He was very open and challenging and he said you have an opportunity here, so please take it, that it's going to involve risks, but that they needed to be taken. The biggest insight I got from him was when he said that in negotiations the toughest discussions are not with your adversary across the table but with your own side. In other words, it is in your own private rooms where you are actually negotiating, and that's the toughest one because you are facing two issues: having to placate or bring on board your own people, but also having to do it on the basis of a position which is likely to be credible in the negotiating room and therefore cannot be absolutist; that now you are dealing with the art of the possible. So the moment you leave the negotiating table and go back you are effectively representing your adversary, and that was a great insight.

So you become in a way an advocate for your adversary?

Pretty much. In effect, when you are negotiating with your adversary, you are representing your own side, but when you're back with your own colleagues you are in effect representing your adversary. You can see the demands that that places on the negotiator. As I say, it was a very revealing and valuable insight.

Do you think that Sinn Fein learned from others in ways which they would not have done otherwise?

I would think so. There is something about being in a discourse where you have a chance of influencing others and being part of a wider process where you are actually being validated for your position and trying to argue your position. But you also have to leave yourself open to being influenced by others. In no negotiations do you get everything you seek. But when you have come from a place where you have never had to negotiate anything, but rather just articulate your own maximalist position, that is quite a shift. That was all starting to happen for Sinn Fein in the Forum. And, of course, there was a similar process involved for the other parties.

Is it the case that you met Seamus Mallon and Sinn Fein after each Forum meeting to review?

That was more an informal thing, and certainly didn't happen after every session. But when it did happen it was a bit like the video analysis after the match. The team came in and they basically dissected the performance, analysed what happened and how to do better next time. Basically that is what we were doing.

Was it just with the SDLP and Sinn Fein?

We were obviously close to the SDLP, the Irish Government had been close to them throughout, and then there would have been a personal relationship with Seamus on my part, a man, as I said earlier, for whom I had (and still do have) the highest admiration and respect. The SDLP were still the primary partner, so it was very important that we heard their private views and what they felt. We were constantly refining the position so that we could be more effective the next time. But we were talking privately to the other parties too. For instance, Dr John Alderdice (now Lord Alderdice), then leader of the Alliance, had an important role to play, both in his own right but also as an interpreter of unionist thinking in the absence of the unionist parties themselves. So we would stay in close, private ongoing contact with John and his colleagues in the Alliance Party, and they were very helpful to us.

The final report never came out because of Canary Wharf and has never been seen, is that so?

There was a draft in play but no final report was published. However, let's go back to the context. The Forum was devised as an interim structure to provide a platform for engagement ahead of full-blown negotiations. To a certain extent the Forum was a staging post, and only that. To that extent, it was more about the process than the outcome, and in that respect the fact that it did not produce a final report was not a huge issue; in effect it had served its purpose.

But if the report had come out what would it have achieved? Would it have created leverage, come the full negotiations?

I think it would possibly have laid the ground a bit more and it was preparing for that. Perhaps, too, it would have helped lock Sinn Fein more into an irrevocable commitment to exclusively peaceful means. But that was not to be, and, as I say, broadly speaking it served its purpose.

Did Sinn Fein have problems with the concept of consent?

Theologically it was a contradiction of their long-standing position. In their canon they did not recognise partition and a united Ireland was the unfettered right of the people of the whole island of Ireland. Giving Northern Ireland or the unionists the right to withhold their consent – and therefore hold a veto – was a breach of that theology, and that was a real concern. If you introduce the principle of consent into the equation where a million people in Northern Ireland regard themselves as British, and basically the principle of consent says you can't change the constitutional status of Northern Ireland without the consent of the majority in Northern Ireland, then there were fundamental contradictions at play for them.

So how did you discuss that or try to get around it?

That was a very serious issue, and if Canary Wharf had not intervened I'm not sure we would have got a full agreement on that. Effectively, Sinn Fein ultimately signed up for the principle of consent by acquiescing to the Good Friday Agreement and are now implementing it. But by February 1996, my sense is they were not yet ready to make that leap.

What about self-determination? Did they have the same problem with that?

Yes, they are effectively part of the same thing. The theological compromise of Good Friday was that self-determination should be defined by the people of Ireland, but semi-colon, not full stop; that right to self-determination is qualified by the requirement of the consent of a majority in Northern Ireland, so that was the trade-off. The frame of self-determination overall is the island of Ireland, but it will be executed through the portal of the consent of a majority of people in Northern Ireland. That was how that constitutional circle was squared in the Good Friday Agreement.

Sinn Fein were involved in serious discussions in the Forum and then you had Canary Wharf. One would assume that those involved in the Forum could not have known this was coming, because if so, what would have been the point? And secondly, even after Canary Wharf, when the Forum stopped, why did it not continue but with Sinn Fein out of it?

Those are reasonable questions. In relation to the first bit, I don't know the answer to that. There was a critical minimum of people who had to be brought along in any given scenario, but from what I could see – but don't know for sure – some of that critical minimum went beyond Adams' and McGuinness' influence. Our sense was that there were people in the shadows behind. So there was the front line of people who were the negotiators and then there were those behind, and this is what I mean by the grey zone, the twilight zone, which was there then and which had to be moved beyond. But then again, maybe that was all tactical – we just didn't know for sure. Canary Wharf was a classic twilight-zone moment because you had these people supposedly involved in good-faith negotiations in Dublin Castle about exclusively peaceful means, whilst others from their movement were planning the old ways. Whatever the reality behind the scenes, it was all pretty shocking and very depressing at the time. And, of course, there was the personal tragedy of more lives lost.

What did the SDLP and the others say? Were they in agreement that the Forum should stop, or did they want to carry on?

I think nobody could quite come up with the answer to that one. It was a difficult question and, as I say, frankly we were all in shock.

It indicates though that the Forum was really for Sinn Fein?

That's a fair point. I think a better way of looking at it was that the thinking behind establishing the Forum was that what was needed now was a comprehensive approach that involved the widest spread of views, and that if you could not have that, better to pause. In reality, constitutional nationalist Ireland had already settled these questions for itself. The other parties didn't need a Forum to come to an outcome that they had already reached themselves. You could say the purpose of having the Forum was to try and bring Sinn Fein into that wider consensus. There was no way that constitutional nationalist Ireland was going to move away from its view that peaceful, democratic politics, with consent at the heart of it, was the only way forward. The key question was whether Sinn Fein could reach an accommodation with that reality.

The SDLP described the Forum as 'an opportunity for the analysis of problems', but in your view was it about clarification rather than giving anything? Did Sinn Fein make any significant gestures in the Forum, or were they just there to see what others were up to?

It all comes back to whether you accept the bona fides of Sinn Fein as being on a journey. Now if you accept the bona fides that there was a view amongst the leadership at least to accept a need to evolve forward, because the conditions exist in Ireland to enable that, then one had to explore that. Everybody was agreed that this had to be happening in the context of a possible and comprehensive new political settlement. And it's back to the old one of can you achieve maximalist goals on your own, and if not what are you going to do? Do you just keep fighting on in the belief that some day it will happen, or do you start to say there has to be another way and we need to start building alliances? But the moment you decide to build alliances is the moment you have to reach out to others, and the moment you reach out to others you have to take on board what they want, and the moment you take on board what they want you have to start accepting some of their premises. Sinn Fein were starting to say things like 'We need to be on the ground. That, of course, for us the national question is the primary issue, but we also need to be on the ground in communities around the country, dealing with the issues that are of concern to people in their daily lives, even if those do not have anything to do with the national question.' That was a shift towards ending isolation and beginning to make themselves more relevant in a broader political sense, and that meant listening to other perspectives and engaging in wider topics beyond the national question. All those factors and considerations were in play.

The challenge for them was attaching an ideological consistency to this shift, then?

Yes, and as you begin to engage more fully and comprehensively in that kind of a process with other stakeholders that is the internal argument, how to marry the old with the new.

Were the unionists outside the Forum trying to denigrate it?

The unionist position, I think, was indifference. They did not regard the Forum process as relevant to them. They were not yet in negotiating mode themselves, and that would come a couple of years later.

But if you have that position and move you look weaker for it?

Well, that is always the conundrum isn't it? What has interested me is how resolute unionism has been over the years in setting its face against any attempt to put an intellectual rationale on the table and reach out in an express way to nationalists and Catholics. That has always puzzled me. Because, to be honest, I do believe that in the Irish historical context an intellectual rationale can be made for unionism – but it just didn't seem to be a road any unionist leader wished to go down. That started to change somewhat with David Trimble, and was, surprisingly, carried on later by Ian Paisley, and by Peter Robinson, Mike Nesbitt and now Arlene Foster. That is an interesting and, in my view, positive evolution that has taken place inside unionism over the last twenty years.

One wonders if the Forum exerted a degree of leverage on unionists that they did not want to admit because how could they ignore it?

To be honest, I am not sure in late 1994 and into 1995 unionists were paying that much attention to the Forum, other than some perhaps privately noting what Sinn Fein were 'up to'. Don't forget that at that point the Ulster Unionist Party was having an internal process of its own, as the tenure of James Molyneaux as leader was coming to an end, with David Trimble taking over in 1995. That was to have a profound impact in its own right in due course.

By the time the Forum collapsed, and from the moment it started, where had Sinn Fein got to in your view?

It was about sixteen to seventeen months, and what they did was advance themselves very significantly in terms of what engagement in a political process entailed. That's what the Forum brought them.

That Forum has come and gone in the literature, but what you seem to be saying is that this performed an important role?

I suppose, as somebody involved directly in it, I'm a bit biased, but I do hope that over time history will judge it as a place and space which enabled important evolutions to happen, which were needed and significant in their own way. Looking back on it, I think you could say it served as a kind of way station between the ending of the main paramilitary campaigns (the loyalist ceasefires followed in October 1994) and the start of formal, comprehensive negotiations towards a peace settlement. It was an invaluable preparing ground for full-on negotiations later. And don't forget it wasn't just about Sinn Fein. Apart from the Northern parties, it also served to bring the Southern political parties into the political process in a more active way as parties also. Up to that point, Southern political parties tended to be most actively engaged in the Northern process when they were in government in Dublin themselves, and other than in the previous Forum in 1983 to 1984, tended not to have a sustained involvement in the Northern question on an ongoing basis, qua parties. Also, I think relationships began to be formed at political level which were useful in the full-blown negotiations which started a few years later. From our perspective as officials, we were also learning how all of this worked. That is, how to deal with people who had been involved in armed struggle and who now had to be treated with respect on the basis of their democratic mandate.

What did you take from that process?

As I mentioned earlier, there were three of us at an official level driving it at the outset. There was Wally Kirwan from the Taoiseach's Office, who was the Secretary, and I was the Deputy Secretary and Rory Montgomery (later Ambassador in Paris and the EU) was the Assistant Secretary. We did all the prep work on behalf of the Government in terms of figuring out the process, the structures, the substance, the papers etc., but we also learned about sidebar negotiations, that is, developing texts for compromises, advancing this or that, taking another way of looking at things. It was a great dry run for us too in relation to what happened down the road. It was especially valuable in terms of developing our skills as drafters. Before you put a piece of paper on the table everything is possible, but the moment you put a draft down everything narrows in, and so getting that first draft down and as right as possible in terms of where agreement might lie was very important. Dermot Gallagher was a tremendous teacher and mentor to us all in this regard. I should also mention that there were a number of other colleagues involved in the Secretariat and they did a great job, such as Anne McGuinness, Pat Nolan, and our irrepressible Press Officer was Dan Mulhall, who subsequently went on to become Ireland's distinguished Ambassador to Berlin, London and now Washington. He did very important work getting the work of the Forum out to a wider audience.

On the informal, did the Irish put a lot of value on the lunch, the dinner and the social context?

Very much so. When we finished the sessions every Friday with the Forum for Peace and Reconciliation we had drinks and some food to end the day. We started in the morning with a bit of hospitality when members arrived, then we had the meetings and then we would do a round-table lunch with tables of ten. As I said earlier, that turned out in design terms to be very valuable because everyone could be included in a conversation. Ten is big enough to hide a bit but small enough so that everyone can hear everyone else. What happened was that for a while people would just be sitting with their own people, but gradually they began to break up so things could start to take place over the lunch, then back into more meetings and then finish with drinks at four o'clock. In terms of all of that together, I think it was all very helpful in ensuring the best possible outcomes.

How many people were in the Forum at any one time?

From seventy up to maybe a hundred.

How did republicans traverse ideals of rigid principle and this new world of compromise and movement? How did they manage the shift from being puritanical to being pragmatic?

The puritanical approach went with ending isolation. You can keep the purity of your own position if you don't have to engage with anybody, because then there is no challenge to it at all and it's very simple: you articulate it and you re-articulate it. However, once you decide you are going to have to build alliances and engage with others, then that means you are building a journey of not defining everything on your own terms. If engaging with others and building the confidence of others is part of your strategy, that means you have to understand where others are coming from as well, and you have to build confidence in the others that you are serious about engaging with them. Here this included the Hume–Adams dialogue, with the famous phrase 'pan-nationalism', which for Sinn Fein started with the SDLP, then included the Irish Government and then included Irish-America. They were the three constituent pieces of it. Once you start engaging with others, then this is where managing the ambiguities can get very difficult, because another principle of the Adams leadership was ensuring there was no split. One of the hallmarks of republicanism historically was splits, and it seemed to me that one of the key principles of the Adams leadership was we shall not split, not significantly in any case, so bringing people along was crucial, and the problem of making progress on these things, but not losing significant people, was a priority. That was the juggle that was going on all the time, and you could see it being played out every step of the way.

So that line between managing change and keeping the cohort together came from constant, persistent dialogue up and down?

It was clearly a hallmark, and you can see there were constant debates. Whatever value judgement you may use there is no question Sinn Fein were working very hard on the new journey, so therefore everything was a matter of debate and everything was moved back and forth. If your policy is to end the isolation of republicanism and to create alliances then you need to be winning the confidence of others who are adversaries, who completely disagree with you in terms of the use of violence, and you do that by engaging with them, which is a constant tension. In the late 1980s the Sinn Fein political struggle continued, but so did the armed struggle, so it was two things, a cutting edge which differentiates you in one way and keeps you driving forward with a political constituency, but, on the other side, it's a ceiling in terms of the level of support you can win, and there were certain constituencies who would never vote for Sinn Fein as long as Provisional IRA violence was in place. That was the dilemma they were managing as they grew politically through the 1980s.

Presumably the serious moral dilemma was pushing on with violence for the sake of it or turning it off in order to develop the political project and then the timing of when you do that. This has been described as a 'crablike process' where the speed of change was dictated by the internal dynamics and tensions of the republican movement. What do you think?

I think that would have been dictated by what they saw. Of course, this is why the constant theological debate was going on externally also about whether they were really changing or whether it was all tactical. And nobody on the outside could judge for sure precisely what was going on in the republican movement in those years. What seemed pretty clear, though, was that the Adams leadership was seeking to nudge the movement continually in the direction of peaceful politics, and on the basis that it would not be possible to sustain a serious political party while still attached to violence. But, as I say, there was another principle which related to the design process of this, and that was avoiding a split. Given the historical adherence of the movement to physical force, those were frequently contradictory impulses, but that was what Adams' leadership had to manage.

Creativity is a word not often associated with politics but was there considerable creativity in play here?

In situations of deep conflict, characterised by polarisation and huge suspicion, finding a way to a comprehensive accommodation is highly complex, clearly. In absolute terms, the contradictions are such that agreement seems impossible. Finding an outcome that everybody can live with (as distinct from being happy with) requires a degree of flexibility, nuancing and creativity. Sometimes those words can have a pejorative connotation and imply a betrayal of principles etc. but, in my experience, you will not end conflict if the parties are not prepared to engage on that basis. At the same time, it's about getting the balance right between principle and pragmatism, and that is a difficult outcome to achieve. But that is what was in play throughout this period – trying to come up with accommodations that had sufficient flexibility to allow everybody to live with them, while at the same time respecting what people regarded as their red lines. What is the construct in that particular situation? Let me sketch one example of that kind of complexity. When we were trying in early 1999 to finalise an agreement between the two Governments and the parties on the detail of the cross-border bodies pointed to in the Good Friday Agreement, an issue that arose was whether or not a 'sunset clause' would apply to the bodies. It was understood (though not agreed) that the British Government had the technical power if it so wished to suspend the Executive and Assembly, and the Ulster Unionist were seeking to ensure that in that event the cross-border bodies could be suspended also. The Irish Government and the nationalist parties were not agreeable to that.

A compromise needed to be found. In the end, we were able to come up with language which referred back to the text of the Good Friday Agreement itself which spoke about the interdependent nature of all of the institutions, that the success of one depended on the success of the others, and by putting that into the text of the Agreement on the cross-border bodies this was sufficient for everybody to show the intention involved, even though it was not actually called a sunset clause. In other words, this was an outcome everybody could live with.

Were you surprised by the way some people reacted to bits of text that you thought were not going to be a problem and ended up being a problem? Could you predict problems?

Mostly that's what you are trying to do all the time. Later on, in our work in the North–South Secretariat in Armagh (implementing the North–South elements of the Good Friday Agreement), I introduced the 'principle of no surprises'. My point was that everything we were doing was full of complexities and our job was to manage that complexity. Making no surprises a principle was a practical tool in terms of that task of managing complexity. It was not possible to get things done in a straight line.

The jigsaw is an interesting comparison to straight lines. When one thinks conceptually that way it suggests that one needs to go around problems rather than through them and not lose sight of the overall picture. Is that so?

That's right. One of the images that I like is of a dashboard with different screens, and one of them always has to be the big picture, always on and the one thing that one should never lose sight of.

Do you believe in turning points, or moments of ripeness, in a process like this?

It's a combination, and there is an evolution going on. That's the mystery of it too. One dramatic moment in time, which was a turning moment, was at 4.30pm on Good Friday afternoon when for about four hours the process had stalled and the Ulster Unionist had had profound second thoughts about the totality of what they were being asked to do in the text of the Agreement. The negotiations had been conducted under one roof in Castle Buildings and now David Trimble was shuttling up and down two floors of the building to Tony Blair's office to try to find some means by which he could still proceed. In the meantime, all the other delegations were sitting in their offices waiting. The Irish Government was not involved. Only Tony Blair and a couple of others, and that was when he gave the handwritten note to David Trimble setting out what would happen in six months if decommissioning did not happen. It was a unilateral sidebar letter that he took it upon himself to write as a means of breaking the logjam. It was controversial of course, but David Trimble regarded it as being sufficient and he contacted George Mitchell and indicated he was ready to sign up to the Agreement. A number of members of his delegation refused to follow him and left the building. It was a pivotal moment, for sure. But mostly things evolved on a slow, inch-by-inch basis.

You hear the expression 'bottom line', but how can this be known unless people walk away?

Bottom lines are difficult things when the stakes are so high; everybody is seeking an outcome and everybody understands the price of failure. It's back to what I said earlier about always seeking that intersection point between pragmatism and principle. A delicate balancing act you have to achieve every day of the negotiations, especially at the end. The more you invest into a process like this the higher the number of floors you go up, as it were. So you might be on floor fifteen and hit an impasse. What do you do? Well the choice is to keep going or collapse everything – in other words, the jump-off is fifteen floors. So the higher you go the harder it is to walk away. Every day you stay involved you are investing more in the outcome and the jump that is involved in failing gets bigger. That is why I use the metaphor of floors. Every month you stay engaged with this process another floor is reached, which makes jumping harder and harder. The sense that prevails is 'we have come this far, and overcome all obstacles so far, we have to find a way to solve this one now too'. That is part of the complexity of a lengthy negotiation process. And the same time, everybody has to have a bottom line and know they can walk away if they have to.

To what extent was the peace process about phases?

Unquestionably it was about phases. In personal terms, when Dermot Gallagher called me back into the team in October 1997 it was clear that a new phase was beginning. The ceasefire had been restored, Sinn Fein had just joined the talks a few weeks before and there was a real ramp-up happening in Belfast, because now you finally had all the key players at that point around the table and this was a process that had been going for fifteen months up to then but had not really moved forward. Look at the sequence. In the summer of 1996 George Mitchell had been appointed as the talks Co-ordinator but the Provisional IRA ceasefire had broken down, so they were back in the campaign at this stage and there was little traction in terms of negotiating influence. There was an attempt to keep the process going but Mitchell was trying to deal with the decommissioning issue and had established the Mitchell Principles around that time. Then in the spring and summer of 1997 significant political change happened. Tony Blair became Prime Minister in London with a big majority and suddenly the British Government had freedom to move on Northern Ireland. Bertie Ahern became Taoiseach in Dublin and he and Tony Blair quickly established together that they both wanted to use the early stages of their tenure to have a real go at getting full-blown negotiations going. By the way, that is no criticism of their predecessors, John Major and John Bruton and Dick Spring, who all put a big effort into trying to make progress on the North. But the political wind was against them. Now, in the summer of 1997, that wind changed direction and was suddenly behind the process. A new Provisional IRA ceasefire was called in July, and by September the George Mitchell-led talks in Belfast took on a new urgency and momentum. These led to an agreement on the make-up and terms of the negotiations, as a result of which a comprehensive framework was agreed by which Sinn Fein would join the talks, and as a result of that a number of the unionist parties withdrew, but crucially the Ulster Unionist Party (then the largest unionist party) and a number of the loyalist parties stayed in. From that moment it was game on.

How did the British engage with such things in comparison to the Irish? What was your observation about how the Irish went about their business compared to the British?

To be honest I wouldn't want to make too much of the difference. That might sound a bit boring, but in truth it was a case for all of us of getting on and making the best of things. We saw the British side, certainly at official levels, as being like ourselves – backroom people whose job was to get on and make things happen based on political direction. Of course, yes, there were differences in nuance and style between the two services. And certainly there is something in the cliché about British expertise in order and structure. But there was a real sense also that we were all in this together and neither side could achieve a good outcome without the understanding and support of the other. In my first posting in Bonn I learned the word 'calculability' – in German that word became associated with managing détente between East and West Germany, that relations were about being calculable, being predictable. In other words, if East Germany said A and West Germany understands what A means and that it is not X, Y or Z, then that is calculability. The British and Irish sides were very much in the mode of calculability at this point. That didn't mean that there weren't significant differences of perspective between us. There were, but both sides knew that we needed to understand and get through those differences.

Was it the British who tended to get the pen on the paper first?

Well, let's say both sides understood each other in terms of the importance of the early drafts. But we also knew there was no point in trying to pull a fast one because what we were involved with was a marathon, not a sprint. The British and Irish sides would spend quite a bit of time at the start of each issue getting the drafting worked out, because each side knew whatever went down on paper had to be something that everybody could live with.

At a political level between the British and Irish was there a competition to put the first draft on the table?

Let's say both sides were good professionals and understood what was needed. Clearly our side wanted a draft that best reflected how we saw things and what was likely to achieve agreement. Our British colleagues were no different. But, to repeat, we also knew there was no point in slapping down a maximalist position which had no chance of securing the agreement of the British side or the unionist parties. The task was to try to capture on paper something that contained what we needed but was constructed in such a way as to accommodate the realities of all sides. Back to that phrase of 'something everybody could live with'.

As the lead Department of Foreign Affairs official in the talks, Dermot Gallagher played a pivotal role in the negotiation of the Good Friday Agreement. He, Paddy Teahon, Secretary General at the Department of the Taoiseach, and Tim Dalton, Secretary General at the Department of Justice, formed the core leadership group at senior official level, supporting the Government led by Bertie Ahern and his central ministers involved, David Andrews, John O'Donoghue and Liz O'Donnell, with Attorney-General David Byrne and Special Adviser Martin Mansergh the other key leadership players at political level. I formed part of a senior officials group at the next level supporting the above, but I think we were all agreed on the central contribution of Dermot Gallagher. In personal terms, he was my boss on and off from 1987 till the close of my public service career in 2010 and I can never thank him enough for his inspiration, encouragement and mentorship. I mention him particularly in this interview because he had a deep understanding of the power of words and the importance of a good (and early!) draft and I was one of a team of people involved in the construction of those drafts. The cause of peace in Ireland owes a great debt of gratitude to Dermot Gallagher.

If you have too many words presumably you get problems, and if you don't have enough you get problems as well. Can you summarise this dilemma by saying something about how you saw the British interpretation of words compared to the Irish?

Culturally the British approach is systematic and well structured. The Irish approach probably places more emphasis on qualities like flexibility.

You talk about the British concern with structure and process, but what was the Irish concern?

The Irish position, and I am caricaturing this a bit here, was that during all of this there was a focus on trying to manage the irreconcilable positions involved that were really in logical terms incompatible, so to be frank that was the scale of the task from the off. If we were trying to design a journey of seeking agreement the question was, where do you go? Or, more specifically, what can people live with? That became the key. It's not so much what people agree on but what people can live with, so you were seeking to find whether there were pieces of ground on which people could stand, and that was a really important piece of the journey. I think however much reluctance everybody had we were able to move on that basis. I suppose in any document, in any process, you had things which people were happy with, and then stuff where people disagree, so you are moving from disagreeing onto a space which they could cope with. This may not be a preferred position or preferred description of the situation, but being able to live with this process meant a certain kind of acquiescence. And people will only acquiesce if, despite the fundamentally irreconcilables, they recognise that they have to find some movement towards establishing an accommodation. That was the famous Humespeak on 'accommodating difference', so we had to keep reminding ourselves of that and keep asking the question whether there was some kind of way in which the position of others could legitimately be accommodated, even though such a position might be a fundamental contradiction to others.

With regards to text, how much attention or contention did you bring to the exact wording, compared to the British?

I think it is important to reiterate here that while the British side and ourselves had our own separate interests and constituencies, we operated throughout on a collegiate basis, recognising that a successful outcome could only be achieved by the closest working together between us. At a personal level, relationships were good and a considerable degree of trust was built up over the period. That was the big picture in terms of how we approached particular tasks such as drafting etc. Yes, getting the documents right was hugely complex every step of the way, where we had the negotiation and then the words. But, in the end, a document had to stand and had to be at minimum lived with, so there had to be enough acquiescence by all sides to achieve a 'critical minimum' of support. I don't say the majority but a critical minimum on both sides.

Where is this critical minimum and who are we talking about?

It's probably a combination of quantum and quality of particular people at any point. A critical minimum is not five per cent, but it probably isn't fifty-three per cent either. It might be forty-six per cent, so you have to have a certain quantum in numbers and then you have to be certain that those people are prepared to move. For conflicts that involve two sides, change happens or the deal gets done when you move from the prevailing status quo to a position where both sides consider that their interests are best served by a deal now rather than sticking with that status quo. That is the moment.

Is that the same as sufficient consensus?

It's a variation of it. What I am trying to get across here is that it isn't just a straight, simple-majority, win-lose idea. It is more subtle and complex than that, and it's about judgement calls on where interests lie. The shift today for my self-interest might be yes, my self-interest is better served by the risk of a deal rather than staying with the status quo, and the most clear-cut example of where that condition was not met is Camp David 2000 with Yasser Arafat when, in the final days of Bill Clinton's presidency, huge pressure was put on to get a comprehensive deal. Oslo had come apart and now there was this chance to put it all together again so Bill Clinton could complete his presidency as the man who copper-fastened peace in the Middle East, and it was within touching distance. But, in the end, Yasser Arafat came to the view (as he was entitled to) that the status quo was a better place for him and the Palestinian people than the risk of the deal, and so he walked away. There is an example of where that condition was not met.

The preamble of a document like the Good Friday Agreement, the foreword, is often about setting out the mood, tone and spirit. Why?

Because we always knew this was not a transactional moment or some kind of technical, contractual document but a potentially profound turning point in the history of these two islands and between the peoples of these two islands and traditions. In that sense, it was a sacred moment that needed to be acknowledged.

So was there a religious ethos about that preamble as well?

In particular, we felt it important at this turning-point moment to give voice to the human cost of the conflict that we were seeking to bring an end to. We were taking a moment to remember that and to understand that is partly why we were there. So it was important to acknowledge the deep and terrible sacrifice of all the victims and their families and to state that this Agreement was being reached in order to stop this happening again.

Did the British have a role in the preamble, or was it written by the Irish?

I think it was something we felt strongly should be there, but the British side were also comfortable with the concept too. The power of something like this is in the diversity. It's like an intricate series of knots that together create a solid structure. British pragmatism was focussed more on getting on with it. But they saw the value of an opening shaping statement. As I just mentioned, I would say between the British and ourselves at an official level, and at that stage, there was solid trust which had been built between both, as well as a firm understanding of each other's role. They worked closely to ensure that the unionists could live with what was emerging and we sought to do the same on the nationalist side. It was simply a pragmatic division of labour based on who was best placed in any given moment to ensure we kept moving forward towards the agreed desired outcome.

When the British under John Major insisted on the word 'permanent' for the Provisional IRA ceasefire what was the Irish reaction to that demand?

We're back to John Dunlop's famous observation about Protestants reading the lines and Catholics reading between the lines. But let us not forget that this dispute was over a piece of land. Now if part of the settlement means me saying I will never ever bid for that bit of land ever again, permanently, you have a problem. Most would respond by saying I'm not doing that and why introduce such a condition now anyway? For us it felt like an unnecessary additional complexity was being added to the equation, but, in fairness, at another level it was simply one further demonstration of how far apart people were and how different people saw the same situation through such radically different lenses.

Do you remember other occasions when that happened too?

That sort of problem was coming up on a pretty regular basis. Everywhere there were differences of view, for example, such as with suspension. The Irish response was not to do it, and the phone was put down in anger over that. It was seen by us as a very crude instrument. Here's this intricate situation of building a process where one side is saying if we believe it necessary we can just pull the lever unilaterally. We were saying no way, and then they did just that.

What happened when they did?

Well, it was a tough moment. We understood in pragmatic, intellectual terms why they were doing it, but we thought it was a terrible mistake. We also knew we would just have to come back again and work on that, which is what we did. There was also concern that maybe here we had something which did not have a solution and that because of that we might have to walk away.

Were you thinking about just solving each immediate problem, or were you thinking about how all problems locked into other areas? Were you always thinking strategically, in other words?

Of course, you were always thinking about it like a bank of screens, or a dashboard as I mentioned earlier. One screen is the big picture, always on and pulsing, but that is alongside individual screens, each dealing with particular issues. But those individual screens had to be made sense of in the context of the bigger picture that is feeding everything. So you have to multiplex all the time.

Did you have to take risks?

Of course.

Did you see those risks best dealt with by using particular techniques of presentation?

There wasn't always time for it to be as logical and choreographed as that. It was more often a case of quick decisions about how best to act now to prevent everything from falling apart. This often involved sidebars with one or other of the parties to establish precisely where they stood following the development and what they could or could not live with in terms of a counter step. If they gave you something, then you became more of a persuader to your own side. Because you would never get someone to say in clear, categorical terms I will agree that, generally it was a matter of getting people to agree through tweaking certain things and making a judgement call about how far they could go. Then you had to go back and sell the tweak to your own side, and to the British as well.

You seem to have seen the process as a design exercise where nothing was agreed until everything was agreed?

I think what was agreed between all sides is that there is a moment and an opportunity here to do something and that moment will pass and if it passes without agreement, the consequences could be terrible, people could die again. So we, who happened to be the key people in terms of the holders of responsibility right now at that moment (and I put it no stronger than that for all of us), had an obligation to take this moment to its ultimate – to stretch in every way we could to salvage the situation and at the minimum to keep it from falling apart. Because history showed that when things fall apart it can take a long, long time to put them back together again. We thought back to our predecessors negotiating the Sunningdale Agreement. There were high hopes for that at the time back of 1973 and 1974 – but by May 1974 it had all come apart and it took nearly a quarter of a century to put a comprehensive process together again. So the stakes were very high and we all knew it. That was the overall picture and the pulse of the reality. But, just to remind again, at that point nobody knew precisely what success looked like, since sustained success had never been achieved before (and Sunningdale, though a noble effort, ultimately failed). So there was a fair degree of simply keeping at it with a kind of dogged determination not to fall back into the past. Because we *did* know what that looked like and nobody wanted to go back there. I suppose one analogy might be we had a map (the desired destination we were seeking to reach) but no compass. So you knew where you wanted to go but you did not really know for sure at the time if you could actually get there or if you were on the right pathway. It was determination not to go back, and not to pass up the opportunity we all knew now existed, that really kept us all going. Now from this remove, almost twenty years later, it all looks a bit clearer, and thankfully it turns out we were broadly heading in the right direction. But I can assure you, at the time it was all a lot foggier.

One reads in conflict resolution theory that for a peace process to succeed there must be a moment of ripeness. Were there moments during the process that were not ripe and moments that were riper than others?

Yes, of course. I call it the 'eleventh-hour moment'. Where there is a dispute of any kind going that is seen in terms of an opportunity at the eleventh hour. In our case, one dimension of that eleventh-hour syndrome was the view that Sinn Fein could not keep going on with one leg in and one leg out of the process, and particularly since this was still the case some three years after the ceasefire. With his introduction of a deadline by which negotiations must close, George Mitchell turned the situation at that point into an eleventh-hour moment. That this dispute was only going to get resolved at the eleventh hour, and the eleventh hour was then.

Were Sinn Fein better at making this happen than the unionists?

I'm not sure it is helpful to see it as a kind of contest of who was up and who was down, who was good at this and who was less good. The truth is, everybody (the Governments, the parties, George Mitchell) was in a great unknown, where in the words of *Star Trek* nobody had gone before. So nobody knew for sure how this was going to work, whether it was going to work and what needed to be done to get agreement. Everybody knew what their own positions were. But that was the easy part and nobody had any difficulty going to microphones to express that. Again and again! But the real question was how are you going to convince the other side, who have a completely different view, and, more crucially, what are you prepared to compromise on regarding your position in order to get agreement? In those stakes everybody was struggling – the Governments, Sinn Fein, the unionists, the SDLP, the Alliance, the lot. Because nobody knew in advance where agreement really lay, because agreement had never been reached before, so the journey was about finding a way to that complex, magic point that everyone could live with. In terms of Sinn Fein, they were relatively new to all of this so they would have been focussed on certain things that they needed themselves and that were important to their own constituency. They knew their own issues well and they concentrated on those. But I don't think it would be correct to be framing this as a case of some folks within the process knowing precisely where it was going and others not. It just wasn't like that.

And Sinn Fein knew the power of symbolism too?

They did.

They knew the importance of having Joe Cahill be seen to enter the US, or for Gerry Adams to be seen with Albert Reynolds and John Hume in Dublin?

Yes, but they also knew they were only one player in a big equation. On the Thursday night before Good Friday they were feeling very excluded from things and were sitting in their room down the corridor because a big part of the work on the Thursday evening was between the SDLP and the Ulster Unionists working on Strand One. So for a number of hours they were feeling completely outside what was happening and they were unhappy with that. By midnight they were ringing the White House saying they were getting ready to walk, and then the White House started ringing the two Governments. So after the Strand One stuff got resolved and we had a broad agreement reached by 1.00am, the focus shifted to Sinn Fein issues.

Would it be fair to say that they were too ideological and did not focus on the detail enough?

Everything is relative, so if they don't get agreement on their core issues then there is no other stuff to be dealt with.

Why did unionists tend to depict a success as a failure?

This is to do with the positions of nationalism and unionism in Northern Ireland being fundamentally different from each other. In very simplistic terms, unionism held the ground and nationalism didn't. If you are going to move towards sharing, towards equality, then in a strict mathematical definition of things unionism has to lose. If I have one hundred per cent of the chips and you have none and we are going to move towards a co-equal sharing, then I have to lose fifty chips. A lot of unionists believe that they were forced into that position by the politics of the previous half century, and that was the reality of Northern Ireland during the Stormont years of 1922 to 1972. In that analysis, it wasn't personal, but rather just the way things were, and the only way that reality could be retained is by holding against it. As I say, if I have a hundred chips and you have none and we need to reach a point where we have fifty, or even sixty–forty each, then I lose.

Is this to do with Catholicism and the journey and where ambiguities are fine as long as you are going in the right direction?

I mentioned already that Reverend John Dunlop has said that the Protestant reads the lines and the Catholic reads between the lines. Yes, some of this is cultural, even religious. In one reading of things it is about straight lines, mortal sin, heaven–hell, black–white, that is a way of looking at the world. It is clarity and certainty. If you commit a sin, a mortal sin, and you die now, you go to hell. There's hell and there's heaven. There's sin and there's virtue, there's right and there's wrong, there's black, there's white, there's night and there's day. That is a particular way of living that has tended to be associated with a white Protestant view of the world – you see examples of it, for instance, in America and the Christian Right.

For someone who reads between the lines, what are they reading?

They are trying to find out whether there is a way of working with language in a way that gives you enough of what you need and gives me enough of what I need without either of us sacrificing on fundamentals. It's as simple as that.

That is similar to the nothing is agreed until everything is agreed approach?

It is.

Is there any substance to the suggestion that unionists and Protestants are of the word, while republicans and nationalists are more about frameworks and process?

These are complex things and it is important not to over-simplify. At the same time, a cliché usually has some ring of truth to it. I suppose a lot of the Catholic experience over many decades would have basically been about being a colonised people, so Catholicism was tied up with living in a kind of subjugated state where you have to make your way through your wits and advance yourself through all means possible. There's an old Irish proverb, 'The thing that is small had better be smart', so if your lot in life, in whatever context, is to be small, then you need to be smart. I think that is a reality that was there historically, whereas if you are the dominant you don't have to worry about that kind of thing and you can go about things in straight lines. Fundamentalism is about a world of absolutes and certainties and clarities that divide neatly into lines, so there is no need for greys if that is your political and religious philosophy in terms of how you live life. Whereas, if you are more receptive to terms like complexity and ambiguity, ambivalence and greyness as a means of navigation, then that speaks to a different view of the world.

Did those different ways of looking at things affect the relationship between the Ulster Unionists and Sinn Fein? Did the Ulster Unionists become so fixed on the Provisional IRA that it formed their negotiating strategy?

I wouldn't see it in those terms. That was their view of history, the world they had experienced, so when they look across the table their fears are right in front of them and that history as they see it is immediate and confrontational. Also, as a fairly besieged community, they had to be strong in their own interests and outlooks. That, for their own survival, they had to be hard, strong and assured.

Is it the case that unionists had a tendency to negotiate right 'down to the wire' and that the most effective moment for them was therefore right at the end, what you call the eleventh hour?

In fairness we need to look back to history and context where unionism effectively just 'was' and Northern Ireland, in political terms, was unionism. If you see yourselves in charge, then why negotiate? If unionists run this place, and that's the way it has been historically, then where is the need for negotiation? You sell yourself on the 'we will never relinquish on that', 'we will never surrender', and that is a non-negotiable position, so negotiation in fact equals surrender. Because of that there was an atmospheric inside unionism that even a propensity to consider negotiation was teetering close to surrender, so you don't prepare your people for anything. The record will show that there is very little evidence of unionist leaders preparing their people for change and compromise over the decades before 1998. There was no real appetite for preparing people because it was not in the psyche, and indeed if you try to do that then you are preparing to sell out. The problem they were up against was if they went out to talk to their people too early they were nothing other than a Lundy, because, just to remind what De Klerk said when he came to the Forum, in negotiations the most difficult discussions are not with your adversary across the table, but with your own people before and afterwards. That is because the moment you enter into that process you risk becoming – and indeed, soon enough, *have to* become – an advocate for your adversary. That is a huge insight. Remember, the idea of not negotiating was tied in to the purity of your position, and your big risk was that negotiating equated with 'talking to terrorists who murdered your own people'. That was a huge challenge, culturally and politically. Your adversary was effectively a terrorist. How could you take them seriously without betraying your own core principles and moral code? The moment you talk about preparing your people for compromise, you are effectively moving onto a slippery slope. Especially since, by definition, agreement has not yet been reached and you cannot even guarantee the outcome you are seeking to sell.

Which means for unionism there never was or could be success because you have already got it?

You have just nailed the really difficult paradigm for unionism. If you are a unionist in Northern Ireland, how, psychologically, can any move towards the nationalist position be anything but a fundamental dilution of your basic philosophy.

What core lessons and principles would you take from this process?

You are in a deep conflict and there is a fundamentally contested space going on. A peace deal will only happen when there is a critical minimum, and not a majority, on both sides who come to the view that their selfish best interests are better served in a deal rather than staying with the status quo. That is the test you can apply.

Principles cannot be applied rigidly like lumps of stone, though, can they?

No, but you have to operate in a very conscious mind-set of sensitivity. A sensitivity to the reality that others engaged in this process see the world in very different terms to you and simply articulating your own position is never going to advance agreement. As I said earlier, you are all the time scanning for shifts and adjustments, no matter how subtle, that can help move things forward, and then using those shifts and adjustments in a positive way with the other side. I appreciate that this all sounds very labyrinthine and complicated, and it is, but if it were simple all would have been resolved a long time ago. My experience is that when people say some aspect 'is very simple' it usually transpires that it is simple to them but anathema to someone else and, as I say, doesn't advance agreement. My response usually is 'What you have just said is a very clear enunciation of your own position, but the actuality is that position is not accepted by the other side; the question therefore is how do you propose to contribute to finding agreement with the other side on this issue?'

Clearly, you need to give people space, but how do you gauge when to apply pressure? How is that judgement made?

It was being made all the time. Remember, none of this ever goes onto automatic. The process is always on manual and you are operating that way all the time, for the reasons outlined. You never know the issues that might arise and where, and particularly when everything is on shifting ground, but you have to be able to react quickly and manage the situations that arise. So you are always going from the general to the particular and back up again, but understanding how they are completely in relationship with each other too.

Is it the case that the value of the three-stranded approach was that it pulled the areas together in a triangulation and that when you were not making progress in one area you could move to another and then go back?

They are not alternative tracks, though they are parallel. Each track had its own integrity, separate from the other, but what made them in design terms very smart is that they were a reflection of the totality of relationships.

So, if things are going wrong in one it is likely they are going wrong somewhere else?

What I am saying is no relationship was more important than the big picture. What's going on in Strand Three meant that what was going on in Strand Two couldn't be a counter to that. They were operating from the same big picture, which was to get on with it, make it happen and get people talking.

One of the elements of negotiation emphasised in key works on the subject is that positional bargaining is often counter-productive and you need to look at the interests of people rather than get worked up about positions. What is your view?

They are interrelated. I would describe it as the basic landscape of trust or no trust. What is the level of trust involved here? The position must be seen in relationship to that.

Was rhetoric an important part of the peace process?

It was a very important part at different moments and when people were speaking to their own audiences. I can remember David Trimble having a good line after an Ulster Unionist Council meeting in 1999 where his party had agreed to go into government on a particular basis worked out with George Mitchell. It was a trade-off between no guns, no government and the opposite of that is guns, government.

David Trimble then went to the Ulster Unionist Council and got agreement for the compromise which had been worked out, and people voted for it. So when he came out of that meeting he went to the press conference and said something like 'Okay Mr Adams, we've jumped, you follow'. That's rhetoric.

Was there any language that he would not tolerate because it was a step too far?

It was an understanding. But part of that understanding was I am not going to give unlimited rope on this. That I will jump now and we will both go into government because that is a moment-in-time thing that has to happen and I will do that, but it is on the understanding that in a very quick period of time movement will happen on decommissioning, and so steps would have to be agreed, starting with the appointment by the Provisional IRA of an interlocutor who would engage with the decommissioning process. That was step one, but, of course, even though step one does not mean a single gun is handed over, it's still a step that is a confidence-building measure. David Trimble was prepared to allow for a certain amount of rope on that, but not unlimited rope.

Did that ever come to light?

Well there was a basic understanding that everything was conditional and nothing was unconditional.

Did people over-read a situation because of their perceived fear of others, and did they make unfounded assumptions because of that fear?

You are always up against that possibility, but it was a space where everybody is contesting. Everyone has a different set of interests, so every day when you walked through the door and into the process you were in a contested space where each had their own interests to defend, and at the same time nobody wants the process to break down, and most certainly nobody wants to be seen as responsible for the process breaking down. In other words, we all knew we were on a journey towards a potential agreement in that period of 1997 to 1998, so everybody knew there was something building. The question was how could you best shape the outcome to protect yourself and get the best result you could, and if it was to go down how could you make sure you were not the one left holding the blame. They were factors in play every day.

A lot of the Irish officials talk about metaphors. Were they important?

Metaphors, like beauty, are in the eye of the beholder. A metaphor only has an impact if it is meaningful to the receiver as well. If you are trying to communicate you need to think of the audiences who are going to receive that communication. And you shift the emphasis accordingly while staying true to the overall objective.

Do you have any closing observations?

Yes, I would like to say something contextual to finish. I wish to reiterate clearly that my role over the years was as a civil servant supporting the work of the Government. While this interview has been about the particular role I personally played, I do want to make clear that the leadership in all we did was driven at political and ministerial level. Our task was to support ministers in the carrying out of their mandate. That may seem like a pedantic and defensive point at the end of a long interview, but it is an important piece of context to remind about again as we close. In other words, I had no locus in any of the above in my own right, only that conferred on me by virtue of being an official of the Irish Government, and I and my official-level colleagues were very conscious of this at all times and points – and if we ever gave a hint of forgetting it (and we didn't), Dermot Gallagher was there to remind us of the reality of things. The direction was set by the Taoiseach and his ministers, with advice from us, and then our task was to execute the policy agreed on any particular issue to the best extent we could. Of course, in the twists and turns of a very intense and tense process there were frequent times when one had to improvise and use one's own judgement, but you did so always within the compass of the policy framework set at political level. And the other point I would like to make (and it is related) is about the people operating at political level. I never forgot the reality that these were the people with the electoral mandate, not us the officials. They were the ones who ultimately would be held accountable to the people, and more specifically to their own electorate, at the ballot box, not us. I felt a strong sense of respect for the elected politicians across all the parties, nationalist and unionist, whom I could see were working very hard both to do the right thing, and at the same time get the best deal they could for their own side. So anything I have said in this interview should be seen through that prism. The political figures involved, both at leadership level and throughout their delegations, had a huge responsibility and there was a deep consciousness of that throughout. Our task as officials was to support them in the best way we could in the discharging of that responsibility. It is important for me in personal and professional terms that my comments here are set in that overall context.

8

The management of dialogue: an interview with Dermot Gallagher

Graham Spencer: *You were Ambassador in Washington from the mid-1980s. What were you doing then?*

Dermot Gallagher: From 1987 to 1991 I was in charge of Anglo-Irish Affairs, after which I was replaced by Sean O hUiginn in 1991, before we then switched in 1997. I became Ambassador in 1991 and in 1997 he went to Washington. I came back in September as Second Secretary in charge of Anglo-Irish Affairs. I was there for four years and then I became Secretary General in 2001 until I retired in 2009.

What involvement did you maintain in the peace process across those three very different roles?

From 1987 to 1991 I was very close when things began with Hume and I was a good friend of Father Alex Reid, but the talks broke down at that stage and then I went to Washington. I concentrated exclusively on two things: Northern Ireland and inward investment. Dick Spring was the Foreign Minister from 1993 to 1997, and he visited Washington about thirteen times and every time saw Clinton. Prime ministers and presidents could not see him, but every time Clinton saw Spring. If it wasn't a formal meeting he would be with the Chief of Staff, Deputy Chief of Staff or Counsel to the President and they would bring Clinton into the room to see him, and that was unique. When the ceasefire was announced I got Dick Spring to fly to where Clinton was on holiday, which I think was Martha's Vineyard, to thank him. Clinton never received anyone on holidays but, of course, he received Spring on that occasion. When I came back in 1997 we set up a small negotiating team in Foreign Affairs. Rory Montgomery, Tim O'Connor, Ray Bassett and Eamonn McKee were on it. In 1997 I took over for a year from Paddy Teahon as Secretary General for the

Taoiseach, and then the Secretary General position in Foreign Affairs became vacant and I moved back to that.

You constructed a speech for Haughey in 1990 where he moved from rejection of the Anglo-Irish Agreement to accepting it. Can you offer some background?

He made a speech in January 1990 and there was a whole series of parliamentary questions afterwards. The discussion went on but nobody could dissent from it, and I would have thought that the authors of the Anglo-Irish Agreement had this in mind anyway, because the Agreement speaks in several places about the impact of devolution and the change that will bring. My first meeting with Haughey would have been about September 1987. When Haughey became Taoiseach it was recommended that I be Assistant Secretary in charge of Anglo-Irish affairs. Haughey had opposed, very wrongly in my view, the Anglo-Irish Agreement when in opposition and I saw this as opportunistic because the Agreement, for the first time, gave Dublin formal influence on developments in Northern Ireland. The Agreement also talked about devolution being achieved. Haughey asked me for my views and I said in very strong forthright terms that the Agreement was of huge significance, that it gave us influence and that it should be operated fully and effectively until it was replaced or transcended by a future agreement which might be endorsed by the people North and South. He thought about it overnight and he came back the following afternoon and agreed. He said we will implement the Agreement fully and effectively, and the instructions he gave to the Minister for Foreign Affairs and the Minister for Justice were to implement it to the best of their ability until it was replaced and transcended by a further agreement. Then Haughey was interested in reaching out to all sides, and he knew I had particularly close contacts with the unionist community, which he encouraged. The unionists subsequently began to say interesting things in the House of Commons and Haughey began to say interesting things on his side. Meantime the Agreement was being implemented fully, and this led to the various echoes from Dublin and London to a statement which was hugely significant in January 1990. That statement basically said that if a new agreement can be reached by direct discussions and negotiations between all the parties involved the Irish Government would be prepared to contemplate a new and better structure or arrangement to transcend the existing one. Potentially, he was saying if it were possible to have a broader, more embracing agreement which would be endorsed by the Irish people North and South, then that would clearly be a goal. I had very good contacts with the unionists from my time in London, so I had a series of meetings with them and the ground was prepared for Haughey's statement in 1990.

Are such statements primarily to focus the Government or bait to draw others in?

It didn't emerge out of the blue, but reflected 'echoes' between Dublin and the unionists that at some stage we would need to envisage a transcending agreement which got everybody around the table. The unionists had been making speeches saying we have got to move forward and think in new terms and Dublin was responding to that. That speech was to enable the unionists to go further and to come in from the cold, but at the same time it was also talking about all sides being around the table, so it was clearly sending a message not just to the unionist community but to the broader nationalist and republican community too.

Is it the case that Haughey coined the term 'the totality of relationships'?

Yes, that was at an earlier period, following a meeting in Dublin Castle with Margaret Thatcher in December 1980.

How much did you have to convince Haughey of the need for a statement supporting the Anglo-Irish Agreement, and who drafted it?

It was drafted in the Department of Foreign Affairs and I drafted a significant part of it along with the Irish Ambassador in Washington, Ann Anderson.

And when you presented this text to Haughey did you have to change it, did he demand modifications?

It was almost the identical text. He went through it forensically.

Did you have to convince him of its merit?

No.

What about the potential contradiction that he could face where one minute he rejects the Anglo-Irish Agreement and then he accepts it?

That convincing was done in September 1987, and he made his position clear from taking office and early on. As I said to you, my first meeting with him was difficult, but he was testing me and then the following day said that the Anglo-Irish Agreement was going to be implemented fully.

Was this a foundational speech for the peace process in a way?

That might be putting it too far, but he said 'We need to put aside ancient quarrels and focus on contemporary realities.'

What was the British reaction to that?

I think they welcomed it. Clearly it was in the British interest as well to bring the unionists in from the cold and to have an all-embracing agreement, and I think they must have known we were working towards this anyway.

When did the peace process take on a formality and intensity?

I think it was in the period from the Downing Street Declaration that the intensive work began. There came a stage when both Governments needed to take absolute control of the situation and needed to trust one another. They needed to agree on certain principles and how to take those principles forward. That ran into trouble from time to time, particularly on decommissioning, where the British got themselves on a hook about where to place disposing of weapons in the sequence of events. But the agreed position was that the Governments realised that the situation in the North had become stalemated. The British were able to contain the situation but they weren't able to win. Sinn Fein and the IRA leadership realised that they were not going to win it either. They were getting older with the long war, and with no conceivable winners at the end, although they had the capacity, as they showed when the ceasefire broke down, to activate a team. The two Governments realised that they had to lead from the front, and that was set out to a very significant degree in the Downing Street Declaration. The key was bringing the extremes into the centre and actively into democratic politics. The consent principle was central. Once you establish principles then it became a question of putting in place, in a pragmatic way, a sequence that would deliver trust and confidence on all sides through those principles.

To what extent did being a businessman shape the negotiating style of Reynolds?

He told the Shinners to get lost when they spoke about a temporary ceasefire, and he understood the North very well. He travelled there a lot and had a lot of business contacts in the pet food business, and a close friend of his was a leading unionist who had shops across Northern Ireland. Albert was always focussed on how to achieve the most profitable outcome, and it was a good strategy. He liked Major and they were very similar in that neither had baggage. I think he found British officials too cautious initially, but then Major was constrained by the lack of a majority. Albert liked to be very open and he was taken aback when he discovered that the British had a back-channel and didn't tell him. Albert would have been frustrated with the pace of implementing an agreement, but sometimes agreements are more difficult to implement than negotiations.

Do you think the Downing Street Declaration set the foundations for the peace process?

It was hugely important in balancing and reconciling a number of principles. The unionists probably had enough for them, but at the same time it showed Sinn Fein that a new beginning was possible because there would be full equality in Northern Ireland and a new North–South dimension. The Downing Street Declaration was, of course, followed by the Frameworks Document, which the unionists found more difficult because of the emphasis on full equality, not just in employment but politics and policing and the administration of justice. What it did signal was that there was going to be a new dispensation, a new beginning, where everything would be on the table and the British were going to act in a benignly neutral way.

Was the Frameworks Document that important? Why did you need it between the Downing Street Declaration and the Good Friday Agreement?

You needed something to give a sense of what the institutions would be like. The Downing Street Declaration set out the principles to bring Sinn Fein further down that road but you also needed to give them a sense of the structure or architecture that would give substance to the Downing Street Declaration.

The unionists did not like the word 'harmonisation', though, did they?

No, but if you go back to Sunningdale and the Council of Ireland there was a problem with a North–South architecture, and so it was always going to be a problem for the initial draft of the Good Friday Agreement too. But, if the process was going to be manageable then there was a need to allow for some flexibility in the structures and the detail, so long as you had the architecture.

Here is a process built on three strands which, it seems, Sinn Fein never really got involved in, and most of the negotiation was with the SDLP. Is that so?

Strand One was done with the SDLP and the unionists but Sinn Fein kept an active eye on it. Everyone knew that there had to be power-sharing and it was not going to work unless there was full political equality. Seamus Mallon really negotiated that and did a brilliant job.

And yet you have two ways of thinking about the Good Friday Agreement which are very different. The unionists maintained it copper-fastened the Union and Sinn Fein said it was a stepping-stone to a united Ireland, so one sees it as a finished deal and the other sees it as a starting point?

The aim was to reach a deal where each side got what they wanted. Trimble got consent underpinned by constitutional change in the South, but I don't think the Ulster Unionists more broadly thought of future elections. It was self-determination on the island, as reflected in Hume's brilliant conceptual thinking of joint referenda on the same day on the same issue, but also where a majority at some stage in the North, if they wished it, could move in another direction, and the possibility of that path was important.

You have said with reference to the 'big picture' it is important in negotiation to keep the detail under control, so is it about keeping in view the end of the process?

The big picture and the text are latticed and interrelated, otherwise you might not get the big picture delivered. You have to be very careful in drafting the text that there is nothing there that would undermine an agreement on one side or the other. On that basis everybody had to sign up to the language, so the big picture and the detail are interwoven.

And yet the language of texts, even if ambiguous, has to be clear, with short sentences etc?

That is why you have short sentences, otherwise there is the danger of opening up to more problems you don't need.

So text opens up the risk of more and more problems and you need to keep it as lean as possible?

Yes, even though it might not have been the most grammatical in places.

What about metaphors being used like the 'train leaving'?

And the 'lobster pots'.

Or 'a new dawn' or 'the abyss' etc?

I said if I heard 'the lobster pot' again I was going to walk out of the room, although I said it as a joke. There was the Mitchell Principles and trying to get rid of punishment beatings, and I think it might have been Mark Durkan who raised 'punishment meetings'. Everyone had certain skills sets, and between the British and us there was a common language. You can imagine in the Middle East how, because of the deep linguistic and cultural differences, this would be a significant problem to deal with, but with the British and us nuances are similar. On occasion each was trying to outdo the other on metaphors.

Did Irish officials have a much bigger emotional association with the problem, and if so did that influence your approach to dialogue and negotiation?

You have to leave emotion outside the door. I think you also have to develop trust and almost to like the other personality. I liked the British, and I trusted those like Bill Jeffrey and Jonathan Stephens. They were very open on all issues. All of us abhorred that we were living in two states where there was still a continuing conflict which we felt was a reflection on all of us, and we had a responsibility if we could to try and bring it to an end, so there was no emotion about it. The only emotion, if you like, was when Albert had a go at John Major because of the back-channel and that was a breach of trust, but they quickly got over that and so we had a common purpose with a common set of principles. At times, we were perhaps too close to the SDLP and Sinn Fein, because obviously we understood them fully and we had the same policy goals. It was essential that we looked at ourselves and saw that we were part of that problem, that there were things that we had to give up unemotionally if we are going to get an agreement, like Articles Two and Three.

Was dropping Articles Two and Three the big concession to unionists?

David Trimble was a good negotiator and went into the talks with that as his priority aim, and it had not been delivered previously. He achieved that even though he could have sold it more effectively. Seamus Mallon always said the Good Friday Agreement was Sunningdale for slow-learners. Well it was and it wasn't. You can see a similar architecture but you didn't have Articles Two and Three removed at Sunningdale, which was a process designed to marginalise the violence and remove any cause for violence. The Anglo-Irish Agreement was similar in that regard, whereas the Good Friday Agreement, on the other hand, was designed to bring everyone into the centre and democratic politics, so in that sense it was the opposite of trying to exclude the protagonists of violence.

Is there a moment of ripeness when you can see that realisation sink in. Can you pin that down to key moments?

Yes, there was a subtle shift in the attitudes of the Governments when back-channels opened between the British and the republicans, and also with Alec Reid and Hume–Adams. Both countries are members of the EU and have a continuing conflict, that's the first point. Hume conceptualised that too and reached out to Adams. At the same time Adams and McGuinness were not getting younger, realised that the war was not winnable, from their point of view, so they were opening up and seeing the need to look at another way forward. Those three things coalesced and happened at much the same time. The two Governments opening up to them, Hume bringing them into the centre, then Reynolds and Major having a relationship, with Reynolds coming into office and making this his priority and being very determined and almost one-dimensional about it.

Was Reynolds working every day at this?

Yes, and he was working at various levels as well as being in contact with the IRA to develop an identity of interest and approach with the British, and then using Washington to facilitate and deepen this opening by giving Adams enhanced status and bringing the Americans into play as a facilitator.

With the Irish system you have a Taioseach that you could meet face-to-face to do business with very quickly, but, in contrast, the British system is much more hierarchical and highly structured. Was it more remote and less responsive because of those layers?

It is much more structured, and I suspect that is reflected on paper. Reynolds could call one or two officials and they would be with him in two minutes. Reynolds was not so worried about the past. He knew it had to be taken into account but also thought let's get a deal on this and ensure that the violence is removed from the political scene and how do we do that? But what was crucial were the sets of underlying principles that were set out in the Downing Street Declaration, where you have established definitive structures that are designed to bring people closer and closer.

What did you think the differences were between the Irish and British official civil servants and systems involved in this process?

Remember, the educational background would not have been greatly different. The language we used and the nuance we used and the signals we sent were easily decoded. The skill sets were not significantly different and we became quite collegiate. I remember meeting all day and then going off and having dinner or flying over to London, where dinners would be very frank, and I suspect that initially the British probably felt that they had two communities. They had the SDLP and the republicans on the one hand and unionists on the other, and they had a responsibility to both, as well as a constitutional responsibility to both, but they were probably conscious that the unionists didn't have the backing and saw at the beginning that the nationalist side had the backing of Dublin and its officials, so the unionists were somewhat vulnerable. As the relationship between the sets of officials grew they became conscious, and also appreciative, that we were very aware and conscious of the unionist position and how it was important to reach out directly, as we always tried to do. They were particularly conscious that the unionists, just like the nationalists, had to get up from the table with enough to be able to sell it in a referendum, so we had to think beyond the border and the wider nationalist community to reflect on what the unionists needed as well.

When you say that you sent coded messages and they knew what they were, what were they?

In any negotiations you might not want to say straight and directly what the issue is but you would have an oblique reference that we are getting into difficult territory here and maybe we need to reflect a little more away from a formal negotiating session and talk it through. You could say that in a very indirect way and they would understand and not push it. If you take the Americans and their use of language, it's much more direct, whereas we and the British understood one another perfectly and decoded one another perfectly when it was necessary. We also had a little intellectual jousting from time to time, but that's a good thing.

You mentioned before that the first draft of a document is important, so was there a rush between the sides to produce that draft?

Yes, but I think less so as the process developed because there were so many other players, and it was important that whatever text went round that you talked to everybody. With Sinn Fein sometimes you got texts saying they had difficulty, but it wasn't very clear what the difficulty was, which was challenging, but as the process went forward the British and ourselves realised that if we were not frank with one another and work closely to try and develop a common position then the process was unlikely to be successful.

Were there disputes within the Irish camp about getting rid of Articles Two and Three?

No.

Was it expected then that that was going to happen?

It was seen as essential.

Do you remember when it was first flagged up?

I think Albert Reynolds first flagged up that everything had to be on the table. Reynolds was a very good negotiator, in that he was a business man and had the capacity to see that everybody had to be, to some degree, satisfied with the outcome of the process. There was no dissension from that.

Principle and pragmatism are obviously important, but if you have something like decommissioning and you keep shifting it for pragmatic reasons does it not become a point of distrust and a destabilising issue?

You had to be able, to the greatest degree possible, to read the other negotiators' body language, their thinking, how much they could deliver and when they could deliver it, and if they were to say to you, particularly in a one-to-one or a very small group, that creates enormous problems for us, or I don't think we can do that, you have to take that on board. You do not change the principle, so taking arms out of the equation at some stage was important. However, we saw this as something that had to come at the end of a process, because if it came too early then what you were asking people to do was to put up a white flag and surrender. In the theology of the republican movement that was not going to be achieved. It wasn't achieved eighty years ago, when they buried their own guns, or at the end of the 1956 to 1962 campaign, when they dumped arms, so they were not going to hand over in 1998 and, indeed, to insist so would have wrecked the whole process. Not that you renege from the principle, but if you insist on it at too early a stage you are stacking up problems for yourself. We always felt that it was going to be made much easier if the republican movement encouraged their people to join the police force, because if you had a police force that was acceptable to the republican movement and that they endorsed, and encouraged their constituents and supporters to join, then clearly you don't need guns. So it was a question then of how to deal with that. We were asking people to study how it was done in other countries, and a number of options came up. One was when Archbishop Makarios got rockets and quite important arsenals from the Soviet Union, and the UN took control of them and they were put in a UN base but were guarded at the time by Norwegians. We opted for this taking place on an interim basis, where arms were placed in dumps that were sealed and this would be confirmed by an international grouping.

When Patrick Mayhew introduced the decommissioning condition in Washington did that come as a surprise you?

Although I was Ambassador at the time in Washington it was not run across us, so, in that sense, it was a bit of a surprise.

What was the Irish reaction?

We thought it was a very serious problem because it was not achievable. Everybody at that stage knew that if there was going to be deep, meaningful and ultimately successful talks which would take the gun out of politics and bring the extreme into the centre, then Sinn Fein needed to be part of that, and that would be impossible if decommissioning were to be insisted on as a requirement for Sinn Fein to be involved. They couldn't deliver that. You had to make a judgement, and we spoke with the British very openly about that. We had informal meetings over dinner and we spoke quite assertively about how this was not achievable. Both of us made a judgement as to the degree of influence that Adams and McGuinness had. There were jokes about them going into the next room and talking to the mirror and coming back and saying we have consulted, but it was much more complex than that. I remember at times being with Gerry Adams having a meal in Castle Buildings, and he would say I will be out of touch for twenty-four to forty-eight hours. He would then resurface forty-eight hours later, so it wasn't a case of just going in and telling the Army Council what they had achieved and they would tick the box and agree to it. You had to make a judgement at any one stage of what they were capable of delivering. In fairness, I think the British quickly realised that and began to see how they could unhook themselves from it.

Do you remember whether there were heated exchanges with the British when Mayhew said that?

No. Negotiations are tough but there was great respect on both sides, and I think great credibility. I was in Washington at the time, so a lot of that discussion would have been back in Dublin, but we trusted one another and as the process went on there was more and more trust generated. We said in our considered view this is a serious mistake and you will be in danger of losing or excluding Sinn Fein.

Why would Mayhew have made that announcement in Washington and not London? Was it because of anger over the Cahill and Adams visas? Was it an attempt to take a harder line in an American constituency because of anger over perceived American intrusion?

That could have been there, but I could not say that. It was probably related also to his own constituency. It might have been related to some of the people who he reflected on the North with in the House of Commons. It may also have been his wish to steady the unionist camp at that time, but I don't know. That would have been popular with some people in the House of Commons, possibly with some in the security forces too, and it may have reflected disappointment and anger that the Americans had given Adams and Cahill visas, but I just don't know. The British officials were very sensitive and very reflective people and they quickly realised this was a problem. I saw the reports of all the discussions and the meetings, but sometimes they don't give the full picture. You have to get the tone and nuance as well. There was always a sense that once Sinn Fein entered into the dialogue and decided to go down this road and created a ceasefire that they weren't going to resign from it, or walk away. They might step outside from time to time, but remember the military situation was being contained by the British, and it was clear to both sides that neither side was going to win. I think they were political people who did not indulge in it for the sake of indulging in it. They were serious people and they showed subsequently, when they got used to negotiations, which they did very quickly, how skilful and intelligent they were. So it was important that the two Governments didn't do anything that made them step off the pitch and walk away. If you are in negotiations and you know the other side, particularly when they talk to you one-to-one, or two-to-two, or you walk down a road with them, or walk round a field or a garden, you really get a sense of whether something is deliverable or not. There are always games being played but you have got to make a judgement, and if you feel that here is somebody that you trust because when he said he would deliver he did deliver, then that is a verifiable track record. When that person says something is simply not possible you have to take careful note of that.

Why did decommissioning not come at the time of the Good Friday Agreement?

The Agreement was in 1998, and it was clear that there were a number of issues that could not be resolved on that day. One of them was policing, which the Patten Commission was set up to address, and the other was decommissioning. Clearly the two Governments tried to encourage decommissioning as early as possible because it would have helped the process, and as an interim there was a sealing of arms dumps. But after the Agreement in 1998 it took quite a considerable time for the structures to come into being. That is, the Executive in the North and the all-Ireland bodies. Sometimes the implementation of an agreement is almost as difficult as the negotiation of that agreement. There wouldn't have been an agreement if there had been an insistence that it should happen that night. It was important to get the arrangements for the institutions in place first and then allow those institutions to come into being before decommissioning. That had to be the sequence. Clearly, the republican movement was not ready for it on Good Friday. There was a long drawn-out, complex process with de Chastelain and it ultimately led to comprehensive decommissioning. I thought that some decommissioning might be possible at the time the institutions came into being, because that would send a powerful signal to all sides, including to the IRA, but I was wrong on that.

Was much of the decommissioning issue discussed with the Irish rather than the British because the British would have been seen more as the enemy?

It was primarily, but remember the British came to be trusted as well, and in the latter stages of the negotiations and for quite a period Blair and Powell 'transcended' that. The Shinners would always be suspicious, but they saw Blair and Powell as honest brokers who genuinely wanted a definitive, comprehensive deal and were prepared to stretch to accomplish that. If he wanted the British to do something Adams would say to Powell look you might give me a hand in drafting something or maybe send me a text that I would look at and that went beyond the colonial thing. The Shinners would always be suspicious about what they called 'the securocrats', but they certainly didn't consider Blair and Powell to be securocrats.

But do you think the closeness of the two Governments was important not just because of the success of the process but because it made it less possible for others like Sinn Fein to exploit what they may have seen as splits or potential differences between the two Governments?

That's true, but the Shinners also wanted a deal as well. Remember, they were a considerable distance down the road and it would be difficult to turn back from that. Also, because they wanted a deal, it would not have been in their interest to play off one against the other. If it was essential for them they would say we need to get Blair over the line, or need Blair's help on this, and we would argue on that with the British, but at the same time we would have to stand back and look at what the Shinners were proposing, and some of this might not be helpful. Others might become more concerned about the process and we would have to question whether they would stay with it, but it wasn't in their interest to try and get the Dublin Government to put disproportionate pressure on the British if that were to drive others out of the process. We had to assess what each side was asking and question whether it fitted into the framework and helped the process or whether it was designed to drive someone out of the room.

How do you stop discussions getting out of control and keep them focussed on the core issues? You mention framework, and it's interesting where the edges of that are and when you are moving outside that, so is it instinctive?

You would have a working session in the morning and afternoon and then you would go through things and go and have dinner in a restaurant somewhere to discuss more informally where things were at. That gave you a better sense of things, and if you go back to the text, where you need to adjust it a bit to bring all sides with you. The British and ourselves had a lot of informal dinners together, and that was very helpful not just in exploring and bringing our own positions closer but getting a common and agreed sense of where we needed to push one side or the other and how we maintained a common position on that.

What is your perception of the American understanding of this, and is the American perception of negotiations similar to the Irish and the British or is their logic different?

The Americans look at the bigger picture. We were very close to Clinton and his advisors. He thought of appointing an envoy for Northern Ireland and he was giving thought to it around St Patrick's Day 1992, and I discussed this with Reynolds when we were planning how to choreograph that first St Patrick's visit. I said to Albert there had to be a consistent relationship built up between the Prime Minister and the Taoiseach and the President. I explained to Clinton's people that this relationship was now going to be different from what it had been for years with previous presidents. We had the traditional presentation of shamrock and we had a meeting with Clinton for about fifty minutes, which had not been possible before. I organised that Clinton and Reynolds travel down together in the presidential motorcade to the Speaker's lunch, and we prepared this. Reynolds said he did not want an envoy because that would complicate things and he had a strategy, and this is what I had been saying to the Clinton people. Reynolds believed he could deliver a ceasefire that would lead into full-blooded talks involving Sinn Fein. Clinton bought into that immediately and didn't appoint an envoy at that stage. He realised that the two Governments decided that they weren't going to allow this part of Europe to have an ongoing conflict indefinitely and that they were going to seize control of it and try and bring it to an end. Clinton realised that Reynolds' strategy was to deliver peace within a certain period, but he needed the support of America not so much on the detail but on giving an international dimension to it, which was particularly meaningful in Ireland. Further, if we managed this properly this would give an enhanced status and credibility in his community to Adams, and that was the line we took in the case of the Adams visa. So it wasn't so much the detail but broader and symbolic support. The making of access available to the White House was the important thing, and not so much the nuance or the detail of a document. Particularly for Sinn Fein here was a benign, concerned, engaged, encouraging White House with all its authority and power and credibility, and the Irish-American community was very supportive of that. Also, the Americans would provide the Chair for the talks, because there was always this fear that the British would go to someone in the old white Commonwealth and ask them to chair, as they had done in previous talks in the late 1980s which were chaired by Sir Ninian Stephens from Australia. But, of course, Senator George Mitchell was appointed as the Chair.

What is the value of access, and what difference does it make?

The White House means an awful lot, and I suppose Trimble liked to be able to go and see and be received by the most powerful politician in the world too. Remember, it had been part of the theology of Sinn Fein and the IRA that America was the friendly, encouraging and benign dimension, and an international American presence would give both the process and republicanism an added credibility, status and authority.

What difference did the Irish-American audience make, and was it a factor in Clinton's thinking?

They worked very closely with the Embassy and they provided the invitation to Adams to come and address a very legitimate historical association in New York, which was not Irish, but something like the American Committee for Foreign Policy. What was crucial though was the relationship between Reynolds and Clinton, and subsequently Ahern and Clinton, but remember, he was also talking to others. One of his closest friends was Dick Reilly, the Secretary of Education, who came on holidays to Ireland with me, and we travelled about together. He was the Governor at one stage of South Carolina and was the first southern Governor to declare for Clinton. That was extremely important, and he was in charge of the transition. In other words, he was in charge of advising Clinton who to appoint in the transitional period between Bush and Clinton following the election but before he took office. There were people like Senator Pat Leahy, Chris Dodd and Ted Kennedy, and he was talking to them and they would talk to us. Jim Lyons from Denver, Colorado was also important and was probably one of the closet friends of the Clintons, and he was somebody who had a view which was conveyed. But the crucial thing was the Clinton relationship. Once the visa was out of the way there was a very good relationship with the British, and the British are a very influential Embassy in Washington. It wasn't just the Irish who had a strategy. The two Governments were becoming very close and unified in their approach once the visa issue was out of the way. Clinton saw that Reynolds and Major were close, and Bertie and Tony were also very close and that was reassuring for the Americans. The two Governments were taking the thing by the scruff of the neck and trying to move it forward and putting in place confidence-building measures and the Americans did play a crucial part in that.

Was Clinton's grasp of the complexities impressive?

Very much so.

Did he get that from reading or advice? How was he able to do that?

He was fascinated by international affairs and conflicts and he liked to get to the bottom of things, and, remember, he had been studying in England when the whole civil rights movement started in 1968. He had an Irish background through his mother and he had a lot of good Irish friends. They must have been talking over the years that if we ever get into power we have to do something about this. He is also a very good people-person and almost felt his humanitarian duty, if he could, to make a difference, and you could see that when he gave Adams the visa. The thinking was that if this works out it will be well worth it, but, if not, what is lost is only forty-eight hours and it doesn't have to be done again. That strategic thinking and the courage of his conviction and judgement was shaped by the view that if you want to make a difference you have to move, and if you continue accepting the same old advice indefinitely then the problem would continue indefinitely.

Are you of the mind that a good negotiator knows when to apply pressure but also knows when to back off, knows when to give people space and knows when to close that space down?

Exactly, and you can never be taken for granted. You open a door, but if somebody isn't responding as they should then you exert pressure.

In the peace process was the pressure exerted in an intense way or did it work almost like hypnotic pressure, where you would leave republicans and others to ponder? Did you have to keep on it all the time and not give them any room to wriggle out of it?

You have got to put pressure on all sides and you have got to spell it out to people that if this is going to work it means bringing all sides with us, and therefore there is no point in having just nationalists there because it wouldn't get you the all-embracing agreement necessary. You have got to make it clear and emphasise and underline to everyone that there is another person across the table and that person will have to sell the deal to their constituency, so there is no point in having a one-sided agreement because it won't go anywhere. That is part of the pressure that any responsible government, or participant, or governments together, must emphasise.

Clearly there is a distinction to be made between compromise and concession, because every political party in a situation like this knows the importance of compromise but doesn't want it to look like a concession because then it puts them into a position of weakness?

You can always say 'stretching for the good of the process'.

Was that an expression used?

I'm sure I used it on many occasions. You can't have it on your terms. You are in a negotiating process and you wouldn't be in a negotiating process unless you are prepared to compromise. It would be perverse to do otherwise.

And yet no one can really admit that, because as soon as you draw people into talking about compromise they feel like they are weakened by that, so they know it but can't talk about it, or can they?

I think they can. It's acceptable in negotiations to say look, we have given here or we have to make a move there. You can't stay rigidly in one place, and if you look there is progressive movement throughout the process. You have to say look, we believe, as Joe Cahill probably said when he went to the US, that this is the way forward and that it will be a difficult and challenging road but we have to go down it because ultimately this will lead to an all-encompassing political arrangement.

Albert Reynolds had an expression, 'Who is afraid of peace?' Was that discussed?

No, it was Reynolds himself and 'Peace comes dropping slow'. You wouldn't expect him to quote W. B. Yeats. He was shrewd.

Did the British see the American role quite as favourably as the Irish?

Remember that Jonathan Powell was the man in Washington and they fought long and hard against the Adams visa, but in fairness to them they would subsequently admit that that was a mistake and that this made a considerable difference. I have no doubt that Tony Blair and Bertie Ahern asked Clinton to ring, including during the Good Friday Agreement final sessions. I was in Downing Street and Chequers, and Jim Steinberg from the National Security Council was fully engaged, so I have no doubt about the value of the US role.

One of the things that came up a lot in the interviews with British officials is text and documents, and the Irish give the impression that although text and documentation were important the process was more conversational and relational. Would you concur with that?

Conversation and dialogue had to move on to text at some stage, and if you look at the Good Friday Agreement it's probably a model of being both short and clear-sighted. It's not complex and it's very careful, because people parse and analyse words. The unionists were less enamoured with constructive ambiguity than nationalists, and I think it's because of different traditions and different educational systems. Maybe it was also to do with an oral tradition on the nationalist side, as well as not being in power with the unionists and a different religious dimension as well. Important though dialogue, talks and discussions are, you have to move to text at some stage and you have to get it down on paper what the commitments and expectations are and get people to sign up to that. Republicans would always have somebody in the early stages who would be a 'watcher', who didn't participate but was watching to see what the body language was. Clearly, for them, just watching at that stage was an important part of reading the process.

Presumably text is also about building trust, because it must reflect listening to concerns?

It's building trust but it's taking into account where they are and where everyone else is. It's about taking people further down the road that they need to be taken down if there is going to be an agreement. So you have to not just engage but encourage, tempt, cajole and say to people, look if there is going to be an agreement there are certain things that you have to sign up to and accept. At the earlier stages you had confidence-building measures like the Adams visa to get Sinn Fein into the space where serious negotiations could take place and where, to use the Blair metaphor, the train was leaving the station and they had to be on it. Once you got them into talks then you had to move to making a judgement on where they were likely to go, how much influence Adams and McGuinness had, how much they could deliver, what was necessary and where there was likely to be a consensus and agreement at the centre. So it was about getting the people out of the room. I remember at one stage saying to George Mitchell on the three-stranded talks, where there might be five, six or seven in a delegation, that it might be better to bring it down to leader and one other, and that changed the tone and the atmosphere because, if there were six or seven in each delegation, clearly it was being reported back to people and that risked greater problems. I also said to Mitchell you have got to take them out of the hothouse that is Castle Buildings, and so we went across to the American residence in London. We had about five days there and we had dinner every evening there. There was no seat plan so it forced unionists and republicans to sit side by side. Previous to that, in Castle Buildings, there was a canteen where they all sat at their own tables, so moving them out of Castle Buildings was important because they began to mingle.

Would it be fair to suggest that you know you are getting down to business when you have two in the room rather than six?

Yes, but two from each delegation in the room for the three-stranded talks rather than six. Even though for quite a long time the unionists would talk through the Chair to Sinn Fein, rather than directly, the atmosphere was different. When there were six or seven you were playing to your own team and your own gallery, and the atmosphere significantly changed, and mostly for the worst, because of that.

Would Sinn Fein ask a stack of questions not because they were important but because they were playing for time and because it made them look tougher negotiators if they drew the thing out?

No, I don't think they were concerned about appearing tough. If they did that they did it to buy time. Their concern was in keeping their people throughout the country and in America informed so when there was some announcement coming their people were not taken by surprise. There were two distinct operations: with the Army Council, where they obviously had to run things across and get approval or endorsement, and with their supporters in the country and America, who they were briefing. They weren't asking for approval but informing them that things were in place. They were a centralised, coherent outfit, absolutely on message whether they were in San Francisco or in Cork. The text would be almost identical. In contrast, the unionists had as many voices as people. If you go back to 1994 you can see the pattern emerging when the ceasefire was announced. Republicans organised cars and flags and were blowing horns and claiming a triumph. Likewise, whenever there was an announcement Adams came out and emphasised the positives. He always looked upbeat. The Shinners would be out first and positive, and that was very reassuring for their supporters.

Did Adams and McGuinness talk at any length about the dangers of a split?

Adams did mention it and was very conscious of the potential of a split and how that would have been a profound failure. That was a red line and the two Governments had to be conscious of that. It was clear to anybody with any sense of Irish or republican history that that was a line that was not going to be crossed.

What interests me about the US relationship with Ireland and Irish republicanism is that many republicans talk about being socialist, which much of America loathes. How is that to be explained?

It didn't really arise at that time. The ideological position or the socialist dimension of Sinn Fein only emerged when they morphed into a significant political party and opted into politics. Remember, at that time they couldn't be interviewed and were in the margins because they were very much a secondary body and a front for the IRA, so that didn't come up and nobody looked at what their social policies were. They saw this as a conflict and tended to conceptualise it exclusively in those terms. So the question became how do we bring these people from a conflict situation into a position where their political party is the one and only representative of that community? How do we get the IRA to move off into the background and decommission? Those were the kind of vital concerns.

Do you remember what Adams' response was to Canary Wharf when the Government pressed on this?

I was in Washington at the time and he telephoned me with a view to getting the message to the Americans that this had happened. Basically, he said it was unfortunate but we can't be diverted from what we are trying to do. When I spoke to the Americans their view was let this not discourage us from going down this road and from keeping at it, it's a setback but it's not a fatal setback.

Do you remember what you said to Adams then?

I said this is hugely unfortunate and it will be very upsetting for our American friends, and I must have said something like I hope this is not the start of a new campaign, or words to that effect. What can you say?

I suppose with that event you either pull the plug or you accelerate the process?

It's what Tim Dalton calls 'keeping the attic window open'.

What was Clinton asking?

It was broad at that stage, but it was look, you have got to keep at it, we are here to help and if I can do or say anything at any stage let me know. He was encouraging people to keep at it and there was an echo in that.

Did the British see Clinton in the same way?

No. You see, he doesn't see foreign ministers. There were prime ministers whom he didn't see, and I think at one stage the King of Spain found it difficult to get in, but this comes back to the group of seven or eight people who had very close relations, including social relations, with the White House. There were good friends of ours at a senior level and one of them would always go, so the Foreign Minister might not see him in the Oval Office, but they would walk him down the corridor to Anthony Lake's office or whoever was there at that time.

To what extent do ambiguous sections reflect ambiguous conversations? Was there a sheet of paper on the table with the republicans all the time about decommissioning, or was it just verbalised?

They let us put it down and put marks through it but they wouldn't tell us where the inadequacy was and how we failed the exam. The decommissioning sentences of the Good Friday Agreement were our best judgement and, in fairness, the British went along with this, clearly envisaging that they could be brought further at a later period.

The whole concept of 'new beginnings' would have been exactly what republicans were looking for and exactly what unionists were afraid of?

Yes, but the complementary balance is the constitutional change. The territorial claim by the South over the North was withdrawn and there were other balances like the North–South institutions which would operate by consensus, so you had checks and balances. For the nationalists the new beginning, equality at all levels and a power-sharing Executive where you had a First Minister who couldn't act unilaterally provided the kind of balances which gave full equality.

How did you work out what was the bottom line for republicans?

Because of the years we had been drafting papers, and from time to time statements too. Tim Dalton and myself came from rural Ireland and had an instinct as to why Adams and McGuinness might not have been able to sell a text to the Army Council. A text may go back and forth until finally you got a statement, but it had to have traditional language in it. You just couldn't put in forward movement all the time. You had to have language about the causes of conflict too. Remember, we weren't drafting an Irish Government statement, we were drafting a statement for the republican movement, so there had to be a certain genuflection if the text was going to run. You had to have the initial paragraph or two which was traditional republican language, and then you moved to the section which would bring them along, move them forward. After sequencing texts, and maybe on the third or the fourth time, you got it right. Then that statement was issued with the theological and ideological republican language but, importantly, the substantive paragraph would then move them forward, and that helped the process when you came to the negotiations.

Did unionists talk about principles?

Yes. The unionists spoke a lot about the principle of constitutional change, the unacceptability of Dublin having a constitutional claim on Northern Ireland. They also spoke a lot about decommissioning and violence. The SDLP put a particular focus on the principle of a new beginning, a new agenda and a new dispensation.

You mentioned before that the first draft of a document is important, so was there a rush between the sides to produce that draft?

Yes, but I think less so as the process developed because there were so many other players and it was important that whatever text went round that you talked to everybody. As said, with Sinn Fein sometimes you got texts saying they had difficulty, but it wasn't very clear what the difficulty was, but as the process went forward the British and ourselves realised that if we were not frank with one another and work closely to try and develop a common position, then the process was unlikely to be successful.

Was it reciprocated on the British side that from their point of view everything had to be on the table too?

Yes, and the consent principle had to be there, but the British were willing to put difficult things on the table too, as they did at the time of the Good Friday Agreement with prisoner releases.

Can you have a problem with too many principles or not enough principles in a process?

I don't have a problem with too many principles but there had to be core principles, and you sometimes have to look beyond principles, at their implementation. You also have to be prudent and sensible and realise that some principles will not be deliverable at the actual time of the Agreement. That for some principles, if you call them principles, there needs to be a time for reflection, and a need to bring in outside expertise to help you chart those very difficult waters that you have to wade through. Policing and decommissioning would be two examples.

What is the value of outside influence in a process like this?

Sometimes people who have expertise and who are from outside and who have very considerable credibility and who engender trust, who are not actually too close, and understand the detail of an issue but are not too close to it, can see what needs to be done in a more clear-sighted way than direct participants. You can see that in the Patten Commission report, which is a model and still relevant after some fifteen to sixteen years if you want to set up the framework for a model police force.

How apparent were the differences between John Major and Tony Blair, from the Irish perspective?

Remember, Blair was post-Second World War, but one major difference is that Blair had a commanding majority in the House of Commons. Major had a majority of two or three and was dependent on the Ulster Unionists, who could have brought him down, so he was extremely courageous. Likewise, on the Irish side Reynolds delivered the Downing Street Declaration, which opened the door to a wider, all-embracing process. John Bruton took over and he brought to fruition and delivered the Frameworks Document, and then Ahern came in. Cowen was in a later period and was very influential as Minister for Foreign Affairs during the Ahern period, when he had a lot of responsibility for the Dail. But Bertie Ahern and Tony Blair developed a very close relationship, and that was crucial for driving the process. In a sense, both were non-judgemental and both wanted an agreement that was fair to all sides and was embraced by all sides so each could say this is a success and we can work this. Where all could say 'yes' to the establishment of the institutions and 'yes' to the implementation of the Agreement.

Were you of the mind that the longer Sinn Fein stayed in the process the harder it would be for them to walk away?

Yes. I always took the view that once they entered into this process that there was very unlikely to be any turning back unless both Governments made a major mistake, and I think the two Governments were so close and so clear-sighted about the process and what it would deliver that they weren't going to make such mistakes. Now the Shinners and the IRA made mistakes, particularly when the ceasefire ended, but the fact that they were clearly very exercised and annoyed about what they saw as British foot-dragging indicated a desire to get the process back on the road. It was clear that the process would restart again at some stage. There had to be a cooling-off period, but I thought that once the process was underway again there would be no turning back.

On the problem of text can you describe the style of writing that you yourself were involved in. Is it a particular Civil Service kind of approach, very lean, sparse, short sentences, short words, etc.? Explain the style?

Well the Agreement itself was quite short. The more convoluted or complex you make it the more open to ambiguity and to disruptive and critical analysis it becomes, but on issues like decommissioning and in getting Sinn Fein to accept text you have almost to put yourself into their frame of mind and use language, while clear, that they can sign up to. The classical example in my view is 'putting arms beyond use', because that conveys the concept that it is they who put arms beyond use, though it was verified as being beyond use and unusable.

So it wouldn't have been better to say 'put arms and explosives beyond use'?

No, that wasn't a factor, because 'arms' was all-embracing and because it was verified with an inventory. 'Arms' was meant to be all-embracing. It wasn't as if they had tanks, but 'arms' was meant to cover rockets, explosives and everything in between.

To say 'putting arms beyond use' seems a softer way of saying we will destroy arms?

Yes.

Did you have people in the Irish Government who were unhappy about the softening of language?

No. Remember, it was a very tight group and there were no leaks.

In the narrative of the peace process Albert Reynolds and Bertie Ahern are cited as the key figures. John Bruton is often, not dismissed, but not spoken about in the same way. What is your view on that?

Well John Bruton is a friend of mine, as Reynolds was and Ahern is, and I was in Washington in John Bruton's time. You ask about Canary Wharf. Bruton came in with a different background from Albert Reynolds and Bertie Ahern, but he was determined to move the process forward and you saw that with the Frameworks Document. Bruton was determined to drive it on but personally found it a bit more difficult. After Canary Wharf he rightly took a strong line with the republican movement, and anybody who was Taoiseach at the time would have done that.

What is the difference between strategy and tactics?

Strategy is where you keep your eye on what you want to go to, and you might have to adjust the tactics or change the car in getting there.

So, in knowing where you want to go in this situation are you talking about a peace settlement or something else?

Strategy varied from time to time. The ultimate strategy was an all-embracing peace settlement, but if you go back to Sean O hUiginn the strategy was to get the British and ourselves to sign up to a declaration that would open the way and encourage and engage people into coming forward to see if the beginnings of a process could lead us into an end game. The Downing Street Declaration would have been sub-strategy at the time and the Frameworks Document followed from that. Then the strategy was to get talks open, but the ultimate strategy is to use interim strategies to get an all-embracing peace deal. The tactics varied, and, at a certain time, in order to deliver on your strategy you had to bring the Americans into play. That was a tactical move and it had to happen.

There seems to be that tension between pragmatism and principle?

Pragmatism is a bit like tactics though. You have the principle there but you are pragmatic in pursuit of it in its delivery and you adjust the tactics.

The Irish political culture seems much more oral; that is not to say that it's not literal, but most officials say that speaking and talking is a large part of the political culture?

The Good Friday negotiations had gone on for X period but then had a deadline set, which was Holy Thursday. At some stage you have to produce a text, even if you know that the initial text is not going to be the end text, because, as in the case of

Good Friday, there were elements in it like the North–South element which gave very significant room for manoeuvre. The unionists found that unacceptable and wanted to take it out and adjust it, but at some stage you have to set text down in writing, let it float and see what the reaction is.

Is that when the problems start, because once you make a public declaration of something, as with a piece of paper, then people start to focus more on what parts they can use for their own ends? And is that what single-text negotiation is about anyway?

If you read that text nobody could object to it because it is essentially saying it's an international agreement and we are working it fully. But, of course, if the people North and South and the two Governments agree a more comprehensive, more all-embracing agreement, then that transcends any earlier agreement.

What is interesting in President Carter's work with Sadat and Begin in 1976 is when Carter says of Sadat that 'His negotiating tactic was never to haggle over detail but to create an atmosphere that made disagreement psychologically difficult.' Is there any comparison here to be made with the Irish when you say there is nothing in there that one can disagree with and that detail is potentially dangerous? You obviously need detail but, presumably, you need to keep it minimal?

Yes, but it is also to set out a framework. Remember, you have a situation where the unionists are not engaging politically, so in earlier speeches you send what you might call 'echoes to one another', and, if you notice, at Molyneaux's instigation some of the unionists said interesting things in the House of Commons, but they're not said in isolation, they are said in order to facilitate a response from Dublin. The whole thing is choreographed, if you like. Then you basically say that the Anglo-Irish Agreement clearly isn't there for all time and that it can be superseded and transcended, so that enables the unionists to move in without alienating anybody else because nobody objected. So you set a framework where people begin to move and where, at some stage, they enter into dialogue and discussion. Coming back to the detail, even with the first draft of the Good Friday Agreement you put it on the table but it's not set in stone, and so it was significantly adjusted and changed. Maybe twenty-five per cent of it disappeared and was replaced by other elements. You might make life difficult for people, but if you say look, if you don't like it come back and tell us what's better and it isn't set in stone but there is enough there, such as with constitutional change, which was particularly attractive to David Trimble, and other elements which were attractive to the Shinners and the SDLP such as power-sharing and devolution, then you had scope for movement while keeping everyone engaged.

Did you see the peace process as a moral as well as political process?

I think it was a political process but with a moral ending. It delivered a moral solution because clearly any political agreement that ends killing and violence and brings people together is a significant moral achievement, but it was a political process and agreement that delivered that.

Conclusion

The interviews in this book provide detail and personal reflections on the shift from exclusive political processes to an inclusive political process in an attempt to achieve peace in Northern Ireland. The failure of Sunningdale, which condemned Northern Ireland to another twenty-five years of violence, revealed the shortcomings of not having joint government participation to support power-sharing and of a lack of will (especially on the part of the British) to make the initiative work. The Anglo-Irish Agreement demonstrated the importance of a collective approach by both British and Irish Governments to Northern Ireland but did not engage the political parties in the process of reaching that Agreement. In contrast, the Good Friday Agreement came about as a result of both Governments (along with the US) and the political parties in Northern Ireland working together (to a greater and lesser extent) to bring the conflict to a close by accepting the value of a power-sharing Executive. In a sense, all were stages in the long struggle to give politics primacy over violence in Northern Ireland, and so chapters in a larger story.

The peace process, which began in the late 1980s, was based on the recognition that an inclusive political agreement would require an inclusive political process to bring it about, and so, in contrast to Sunningdale and the Anglo-Irish Agreement, drawing the extremes onto the terrain of democratic (and therefore moderate) politics. For this to occur, aspirational differences had to be acknowledged and managed through core principles and strands of engagement. The concept of strands was used to triangulate competing British and Irish interests in connection to North–South, East–West and internal Northern Ireland relationships, and key principles provided the space for opposing political ambitions to be contained by the common focus of reaching an accommodation. To achieve the Good Friday Agreement both principles and strands needed some elasticity to accommodate the divergence of political interests, and this was provided by a language environment of constructive ambiguity (Powell 2008: 108).

Such context is given great emphasis here by Irish civil servants, who acknowledge the interdependency of the personal and the textual and see both as key drivers of the peace process, enabling participants to interpret intentions, actions and meanings in relation to each other. The architecture of the three strands helped to forge a framework that drew the participants closer together, while the conceptual power of principles such as equality and consent allowed political differences to inform the scope and detail of negotiations. It was the strands and principles together that facilitated new relationships and allowed a dynamic of exclusive difference to become a dynamic of common concern as each party struggled to define the shape of peace and find its own voice within it.

As with British involvement in the peace process, the respondents here highlight the need for cohesion, collective impetus and intense engagement (Spencer 2015). The emphasis on momentum, based on sequencing informal as well as formal dialogue and negotiation, presents the peace process as representative of the relationships forged within it and the building of trust and confidence as vital for successful outcomes. Although much of the peace process could not be known in advance, and so would emerge as an outworking of negotiations, it is apparent that for those negotiations to be successful, a co-ordination of influences would need to come into play so that wider expectations and anticipations about power-sharing could not only be disputed, but, more importantly, shared.

The interviews reveal the importance of dialogue, interaction, consensus and compromise. They highlight the significance of understanding nuance and possibility and the need to converge influences in order to make the case for peace compelling. The role of the US in helping those such as Sinn Fein, by providing opportunities for symbolic performance and presentation to show emerging political respectability (as with the Adams visa), also brings to light the significance of influence beyond that created by British and Irish Governments (Clancy 2010; Lynch 2004).

The damage and deaths caused by the PIRA ending its ceasefire with the Canary Wharf bomb raised fears that the transformation from militant to political republicanism might not happen, but the underlying view also seemed to be that there would be little advantage for republicans (and, to a lesser extent, loyalists) in ending political engagement and returning to armed struggle, and that participation in a peace process over the long term would be likely to de-legitimise violence and so make any return to it politically counterproductive. Indeed, a resumption of the armed struggle by the PIRA appeared contradictory to the aims of the Adams and McGuinness leadership of Sinn Fein and was strongly factored into the thinking of Irish (and indeed American and British) officials as they considered whether the peace process was worth pursuing at that point or not. Such challenges were representative of the unpredictability of the peace process in its formative stages and indicative of how problems would require an intensification of effort in order to continue. The interviews underline the importance of this intensification and how necessary it was, not just for making progress in the wake of unexpected events but as a form of pressure to deter participants from walking away.

Drawing any specific lessons from the interviews about how to create and then implement a peace process may be tempting, but should be approached with caution. The transferability of such a process into situations with different identities, histories, cultures and politics risks a 'one size fits all' template that may be not only unsuitable, but also dangerous. Having said that, perhaps one conclusion that might be drawn is that peace cannot be realistically achieved without dialogue and negotiation and that both, in taking place over time, are constitutive of a process. This process will shift in terms of intensity, momentum and direction, with obstructions presenting tests for the credibility and authenticity of engagement, but the core concerns of integrity, trust, momentum and commitment remain central challenges in any peace process, regardless of different social and political circumstances.

Importantly, the determination to end violence is not just a political enterprise but a moral one. There may be disagreement about strategic and tactical methods of achieving that end but, ultimately, the saving of human life makes rejection of the peace process a particularly difficult (not to mention possibly inhumane) position to defend. The fact that reaching an accommodation saved many lives in Northern Ireland justifies its validity, however much one disagrees with its manner of delivery or however distasteful one finds the idea of bringing extreme groups into the centre. One thing that is also hard to dispute is that if such an inclusive process had failed it is unlikely there would have been an alternative process that would have been better placed to end the conflict. More likely is that death, injury and destruction would have continued.

Although Sunningdale, the Anglo-Irish Agreement and the Good Friday Agreement represent three distinct and separate historical moments, each has some level of connection with the other. The inclusivity of the peace process was also a response to the shortcomings of not having a joint approach from the two Governments and then of having a joint approach that did not involve the political parties of Northern Ireland. It also required a symmetry of forces and influences convergent to the goal of peace that were lacking with Sunningdale and only tentatively emerging with the Anglo-Irish Agreement. That said, this volume has only touched upon some of the difficulties involved in working to reach a political settlement in Northern Ireland and further reflection is needed to identify the complexity and multiplicity of roles that came into play. The peace process was not only about reaching an agreement, but about realising the promise and possibilities of that agreement through implementation. The challenges this posed for the Irish Government, and not just for civil servants but for political leaders, is more comprehensively addressed in an accompanying second volume.

References

Clancy, M. A. C. (2010) *Power Without Consensus: Power Sharing Politics in Northern Ireland*, London: Routledge.

Lynch, T. J. (2004) *Turf Wars: The Clinton Administration and Northern Ireland*, Aldershot: Ashgate.

Powell, J. (2008) *Great Hatred, Little Room*, London: The Bodley Head.

Spencer, G. (2015) *The British and Peace in Northern Ireland*, Cambridge: Cambridge University Press.

Index